Using

Access 2002

in Accounting

James T. Perry, Ph.D.
The University of San Diego
School of Business

Gary P. Schneider, Ph.D., CPA
The University of San Diego
School of Business

THOMSON

SOUTH-WESTERN

Australia · Canada · Mexico · Singapore · Spain · United Kingdom · United States

THOMSON

SOUTH-WESTERN

Using Access 2002 in Accounting
James T. Perry and Gary P. Schneider

Editor-in-Chief:
Jack W. Calhoun

Vice President/Team Director:
Melissa S. Acuña

Acquisitions Editor:
Julie Lindsay

Developmental Editor:
Carol Bennett

Marketing Manager:
Mignon Tucker

Production Editor:
Salvatore N. Versetto

Manufacturing Coordinator:
Doug Wilke

Production House:
Litten Editing and Production, Inc.

Compositor:
GGS Information Services, Inc.

Printer:
Phoenix Color
Hagerstown, MD

Design Project Manager:
Rik Moore

Internal Designer:
John W. Robb
JWR Design Interaction

Cover Designer:
John W. Robb
JWR Design Interaction

Cover Photo:
Digital Stock

Media Developmental Editor:
Sally Nieman

Media Production Editor:
Robin K. Browning

Library of Congress Cataloging-in-
Publication Data

ISBN: 0-324-19034-4

Perry, James T.
  Building accounting systems using Access
  2002 / James T. Perry, Gary P. Schneider.
    p. cm.
  Includes index.
  ISBN 0-324-18991-5 (alk. paper)
  1. Accounting—Data processing.
  2. Transaction systems (Computer systems)
  I. Microsoft Access. II. Schneider, Gary P.,
  1952– III. Title.

HF5679 .P4195 2003
657′.0285′5369—dc21   2002071953

PREFACE

Traditional methods of recording economic events and accumulating accounting information are giving way to database technology in today's accounting information systems. As we write *Using Access 2002 in Accounting*, we find that organizations increasingly depend on databases that include accounting and other operating data for mission-critical information. Accounting information systems—or the accounting views of enterprise-wide databases—contain much of the information managers use to make decisions and control operations. These databases also store the information that accountants use to prepare the formal accounting reports, such as year-end financial statements that organizations issue to external users. As a professional accountant, you will play a central role in ensuring that the accounting systems you use, audit, and help design will deliver timely, accurate, and complete information. This book will help you learn how to use modern databases such as Access to perform that role effectively.

This text describes how database management systems provide design tools that information systems professionals and accountants can use to build accounting systems. The text assumes that you have obtained a working knowledge of accounting principles and builds on that knowledge. This book will help you develop your understanding of the theory and practice of relational database management systems in accounting settings. With that foundation, the book shows you how to build the elements of accounting systems using Access.

The book begins by explaining how to use the Windows operating environment. It then reviews the history and theory of relational database systems and describes practical uses of Microsoft Access.

Chapter 1 provides a firm grounding in the fundamentals of the Windows operating systems. This chapter may be a review for some of you; for others, this will be your first hands-on introduction to the Windows operating system. Chapter 2 introduces Microsoft Access database management software. You will learn the basics of using tables to store information, displaying database contents, finding answers to questions with database queries, using forms to enter data, and printing database reports. Chapter 3 presents a concise, yet thorough, introduction to database theory. You will learn how to use normalization rules to structure your data in ways that avoid redundancy and data loss. This chapter also introduces user views and entity-relationship modeling. Additionally, you will learn the differences between database accounting systems and double-entry bookkeeping systems, and then you will learn about the advantages of the database approach. You will learn how to classify business activities by level of complexity. You will also learn to identify the business activities that occur in four important transaction cycles. Finally, you will learn how to perform basic database operations that enable you to locate subsets of table rows or columns and to collect information from several related database tables. In Chapter 4 you create several tables and queries—tasks for which we provide step-by-step guidance. You will be happy to know that you can perform all of these database functions *without writing a single line of program code*. When you have finished Chapter 4, you will have the database skills you need to create both tables and queries—the fundamental database building blocks that deliver data to the remaining basic accounting system components. Chapter 5 provides an in-depth discussion of designing and creating Access forms and reports. You will learn how to create forms based on one table and multiple tables. Similarly, you will learn how to design and create reports using the Access Report Wizard as well as to manually create reports based on queries.

We hope you will become an active participant as you read the text and work through the step-by-step examples. You will best retain what you have read by working through the book on a computer. To reinforce your learning, we have included three types of review questions at the end of each chapter:

- Multiple-choice questions, which refresh your memory about key points in the text.

- Discussion questions, which are more general and provide a basis for interesting small group discussions of the topics.

- Exercises, which require you to use Microsoft Access to create your own accounting databases or extend the examples in the text.

By studying the text carefully, working through the examples, and using the end-of-chapter materials to reinforce your knowledge, you will learn how to use database management software to design and build accounting systems that deliver timely, accurate information to managers and financial statement users.

TO THE INSTRUCTOR

Many accounting professors believe that the accounting information systems course is the greatest teaching challenge in the curriculum. One of our goals in writing the books in the *Building Accounting Systems* series is to help make your job of teaching accounting systems easier. Accounting practice has evolved from manual journals and ledgers to database accounting systems—even in very small firms. At the same time, many introductory accounting courses have shifted to financial statement user and managerial decision-maker orientations from the more traditional preparer orientations. Despite this decreased emphasis on the mechanics of accounting in the introductory courses, accounting majors still need to understand how accounting systems record, classify, and aggregate economic events. We wrote this book to help you give your students a solid introduction to database principles *and* valuable hands-on experience in constructing accounting systems. By using Microsoft Access—object-based software that features an intuitive graphic user interface—this book vastly reduces the amount of class time you must spend on non-accounting systems matters. The text's step-by-step instructions can reduce your time and drudgery in the computer lab. The time you do spend with students in class or in the computer lab will not be wasted on mundane "click here and then click there" instructing because we have filled this book with detailed instructions and examples to save you that kind of work. We have designed this *Using Access 2002 in Accounting* edition for use by students who have no background in Microsoft Access. We wrote it in direct response to calls from our colleagues for a book that included the features of our existing editions of *Building Accounting Systems*, but that would also allow them the flexibility to do other things in their courses.

We are convinced that there are at least as many different ways of teaching the accounting systems course as there are professors teaching it. Therefore, this *Using Access 2002 in Accounting* edition was designed to be flexible. In a junior- or senior-level course, this book can effectively supplement any accounting information systems text currently on the market. Adopters of this book's earlier editions have used it successfully with many different accounting information systems texts. We believe that instructors can incorporate this book into their courses in a number of interesting ways. You may want to cover all or part of the book in class. Alternatively, you might assign the book as a series of computer lab assignments or as outside reading. This edition was designed for students who are not familiar with Microsoft Access or have used Access briefly, but not in the context of accounting systems. We believe that some instructors who use their own materials to introduce the software will find this book to be an excellent Access resource.

Many accounting systems courses include some type of systems design project. A number of instructors have used earlier editions of this book as an effective springboard for such projects. Students can extend the book's examples or use them as analogs for the real-world systems they design and build in their projects. Students will feel better prepared to take on the challenge of a systems design project after they have experienced successes with creating the two example accounting systems in this book.

Although we designed this book to meet the needs of the undergraduate accounting major systems class, it is flexible enough to be used in other settings. Many community colleges now offer a computer accounting course. This bo.

would serve well as either the main text or a supplement in such a course. Instructors of graduate accounting systems courses may wish to assign this book as a project for those students who lack undergraduate database course work or as a quick refresher for students whose undergraduate database exposure is dated. Instructors of information systems auditing courses at the graduate level have also found the book to be a useful supplement in those courses. The book includes a number of features that will make your teaching easier:

- An exposition of the database approach to accounting systems that includes a comparison to double-entry bookkeeping procedures.

- A concise introduction to database theory in Chapter 3 that includes thorough discussions of normalization and entity-relationship modeling.

- Step-by-step instructions that guide the student through each example.

- Numerous figures that show the computer screen at key points in each task and that show finished forms and printed reports.

- A Companion CD that contains tables, files, queries, forms, reports, and other information to help students complete the exercises and follow along with the examples in the text.

You will find that many of the tables include comprehensive examples of significant size. By including these very large tables, we hope to give students an experience that resembles working with real-world databases.

The Instructor's Manual is available online at the Perry/Schneider Web site (http://perry.swcollege.com) to adopters. The Web site contains detailed lecture suggestions for each chapter and solutions to all end-of-chapter questions and exercises. The online Instructor's Manual also contains solutions to all computer exercises in the form of Microsoft Access tables, forms, queries, and reports, and contains the text of the Instructor's Manual, in both Microsoft Word and Adobe PDF formats, to help you create customized lecture notes, transparencies, and presentation software slide shows for classroom use.

ORGANIZATION OF THE BOOK

The text contains five chapters that provide a brief introduction to the use of databases in accounting systems. This *Using Access 2002 in Accounting* edition of the text assumes that students have never used Microsoft Access or the Windows environment within which it operates (though most students probably are already familiar with Windows 98, NT, or 2000).

Chapter 1 presents an overview of Windows 98/NT/2000 and emphasizes fundamental operations such as launching programs, examining object properties, and manipulating windows. This chapter will help students that are computer novices attain sufficient Windows proficiency to use any Windows database management product.

Chapter 2 familiarizes students with the Microsoft Access database management system. All major database elements are discussed including tables, queries, forms, and reports.

Chapter 3 presents a brief history of databases; describes the requirements for databases to be in first, second, and third normal forms; and describes how database accounting is different and why firms are using database accounting systems. Chapter 3 also identifies firms as service, merchandising, or manufacturing, discusses the transaction cycle elements that exist in each type of firm, and gives students sufficient grounding in database theory to create well-designed, anomaly-free databases.

Chapter 4 provides students with hands-on experience in building database tables and queries. Beginning with tables and then queries, students learn that tables are the data containers holding all database data. Queries, they learn, provide a vehicle for asking questions and making table-wide changes to data.

Chapter 5 contains a thorough discussion about designing and building Access forms for data entry, data viewing, and designing and building Access reports to supply management with hard copy output. Building on a foundation of tables and queries, the forms and reports discussion provides the capstone Microsoft Access experience needed to completely understand the role of a database management system in producing accounting objects.

ACCESS INSTALLATION NOTE

This book assumes that you have installed Microsoft Access 2002 on your computer. The installation that Microsoft provides as part of its default "Typical" installation option does not install all of the program elements that you will need to complete the exercises in this book. You must include the set of program features titled "Additional Wizards" when you install Access. The installation dialog box in which you make this selection appears in Figure P-1 on page viii.

If your original installation did not include the "Additional Wizards" option, you can reinstall Access by inserting your Access 2002 or Office XP installation CD and selecting install. The options that were selected during the last installation on that computer will appear in the dialog box. Change the Additional Wizards option as shown in the figure and continue with the installation. The reinstallation will not delete any Access files that you have created; it will only update the Access program files to include the additional program features you have selected.

ABOUT THE AUTHORS

Jim Perry is a Professor of Management Information Systems at the University of San Diego School of Business. He is the co-author of over 57 textbooks and trade books and over a dozen articles on computer security, database management systems, multimedia delivery systems, and chief programmer teams. Jim is a charter member of the Association for Information Systems. He holds a Ph

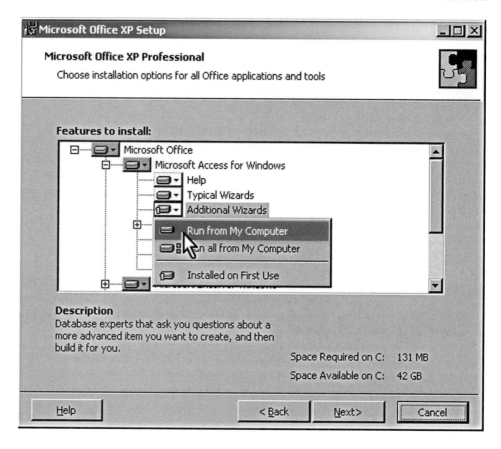

Figure P.1   Installing the Microsoft Access 2002 Additional Wizards option.

in computer science from the Pennsylvania State University and a Bachelor of Science in mathematics from Purdue University. Jim has worked as a computer security consultant to various private and governmental organizations, including the Jet Propulsion Laboratory. He was a consultant on the Strategic Defense Initiative ("Star Wars") project and served as a member of the computer security oversight committee.

Gary Schneider is an Associate Professor of Accounting and Information Systems at the University of San Diego School of Business. The author or co-author of 31 books, Gary has written more than 70 research papers on accounting, electronic commerce, and information systems topics. His work has appeared in a number of journals including the *IS Audit & Control Journal*, *Interfaces*, and the *Journal of Information Systems*. Gary is active in the American Accounting Association and has served as editor of its *Accounting Information Systems and Technology Reporter*. He has provided training and consulting services to a number of major clients, including the Gartner Group, Gateway Computer, Honeywell, and Qualcomm. In 1999, he was named a Fellow of the Gartner Institute. Gary holds a Ph.D. in accounting systems from the University of Tennessee, an MBA in accounting from Xavier University, and a BA in economics from the University of Cincinnati. He is a CPA and practiced public accounting in Ohio for fourteen years before undertaking his academic career.

ACKNOWLEDGMENTS

Creating a successful book is always a collaborative effort between authors and publisher. We work as a team to provide the best book possible. We want to thank the following reviewers for the insightful comments and suggestions they gave us on this and previous editions: A. Faye Borthick, Georgia State University; Severin Grabski, Michigan State University; Mary R. Scott, Grambling State University; and Jerry D. Siebel, University of South Florida. We would also like to thank the many professors that have used previous editions in their classes and have provided us with valuable insights and suggestions for this edition. Students in accounting information systems classes at the University of San Diego and at Georgia State University have used various versions of the manuscripts for this and previous editions of the book. We appreciate the many helpful suggestions these students provided. In particular, we want to thank former students Pamela S. Drotman for her excellent technical editing assistance on the text and accompanying digital media, and Steven French for his terrific job in generating much of the data that was incorporated into the databases.

The authors especially want to acknowledge the work of the seasoned professionals at South-Western Publishing. We thank David L. Shaut, our original acquisitions editor on the book, for his initial interest in and continual support of this project. Dave recognized an emerging need for this kind of book before any other publisher. We are grateful to Julie Lindsay, for her support of the *Building Accounting Systems* series. We extend special thanks to Carol Bennett, Sam Versetto, and the other members of the Accounting Team at South-Western. We especially appreciate the efforts of Martha Wagner, who enthusiastically encouraged and supported our proposal for the first edition of this book. We appreciate the care and attention to detail with which everyone at South-Western handled the development and production of this book.

Finally, we want to express deep appreciation to our spouses, Nancy Perry and Cathy Cosby, for their remarkable patience as we worked both ends of the clock to complete this edition of the book on a very tight schedule. We also thank our children for tolerating our absences from their lives while we were writing this book.

If you would like to contact us about the book, we would enjoy hearing from you. We welcome comments and suggestions that we might incorporate into future editions of the book. You can e-mail book-related messages to us at debit@sandiego.edu. For the latest information about *Building Accounting Systems* and related resources, please visit our Web site at http://perry.swcollege.com

DEDICATION   This text is dedicated to Nancy C. Perry and Cathryn A. Cosby

TRADEMARK LIST   The following trademarks and registered trademarks appear in this book:

1. Microsoft, Windows, Access, Word, Excel, Exchange, Internet Explorer, Fox-Pro, Paint, Office, and The Microsoft Network are registered trademarks of Microsoft Corporation. Any reference to Microsoft Windows, Access, Word, Excel, Exchange, Internet Explorer, FoxPro, Paint, Office, or The Microsoft Network refers to this note. Screen shots reprinted by permission from Microsoft Corporation.

2. Adobe is a registered trademark of Adobe Systems Incorporated. Any references to Adobe Reader refer to this note. Adobe Acrobat Reader is a trademark of Adobe Systems Incorporated in the United States and/or other countries.

CONTENTS

3   DATABASES AND ACCOUNTING SYSTEMS   111

4   TABLES AND QUERIES   165

5   ACCESS FORMS AND REPORTS   221

1 WORKING WITH WINDOWS

OBJECTIVES

This chapter presents an overview of the Microsoft Windows environment available on millions of microcomputers around the world. For those unfamiliar with Windows, you will learn the skills essential for working with it. All references in this chapter apply to Windows 98, Windows ME, Windows 2000, and Windows NT unless specifically noted. Those of you familiar with Windows will probably discover some new techniques while reading this chapter. Several key Windows features are presented. In particular, you will learn how to:

- Understand what objects are found on the desktop.
- Open, close, maximize, and minimize windows.
- Launch an application using the Start button.
- Use a dialog box.
- Exit an application.
- Use Explorer to manage files and programs and to launch a program.
- Create folders in Explorer.
- Get help on the current application.
- Launch multiple applications and switch between them.
- Pass data between Windows programs.
- Create and use desktop shortcuts.
- Modify the Start menu.
- Relocate the Taskbar.
- Exit Windows.

AN OVERVIEW OF WINDOWS

Windows provides a convenient work surface from which you can run applications, manage files, and run your business. By simply clicking the Start button and selecting a program, you can launch Microsoft Word, Microsoft Access, or any of the thousands of Windows programs available. One significant advantage of using Windows is that you can run more than one program at the same time. For instance, you could be writing a memo to your sales manager using your favorite word processing program, Word. When you are ready to summarize last month's sales figures, you can quickly switch to Excel, your tried and true spreadsheet program, to review the sales figures found in last quarter's spreadsheet. Switching between applications is as easy as clicking a button.

Another advantage of Windows is that transferring data between Windows programs is easy. Suppose you want to mail letters to customers in a particular state—Washington, for example—informing them about a special product promotion available for a limited time only. You need to create Word documents for each customer in Washington containing details about the promotion. This would be a daunting task if you had to actually type each letter individually. However, you know that Word can use Windows tools to retrieve information from an Access database containing your customers' names and addresses. Microsoft Word and Microsoft Access work together seamlessly to deliver database information to Word documents on demand. With Windows, Word, and Access, it is simple to create a form letter for each customer as well as mailing labels. Figure 1.1 shows an example of a Word document (bottom), a sheet of Avery 5160 mailing labels, and an Access database (right) that dynamically supplies customer addresses to both forms. This is an example of Windows information sharing between applications employing Dynamic Data Exchange (DDE).

Another way that applications can share information is called Object Linking and Embedding, or OLE. Newer than DDE, OLE actually embeds a *copy* of the data into another document. For instance, you could place a copy of the customer database, or a subset of it, into a Word document. In this example, the Word document is the *container* and the Access database, supplying the database information to the document, is known as the *server*. (You will see this container/server relationship illustrated throughout this text.)

Because of its ease of use and the advantages mentioned, Windows is a well-established standard among PC users. In the sections that follow, you will learn the most important features of Windows—those skills and techniques essential to thriving in today's business world.

Starting Windows

Windows automatically executes after your computer is turned on and has successfully completed some hardware tests. You will first see some introductory screens, and then the Windows desktop will appear. Depending on how you have set up Windows, you may be asked to type a user name and password. If asked to do so, follow the steps outlined in the following section.

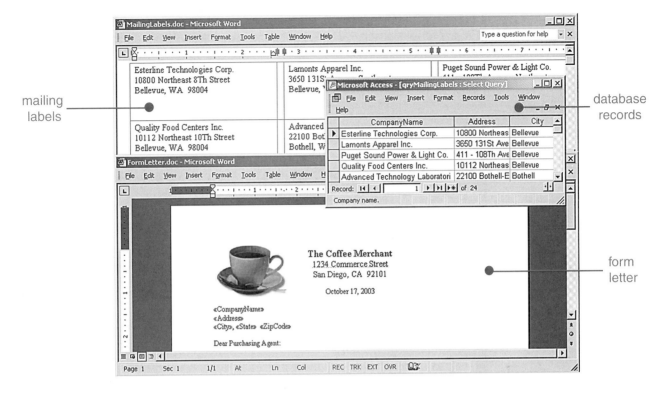

Figure 1.1 Linking database information to Word documents.

Logging On to Windows

If your computer is in a school or corporation, you may be required to log on to Windows. After starting Windows, you will see the Windows logo on the screen followed by a dialog box requesting that you enter your user name and password in order to gain access to the computer. (Windows NT and Windows 2000 may ask you to press Ctrl+Alt+Del prior to logging in.) You may simply enter your last name and a password assigned by your instructor or supervisor. Check with your instructor or the lab supervisor. The actual process of logging on is simple once you know your user name and password. Type your user name and press Tab to place the cursor in the Password text box. Type your password and press Enter to complete the Windows log-on process. Within a few moments, the Windows desktop is displayed.

What's on the Desktop

Windows uses the *desktop* metaphor whereby the computer screen simulates, through icons, one's desktop containing various objects. Everything on the desktop is an *object*, meaning it is a thing having properties or characteristics. Examples of objects on the desktop include My Computer, Network Neighborhood, and so on. You can even add *shortcuts* to programs, printers, and documents. Figure 1.2 shows an example of a Windows desktop. Keep in mind that your desktop may look different because it may contain a varying number of objects that are arranged in unique ways. However, our figure is representative of the major elements found on the desktop.

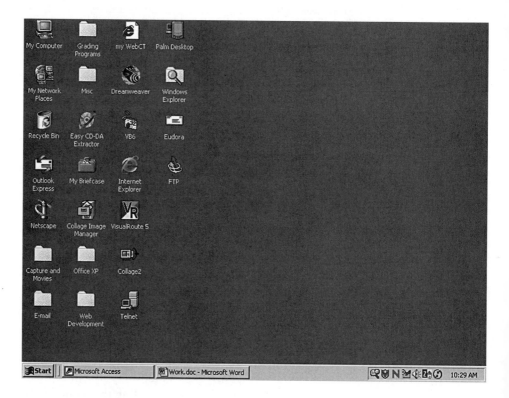

Figure 1.2   Windows desktop example.

Your desktop probably contains the My Computer icon. My Computer is the entrance to all the disk drives and files on your computer. Through My Computer you can examine the floppy disk drive, hard drives, CD drives, and the system configuration.

The Recycle Bin icon holds files and folders that have been deleted. Anything in the Recycle Bin can either be recovered or removed permanently. Once objects have been removed, they cannot be restored.

Your desktop may show an Internet icon. It provides a convenient way to access the World Wide Web (WWW) using Microsoft's full-featured Internet Explorer. Navigating the WWW couldn't be simpler, because it uses a page metaphor to display information.

Desktops can also contain My Briefcase. This icon enables you to keep various copies of your files synchronized and up to date whether you are working on the road, at home, or in the office. When you are finished working on a file on your laptop computer, for instance, you can use My Briefcase to update the file on your main computer when you get back to the office. Files are automatically and nearly effortlessly maintained so that you need not worry about which file is the latest version and which file should be deleted.

The *Taskbar* is the gray area that normally rests on the bottom of your screen. (You can move the Taskbar to the top or sides of the screen if you wish, and you can even hide it until it is needed.) The Windows Taskbar contains the Start button (see Figure 1.2), which you can use to quickly find a file or start a program; buttons representing programs that are currently running; and the task tray. Two programs are currently running, and the buttons on the Taskbar indicate their names: Microsoft Word and Microsoft Access. The *task tray* contains small icons representing programs that are always in memory. For example, the task tray shown in Figure 1.2 shows several icons representing programs to schedule regularly run system tasks, guard against computer viruses, and other important programs. The task tray also displays the current time.

Using the Mouse

Before we examine Windows any further, it is important to understand how to use the essential pointing device, the mouse. Although you can use Windows without a mouse, it is considerably more difficult. Five terms, describing different ways to use the mouse, occur throughout this text: *point, click, right-click, double-click,* and *drag.*

When we ask you to "point to Programs" or "point to Find in the Start menu," we simply mean you should move the mouse pointer so that its tip is directly over the desired object on the screen. Pointing in Windows frequently opens displays, menus, or submenus.

When you are instructed to "click the mouse" or "click," press and release the left mouse button. If you are to "click on the . . . button" shown onscreen, move the mouse pointer to that element and then press and quickly release the left mouse button once. Select an item onscreen by moving the mouse pointer (the arrowhead) to the item and clicking once with the left mouse button. Once you select an item, you can perform various activities. For example, you can move an icon from one place on your desktop to another after you have selected it.

The action of right-clicking is similar to clicking except that you use the right mouse button. For example, if you wanted to learn about a desktop icon's properties, you would first right-click the icon to display a shortcut menu.

Frequently, we will ask you to *double-click* some object on the Windows work surface. When you double-click an icon representing a program, that program is activated. To double-click, quickly click the left mouse button twice. If you don't click rapidly enough, you will simply select the object twice, not activate it.

Another way to use the mouse is to *drag* an object. In a word processing program, for example, you might want to move a sentence from one place to another. You can do this by dragging it. To drag any object, select the object (click it), press and hold down the left mouse button, and move the mouse. It takes a little practice, but you will master it quickly. Dragging is useful in several circumstances. For instance, you can enlarge a window by dragging its border or corner. You can also reduce or enlarge a Windows help frame by dragging a border toward or away from the opposite border.

BECOMING MORE FAMILIAR WITH WINDOWS

Anatomy of a Window

Most windows contain the same elements. Figure 1.3 shows a typical window that opens when you double-click My Computer. A window has a frame or border that defines its outer edges. The My Computer window shown can be sized— that is, the window can be stretched or shrunk by dragging any edge. In the lower right corner is the *size grip*, which is a special handle to make obvious to the user how to resize a window. Along the window's top is a *Title bar* containing the name of the application, current topic, or current document. The current application, My Computer, is displayed in this case. When a window is active, its Title bar is a darker color than the Title bars of other windows.

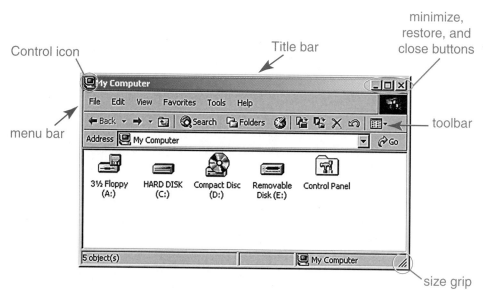

Figure 1.3   Components of a window.

On the extreme left of the Title bar is a *control icon*, which can be opened to manipulate the window with the keyboard. You can close a window by double-clicking its control icon, though you will find it far easier to use the mouse for most actions. Three window buttons appear on the right end of each window's

Title bar. These are called the Minimize, Maximize/Restore, and Close buttons. You would click the *Minimize* button (the button that looks like a dash) to remove the window from view (the program remains running). If the window does not fill the screen, as ours does in Figure 1.3, then the middle button, called the *Maximize* button, causes the window to fill the screen when the button is clicked. If the window is already maximized, then the middle button looks like two overlapping windows and is called the *Restore* button. When you click Restore, the window is reduced to less than full screen. You use the *Close* button in the upper right corner of a window to close the window with one click. If the window represents a program, rather than a group, then clicking the Close button terminates execution of the application.

Below the Title bar is the menu bar. Clicking any of the menu items displays a pull-down menu, which contains commands that you can select. If you click the Control Panel's Edit menu, for instance, you will see the pull-down menu shown in Figure 1.4. A list of commands is associated with each menu of any Windows program. When you select a menu, its pull-down menu is displayed. You can select a menu either by clicking it with the mouse or by pressing the Alt key and the letter underlined in the menu name. For example, notice that the letter E in the Edit menu (see Figure 1.4) is underlined. Pressing Alt and E simultaneously displays the Edit menu. Throughout the text, we use a standard notation to indicate keys that are pressed simultaneously. For example, Alt+E denotes pressing and holding the Alt key and pressing and releasing the letter E to invoke the Edit menu. The key that follows Alt varies depending on the menu to be selected.

When you want to select a command in a pull-down menu, simply point to it with the mouse. The selection bar highlights the designated command. To execute a highlighted command, simply click the mouse. Alternatively, you can use the arrow keys to move up and down the pull-down list of commands, pressing

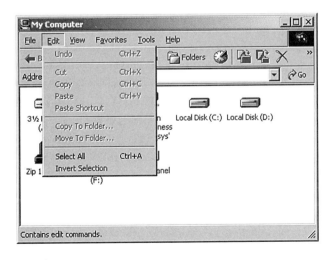

Figure 1.4 A typical Windows pull-down menu.

Enter at any point to execute the highlighted command. Some commands are inapplicable in certain situations. Whenever a command cannot be selected from a menu, it is *dimmed* (light gray). The Cut, Copy, Paste, Paste Shortcut, Copy To Folder, and Move to Folder commands are dimmed in Figure 1.4. All other commands are bold (for example, Select All).

Along the window's bottom edge is the status bar. The status bar displays useful information about the window, such as the number of objects it holds or a description of a command you have selected when the window contains a running application.

When there is more information than can be displayed in the window, *scroll bars* automatically appear on the right and bottom window edges. By sliding the scroll boxes or using the scroll arrows, you can pan the window up, down, left, or right to see otherwise hidden parts of the object within the window.

Manipulating Windows

As with the other sections that follow, this section actively involves you in learning several Windows features. You will manipulate program and document windows in several ways, including moving and sizing them. To help you learn and reinforce these Windows skills, we ask you to follow up your reading with actually practicing each task being described. Two types of activities in which you can participate as you read are the *Try It* tasks and *Exercises*.

Try It tasks are smaller, more easily accomplished computer activities that take only a few moments to complete. For example, a Try It task might be to minimize, maximize, and restore a window, or it might be a description of how to switch between Microsoft Access and Windows Explorer using the Taskbar. The phrase **Try It** introduces a paragraph describing these types of activities. If the task comprises several steps, the individual steps are not numbered.

Exercises are more comprehensive activities that are central to some ongoing and important process or project that is being described in a chapter. Exercises typically consist of two or more numbered steps, the completion of which helps you to achieve some important goal. An example of an exercise is the series of steps that illustrate how to launch several Windows applications, open document windows in each application, and copy information between open windows. Such an exercise strongly reinforces how to implement information sharing between, for example, Access and Word—an essential task in business.

Try It

Let's learn a little about the computer you're using. Double-click the My Computer icon (see Figure 1.2). What happens if you click a desktop icon only once? You simply select the icon. To activate it, double-click. The My Computer window will open, displaying icons representing hardware on your computer and your network similar to Figure 1.3. Maximize the My Computer window. Right-click the icon representing drive C. The *shortcut menu* is displayed. Locate Properties in the menu (near the bottom of the list) and click it. A tabbed dialog box, showing the properties of the selected object, is displayed. Click the General tab, if necessary, to go to the page containing a pie graph. It illustrates how much space is either occupied or available on drive C. After you have had a chance to examine the display, click the question mark button called *What's This?* Notice that the mouse pointer changes to an arrow with a question mark attached to its right side. After clicking What's This?, you can move to any object and click it to obtain context-sensitive help. Move the mouse pointer down to the pie graph and click it. A brief explanation of the clicked object (the chart in this case) is displayed as in Figure 1.5. Click the help box to make it disappear. Finally, click the Close button on the dialog box to close it. Click the Close button on My Computer to close it. The desktop reappears. Moving windows about the desktop, changing their size, and closing them is intuitive in Windows. We'll direct you through some fundamental window manipulation activities next.

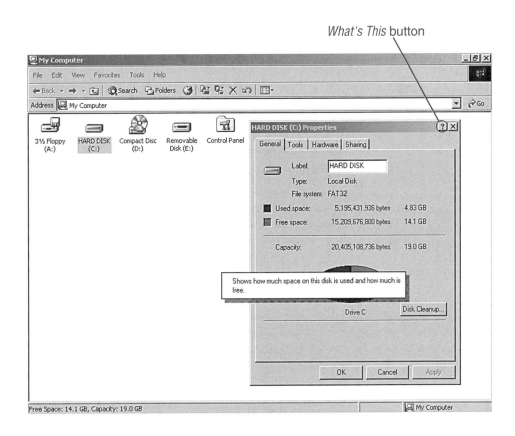

Figure 1.5 Obtaining help with the What's This? button.

Try It

Open the My Computer window again (double-click its desktop icon). Maximize the window, if necessary, so that it fills the screen (click the Maximize button, which looks like a small rectangle). Restore the window so it occupies only part of the work surface by clicking the Restore button (the icon that looks like two overlapping windows or rectangles located in the top right corner of the window). Make the window virtually disappear by pressing the Minimize button (the button in the top right corner of the My Computer window that contains a narrow line or dash). Where did the My Computer window go? When a program is minimized, a button representing it—called a *Taskbar button*—is placed on the Taskbar. Though the window disappears, its Taskbar button remains. By clicking a program's Taskbar button, you can switch from one program to another. Restore the My Computer window by clicking the Taskbar button labeled My Computer. You can change the size of a window that is not maximized. Click and drag the My Computer window's size grip away from its opposite corner to increase the window's size. Similarly, drag the size grip towards its opposite corner to reduce the window's size. You can create an infinite number of window sizes this way. Moving a window to a different part of the screen is also easy. Simply click and drag the window's Title bar to move the window anywhere you want. Move the My Computer window to the top left of your screen. Then, move it so it is approximately in the center of your screen. Finally, close the My Computer window.

Getting Help

Help is available in all Windows programs in a variety of ways. Context-sensitive help provides assistance for almost every object on the screen. Microsoft products have help screens that are actually Web pages. That is, help for Microsoft products including Windows and Microsoft Access are formatted as Web pages complete with hyperlinks that take you to related information when you click them. You have already used What's This? to obtain information about an object on the screen. *ToolTips* are another form of context-sensitive help. ToolTips are small pop-up banners that appear when you briefly hover the mouse over an object, such as a toolbar button. See for yourself.

Try It

Move the mouse pointer over the Start button, which is located at the left end of the Taskbar. After a second or two, a ToolTip appears indicating you should "Click here to begin." Likewise, you can see the date if you move the mouse pointer to the time display located in the task tray.

Windows programs supply explicit help through a Help menu. Extensive help is available on the computer. The Windows Help system provides search features, as well as contents and indexing capabilities. An excellent way to see Help in action is to try it yourself. Windows help, available from the Start button (you will learn more about the Start button in the next section), is an excellent choice. Perform the steps in the following exercise.

EXERCISE 1.1: GETTING SPECIFIC HELP

1. Click the Start button (the Start button is explained fully in the next section). The *Start menu* is displayed.
2. Click the Help menu item on the Start menu.
3. The Windows dialog box opens.
4. Select the Index tab.
5. Type **formatting** into the text box because we want help on formatting disks.
6. The help system highlights the topic *formatting disks*.
7. Click the overview subtopic in the list, and then click the Display button to view detailed help about formatting disks. The right panel in the Help dialog box describes how to format a disk (see Figure 1.6).
8. Click the Close button after reading the help information. That will close and remove the pop-up box.

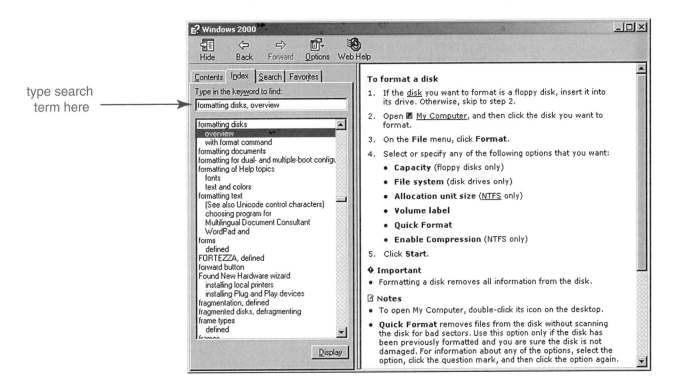

Figure 1.6 Locating help on formatting disks.

THE START MENU

The Start button, located on the left end of the Taskbar, provides the major access point for programs, documents, and other objects. The Start menu is displayed when you click the Start button, and it is a cascading menu. That is, its submenus cascade—logically flow from—the main menu items.

Opening the Start Menu

Opening the Start menu is easy. Simply click the Start button to display its menu items (see Figure 1.7). Standard menu items found on the Start menu are Programs, Documents, Settings, Search, Help, Run, and Shut Down. Some of the menu items have right arrows. These arrows indicate that the menu item leads to a submenu, which opens when you merely point to the menu item by moving the mouse over the item and pausing briefly.

the Start menu

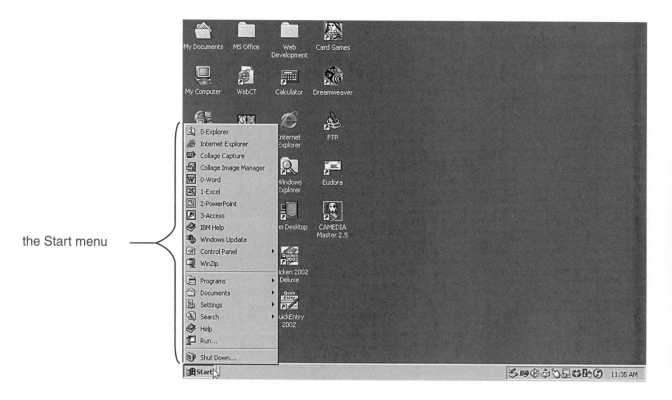

Figure 1.7   The Start menu.

The Programs Menu Item

The Programs menu item cascades to reveal program items and program group items. Only executable items are found in the Programs menu, not data or other nonexecutable objects. Programs include Windows Explorer and other application programs you have installed on your computer. When you point to a group item, Windows reveals more entries. For example, Accessories is a group item that contains the usual collection of standard Windows groups and programs (see Figure 1.8). You simply point to Accessories and then select a program or group item from the cascaded menu. You can close each of the cascading menus in turn by selecting a menu item from a previous menu. Similarly, you can close all menus except the Start menu by moving the mouse pointer to one of the Start menu items that doesn't cascade, such as Run or Help.

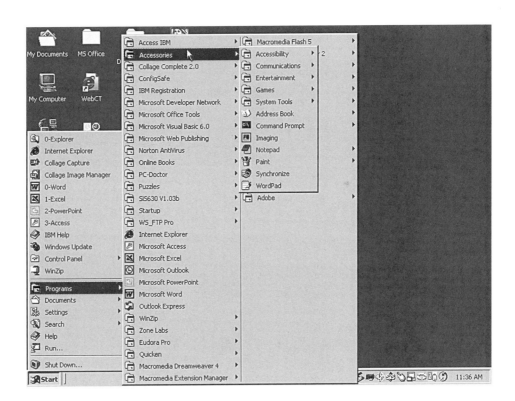

Figure 1.8   Displaying submenus of the Start menu.

Windows provides keyboard alternatives to the mouse. For instance, you can press Ctrl+Esc to open the Start menu. Once open, the Start menu lists items that you can select by using the arrow keys. The up and down arrow keys move up and down an open menu, and the right and left arrow keys move to a cascading menu or the previous menu, respectively. Press the Alt key to close all open menus.

Try It

Open the Start menu and move the mouse pointer to Programs. Pause and the cascade menu opens. Next, move to the right and point to Accessories. Move the mouse pointer down the menu items to WordPad. Finally, close all menus.

The Documents Menu Item

The Documents menu item displays a list of the 15 objects you have most recently used. If you worked on an Access database named *accounts payable.mdb* and then opened Microsoft Word to write a letter you later saved as *New accounts.doc*, then those two document names would appear in the Documents menu item list. The Documents menu facilitates returning quickly and easily to the items with which you have recently worked. For example, you return to your computer after a day's absence, start Windows, click the Start menu button, point to Documents, and then select the document with which you want to work. (In this context, the word *document* refers to a variety of objects, including a word processing document, a spreadsheet, a database, or a graphic image.) This reinforces the notion that you focus on the object that you want to work with, rather than worrying about which program or tool is required to load and manipulate the document— the document "knows" what program is needed to operate on it.

Try It

See what documents people using your computer have recently used. Click Start and point to Documents. The cascade menu will reveal the document names, or *empty* if the list has been erased. (You will learn how to erase the Documents list later.)

The Settings Menu Item

The Settings menu item allows you to change global Windows settings and options. It contains three menu items: Control Panel, Printers, and Taskbar. Control Panel contains icons representing a large number of system settings you can change and actions you can take. For example, you can add or remove programs from the Control Panel group, change your monitor's display characteristics, or alter the date and time. Clicking the Printers item takes you to a group that adds, deletes, or modifies printers available to your system. Taskbar allows you to modify the structure and contents of the Start menu and provides a way to change selected properties of the Taskbar. You could choose to hide the Taskbar or hide the clock, which is customarily displayed in the task tray on the right end of the Taskbar.

The Search Menu Item

Having a document-centric system like Windows aids your productivity; however, it is not useful if you cannot locate the document you want. That's when the Search menu item goes to work. You can use Search to locate files or folders on any disk drive, including floppy drives. In addition, you can find files or folders on any computer on any network to which your computer is attached. If you have opted to use the on-line service Microsoft Network, you can locate files on it as well. If you cannot find a file on your hard disk, you can invoke the Search menu item to search through every file on your hard drive.

Try It

See if you can locate the Windows file called *msaccess*. Search for it. Click the Start button, point to Search, and click For Files or Folders. When the Search Results dialog box opens, type **msaccess** in the *Search for files or folders named* text box and ensure that the Look in text box contains *My Computer*. If it does not, then click the list box drop-down list arrow, scroll to the top of the list, and click My Computer. Click the Search Now button to start the search process. Windows begins searching for any files or folders that begin with *msaccess*. Shortly thereafter, files are displayed in the search results window. After you have reviewed the names, click the dialog box's Close button.

The Help Menu Item

The Help menu item, which you used earlier, provides systemwide help at the click of a button. Select Help whenever you want to find more information on a Windows topic. Product-specific help is best obtained through the Help menu of the product itself, because software product manufacturers supply rich help content along with their programs. If you want help on Microsoft Access, it is best to seek help from the Help menu within Access. Help on creating Windows shortcuts—a topic that is common across applications—can be found by using the Start menu Help menu item.

The Run Menu Item

The Run menu item provides a way to run a program by simply typing the program's name and pressing Enter. Users often apply the Run command to launch infrequently used programs that might not be represented on the Start menu or its submenus. When you want to launch a program from the Run menu item, click Start, click Run, and enter the program's name, including the full path, in the *Open* text box. If you do not know the program's exact location on the disk, you can choose the Browse button and search through folders until you locate it. Or you can use Search to locate the program. If you use the latter method, then you can double-click the program within the search results list to execute it. If you find yourself using the Run command frequently for a particular program, consider placing the program in the Programs menu item or placing on the desktop a *shortcut* to the program (we will show you how to do that later in this chapter).

The Shut Down Menu Item

It is incorrect to simply turn off your computer when you are finished using Windows. In fact, Windows requires you to follow a simple procedure to shut down your computer. Doing so protects files and other data from being corrupted or saved improperly. In short, never turn off your computer while Windows is running. A Shut Down menu item is available as a one-step Windows exit procedure. To shut down Windows prior to system power off, click the Start menu and click Shut Down. A dialog box containing your options is displayed (see Figure 1.9). Click the list box arrow and then choose the option "Shut down" if you want to turn off your computer for an extended period (more than a few hours). If you want to restart your computer, then click "Restart" in the list of choices.

Use caution. If you are using a computer in a laboratory with several computers, you probably should *not* shut it down. Always check with your instructor or an available lab assistant before selecting the Shut Down option. If you merely want to restore the computer desktop to its original state before leaving the lab, then select the option "Restart."

Figure 1.9   The Shut Down Windows dialog box.

WORKING WITH PROGRAMS AND DATA

WordPad, a close relative of the full-featured Microsoft Word, is a word processor that comes with Windows. We will describe and use WordPad to help illustrate several mouse and keyboard techniques that can be used in other Windows products. Perhaps the best way for you to become better acquainted with the Windows environment is to go through a complete cycle: launching a program, opening a document, altering some of the document's text, and printing the final result. We show you that process in the paragraphs that follow.

Launching Applications Directly

The following exercise guides you through the process of executing (sometimes called *launching*) the WordPad program. Subsequent exercises continue the cycle to its conclusion—a finished letter ready for mailing.

EXERCISE 1.2: LAUNCHING AN APPLICATION

1. Click the Start button.
2. Point to Programs in the Start menu.
3. Point to Accessories in the menu that cascades from Programs.
4. Locate the WordPad menu item and click it once. If necessary, maximize the WordPad window. WordPad opens and displays an empty document.

Next, you will use a menu to open a document and make a change to it. Doing this gives you practice using a typical Windows application menu. To read a document from a disk or CD into the WordPad window, you *open* a document. Open is a command found in the File menu of almost any Windows application.

First, let's discuss a few disk-naming conventions we will use throughout the text. The exact names of your internal hard disk, floppy disk(s), and CD drives vary depending on the configuration of your computer; so, we adopt the following disk names to keep things simple and consistent. We refer to your floppy drive as drive A, though it could be drive A or B. We assume you have at least one hard drive (though you may have more than one), which we refer to as drive C. Finally, drive D refers to the CD-ROM drive. So, simply remember this: Drive A is the floppy disk drive, drive C is the hard disk drive, and drive D is the CD-ROM drive.

To prepare for the next exercise, place the Companion CD, which came with your text, into the CD-ROM drive D. If your CD-ROM drive is E, for example, simply substitute E whenever we refer to drive D. Note: If an AutoPlay dialog box automatically opens shortly after you insert your CD-ROM, Windows is trying to help. It thinks you want to install new software from the CD. Simply click the dialog box Close button to remove the dialog box and proceed to the next exercise.

EXERCISE 1.3: OPENING A DOCUMENT

1. With WordPad still open, click the File menu to display its menu. Note that you can also press Alt+F to pull down the File menu.
2. Click Open or move to Open with the arrow keys, and then press Enter. The Open dialog box appears. Dialog boxes require you to supply additional information and, occasionally, make decisions by clicking various check boxes, option buttons, and other objects within the dialog box. A list of file names (if any) found on one of the available disk drives is displayed in the File Name list box. Notice, however, that only files with .doc extensions are displayed. Those files are stored in a form compatible with both WordPad and Word.
3. Click the arrow on the Look in drop-down list box and select the CD-ROM drive (drive D or E). A list of ten folders called Ch01 through Supplement appears.
4. Double-click the Ch01 folder to open it, click the Files of Type list arrow, and then click the Word for Windows (*.doc) choice in the drop-down list (see Figure 1.10).
5. Open the file *FallWashPromotion.doc* by double-clicking it.

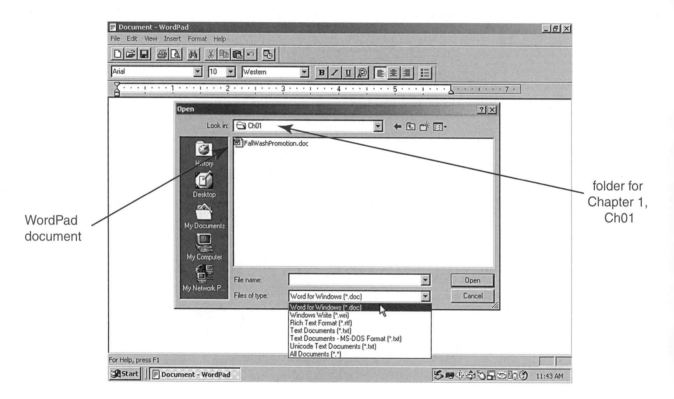

WordPad document

folder for Chapter 1, Ch01

Figure 1.10   Open dialog box.

The document you see in WordPad is a letter to selected customers of The Coffee Merchant. It will be mailed to customers in the Washington state area promoting a special sale for a limited time. The letter displayed in WordPad illustrates a few typical Windows operations and WordPad procedures.

WordPad's Edit menu commands are similar to those found in other Windows products such as Excel or Word. With the *FallWashPromotion.doc* document still visible, let's locate and replace the two placeholder-phrases *company-city* and *company-state* with an actual customer's city and state. There is no need to replace the other placeholder tags that you see in the inside address right now. We just want you to briefly experience a typical replace operation.

EXERCISE 1.4: SEARCH AND REPLACE

1. Select the Edit menu (click Edit or press Alt+E).
2. Select the Replace command (notice the shortcut key combination Ctrl+H invokes replace without first selecting the Edit menu).

    The *insertion point*, a blinking vertical bar, is in the leftmost position in the Find what text box. The insertion point indicates where typed characters will appear.
3. In the Find what text box of the Find dialog box, type **company-city** and press Tab to move to the Replace with text box. (The characters in the Find what text box are often called the *search string*.)
4. In the Replace with text box, enter the replacement string—those characters that replace any or all occurrences of the search string company-city. Type **Seattle** in the Replace with text box.

    Because the search string is long enough to be unique, there is no need to check either of the check boxes (Match whole word only or Match case). Figure 1.11 shows the completed Replace dialog box.
5. Click the Replace All button to replace all occurrences of company-city with Seattle.
6. Click OK when the search ends.
7. Repeat steps 3 through 6, entering **company-state** in step 3 and **Washington** in step 4.
8. Click the Close button in the Replace dialog box title bar to close the dialog box.

EXERCISE 1.5: PRINTING PAGES AND EXITING

1. Click the File menu to display its commands.
2. Click Print. The Print dialog box opens.
3. Click the Pages option button found in the Page Range panel. The bullet to the left of *Pages* is darkened, indicating that it is the current choice among the Print Range options.
4. Type *1* to print only page 1. The completed dialog box is shown in Figure 1.12.
5. Click the Print button to print the file.
6. Click File, click Exit, and then click No when asked if you want to save changes. The document closes, and Windows closes the WordPad application.

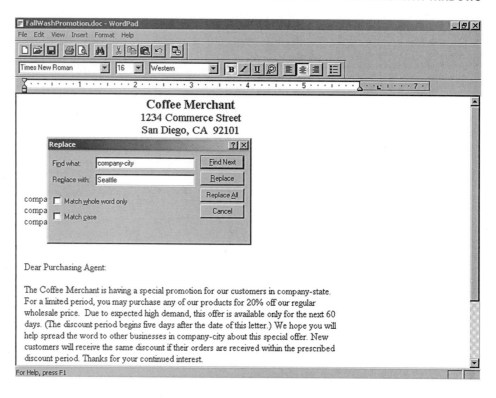

Figure 1.11　Replace dialog box.

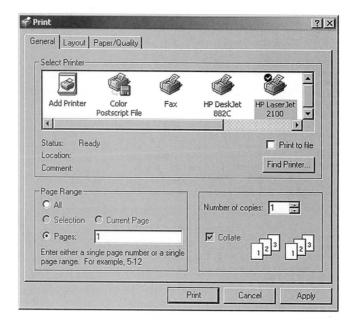

Figure 1.12　Print dialog box.

Launching an Application from a File

Launching a program by double-clicking a data file defines the concept of a document-centric system, which we mentioned earlier. In contrast, the previous section illustrated how to open WordPad and then open a document found on the Companion CD. This roundabout method exemplifies the old *program-centric* approach to microcomputer computing. You will find the document-centric approach much faster, more efficient, and error-free. In this section, we introduce you briefly to this faster method. Instead of directing you to a program and then a file to be manipulated by a program, we'll simply tell you the name of a data file on the Companion CD and ask you to find the data and launch the program that created it. Two questions come to mind. First, how does one find the file—especially considering the size of the CD and the number of files it contains? Second, what program must be launched in order to view or modify the data file? The answer to the first question is that you let the system search the entire Companion CD for you. As for the second question, the system automatically associates a program with a data file as long as the file has a recognized *secondary name* (or extension, as it is sometimes called).

Let's try this approach to computing: find a file and load its associated program. The next two exercises show you how to do just that. In the first exercise, you will use a very helpful program called Find. Find locates files and directories by name on any disk drive. Suppose you know that a particular file is stored on the Companion CD, but you cannot remember where. All you remember is part of the file name—the first part of the file name is *Olympic* and has something to do with the Olympic games.

EXERCISE 1.6: LOCATING A FILE

1. Click the Start button to display the Start menu.
2. Point to Search. The Search submenu is displayed.
3. Click For Files or Folders, indicating you want to search for a file (or folder).
   The Search Results dialog box displays.
4. Type **Olympic** in the *Search for files or folders named* text box.
   This is the partial file name that the Find program will attempt to locate.
5. Ensure that your Companion CD is in the CD drive. Then, click the drop-down arrow on the Look in list box and click your CD drive (drive D in our examples).
6. Click the Search Now button to begin the search. (Keep the Search Results window open because you are going to use it again shortly.)

Within a short time, the Find program locates and displays all file or folder names it found that match, completely or partially, the file name you specified. Figure 1.13 shows that it found only one file on the CD, *OlympicHostCountries .wri*.

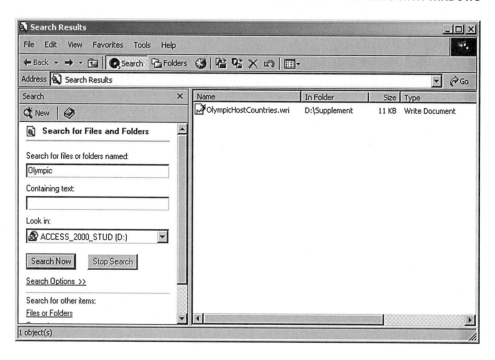

Figure 1.13   Locating a file using Search.

Now that you have found the file, you want to modify it. Suppose you don't know what program was used to create the file. That's okay, because the file name extension (or secondary name) is usually associated with a particular program. Files ending with .xls, for example, are Microsoft Excel files. Similarly, files ending with .mdb are Microsoft Access database files. You don't have to know these facts in order to invoke the program that created the file. The system remembers *associations* like those—file name extensions and their related programs. The next exercise shows you how simple it is to execute the program associated with the file that the Find program just located.

EXERCISE 1.7: LAUNCHING A PROGRAM FROM A DATA FILE

1. Make sure the Search Results window is still available and displaying the located file, *OlympicHostCountries.wri*.
2. Double-click the file name *OlympicHostCountries.wri* located in the list of located files.
3. WordPad, a Windows-supplied word processing program, is launched and the Olympic document appears in a WordPad document window. The document lists information about the modern Olympics, including the host countries and participant information.

4. Personalize the document by inserting your name in the upper right corner: Move the insertion point to the top of the document and press Enter twice to open up two new lines. Then press Tab several times to move to the right in the new, first line and type your name. (The font may be too large for your liking. In that case, select your name, select Format, Font, and select a smaller point size.)
5. Print the document clicking the File menu Print command.
6. Close the Search program, but leave WordPad running, because you will use it in the next section.

The preceding exercise illustrates how easy it is to launch a program from a document. This illustrates the meaning of the term *document centric*. That is, you don't have to first load the program and then load the document. Instead, simply locate the document (*document* is used here to mean any file including a database, spreadsheet, or word processed document) you want to work with and double-click its name. That loads the required program—the one that is associated with the document.

Switching between Applications

Windows is a *multitasking* operating system, which means it is capable of running more than one program at a time. You probably will find that it is most convenient to have several programs running and at the ready simultaneously. Perhaps you are working with accounts receivable files in Microsoft Access and also writing letters to customers using Microsoft Word or WordPad. To appreciate how handy the multitasking capabilities are, you have to experience it. Windows multitasking is smooth and intuitive. To illustrate how easy it is, you will start another program and practice switching between programs. Then you will learn how simple it is for two applications to share information.

EXERCISE 1.8: LAUNCH ANOTHER PROGRAM

1. Make sure that WordPad is still running.
2. Open the Start menu and select Programs.
3. Select Accessories.
4. Locate Paint in the Accessories cascade menu of programs.
5. Click Paint to launch it.

Paint is a graphics creation program supplied with Windows. After a brief pause, the Paint window appears as shown in Figure 1.14.

Now two programs are loaded and available simultaneously—WordPad and Paint. Examine the Taskbar (usually located at the bottom of your screen, though you can drag it to any of the four edges of your screen). Two Taskbar buttons represent the programs. Program Taskbar buttons provide a convenient way to switch

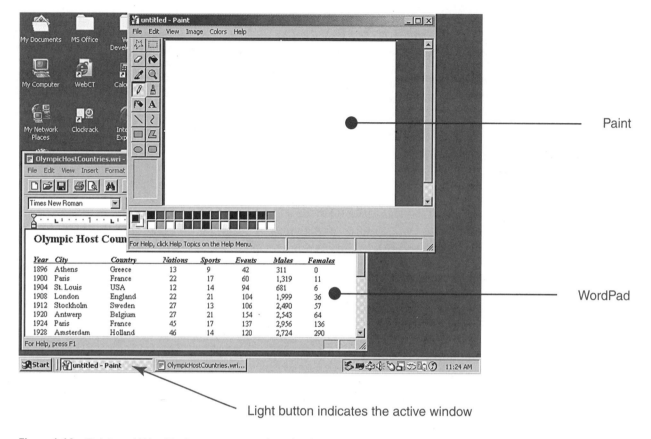

Paint

WordPad

Light button indicates the active window

Figure 1.14 Paint and WordPad programs running simultaneously.

back and forth between programs, especially when programs are minimized. There are three ways to move from one running program to another. Each method operates slightly differently, and you may eventually select a favorite way to switch between applications. The first method uses the Taskbar to switch between tasks.

EXERCISE 1.9: USING THE TASKBAR TO SWITCH BETWEEN PROGRAMS

1. Ensure that WordPad and Paint are still running.
2. Switch to WordPad, which is probably obscured by Paint's window at the moment, by clicking the WordPad button on the Taskbar. The WordPad window becomes active.
3. Switch back to Paint by clicking its Taskbar button.

Another equally effective way to move to another program that is running is to use the keystroke shortcut Alt+Tab. The next exercise shows you how.

EXERCISE 1.10: USING ALT+TAB TO SWITCH BETWEEN PROGRAMS

1. Press and hold down the Alt key and tap and release the Tab key. With the Tab key released, continue holding down the Alt key for a moment. Windows displays in the middle of the screen a marquee of running programs. A border surrounds the program icon that will be displayed if you release the Alt key (see Figure 1.15).
2. Practice moving the border between the two program icons by tapping the Tab key as you continue to hold down the Alt key.
3. Release the Tab key when the border is on the Paint icon and then release the Alt key to move to that program.

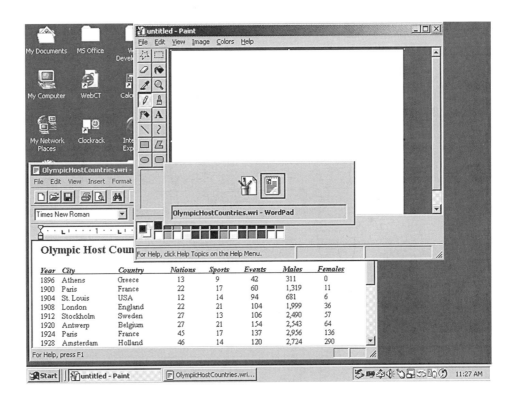

Figure 1.15 Using Alt+Tab to move between running programs.

Using the Alt+Tab key sequence is convenient for touch typists because it allows one to switch quickly between programs.

Occasionally, you may want to minimize all open windows on the desktop so that you can move to one of your desktop *shortcuts*—the icons that represent programs. Minimizing all open windows is simple. Simply right-click the Taskbar (place the mouse in any unoccupied area of the Taskbar—avoiding any Taskbar buttons) and select *Minimize All Windows* from the context menu. Knowing this method can save you time when the desktop is filled with several windows and you want a clear shot at the desktop.

The next section briefly describes how to share information between Windows applications. The particular method, called *object linking and embedding*, or *OLE* for short, simplifies producing mailing labels in Word from a subset of your customers' addresses in an Access database, for example.

SHARING DATA AMONG APPLICATIONS

Data from one program can be shared with another. In this simple but typical example, you will create a graphic in Paint and transfer the graphic to a Word-Pad document. The combined data—a graphic inside a document—is known as a *compound document*.

Try It

First, make sure that WordPad and Paint are still running. If not, launch both by clicking Start, point to the Programs menu item, point to Accessories, and click WordPad to load it. Repeat this procedure, if necessary, to load the Paint program. Switch to Paint using the Taskbar and load the graphic file *WeRecycle.bmp* found in the Ch01 folder on your Companion CD. (Click File, click Open, and navigate to the Ch01 folder to locate the file.) Click the Select tool (the dashed rectangle), and click and drag the dashed line so that it just encompasses the graphic. Then, click Copy in the Edit menu to place the graphic on the Clipboard. Switch to WordPad and load (execute File, Open) the file called *RecycleLetter.wri*, which is also found in the Ch01 folder on your Companion CD. (Remember to set the file type in Word-Pad to Windows Write in the Files of type list box.) Insert a blank line at the top of the document where the graphic will be placed. Choose Paste from WordPad's Edit menu, and move the graphic by dragging it so that it does not intersect any text. Click anywhere outside the pasted graphic to deselect it. Print the document. Figure 1.16 shows the completed compound document. When you are finished, close both the WordPad and Paint applications without saving the changes to any document or graphic.

What is important to remember from the preceding example is that you pass information between Windows applications by *copying* from one application—placing the object on the Clipboard—and then *pasting* the object into the recipient (container) document. This works for all Windows-compliant programs, including Access, Excel, and Word.

embedded graphic

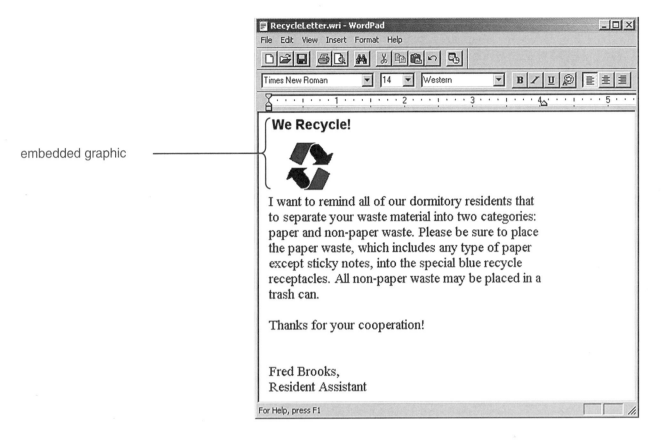

Figure 1.16 Graphic embedded in a WordPad document.

USING WINDOWS EXPLORER

Windows provides an advanced browser and file manager called Windows Explorer, often referred to simply as Explorer. Explorer allows you to perform file management duties, open and close documents, and run programs. In fact, you may find that Explorer is the interface you use most often, because it is frequently more convenient to find a file and work with it by using Explorer. By default, Windows Explorer is found in the Programs group of the Start menu. It may be located elsewhere on your institution's computers, but it is easy to find.

Try It

Launch Windows Explorer so that you can see its interface. Click the Start button, and then point to the Programs item. Finally, click the Windows Explorer item to start Explorer. (You can also launch Explorer by right-clicking the Start button and selecting *Explore* from the shortcut menu. This is probably the most convenient method.)

The Folders pane, also known as the *Tree* pane, presents a tree structure of your entire computer system including desktop objects. Each branch of the tree can be expanded or collapsed, as you desire. In the right panel is the *Contents* pane, displaying the folders, files, and other objects found in the folder that is selected and open in the Tree pane.

Normally, Explorer displays a view of your computer system beginning with your desktop—the "root" of the hierarchical or tree structure of files and devices. Emphasizing the outline structure of your disk file structure, each folder displayed can contain files and other folders. Figure 1.17 shows a typical Explorer window with folders and files.

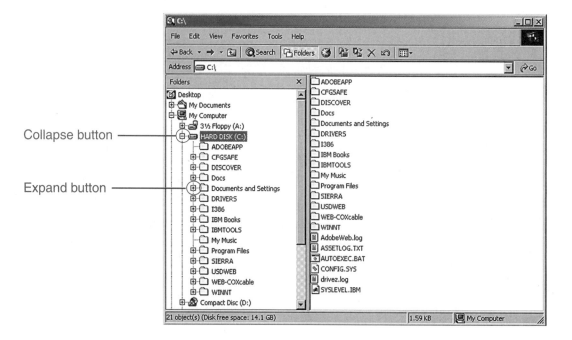

Figure 1.17   Typical Explorer window showing folders and files.

The lines in the Folders pane emphasize the relationships between folders and the folders and files that they contain. Notice the plus and minus signs at the intersection of horizontal and vertical lines in the Folders pane. A small box with a plus sign—called the *Expand* button—indicates that the object contains other objects and can be expanded to reveal further detail. Likewise, boxes with minus signs are called *Collapse* buttons. Clicking a Collapse button implodes the structure, revealing less detail.

Opening Drives, Files, and Folders

The Contents pane can show only one level of detail at a time. Therefore, you must click the Expand button on the particular drive or folder until you reach the particular file or folder for which you are looking. Suppose, for example, that you want to see what is on the Companion CD. Using Explorer, you can "walk" down through each of the folders and files, noting what files are stored in which folders. Practice expanding and collapsing folders in Explorer.

Try It

If Explorer is not running, start it (click the Start button, point to Programs, and click Windows Explorer). In the Folders pane, click the icon representing the C drive. Reveal more information about the C drive by clicking its Expand button. Your display should resemble Figure 1.17, though the exact folder and file names on your disk differ from the figure. Open the folder named *Windows* on the C drive. You may have to use the Folders pane scroll bar to move down the hierarchy of folders until the Windows folder appears. Click the Windows folder to reveal in the Contents pane the first level of folders and files in the Windows folder. Note, the Folders pane never displays file names. File names are displayed only in the Contents pane.

The preceding exercise illustrates the fundamental way you explore the disks and their contents. If you want to look at the contents of your Companion CD, then you simply click the D drive icon—the drive we are assuming is your CD—and look at the Contents pane. If you are curious about how much space is used on your disk drive and how much is left, you can use this shortcut: right-click the drive icon in the Folders pane. Then, click the Properties item on the shortcut menu that is displayed. The Properties dialog box is displayed showing a three-dimensional representation of your disk in two colors. One color represents the amount of space used; the other is the space free. Click OK to close the dialog box.

Formatting a Floppy Disk

One of the useful activities you can perform while running Explorer is formatting a disk. In particular, you can format your floppy disk, because it is highly unlikely you will want to format your hard disk(s) and you cannot format your Companion CD, which contains files, databases, and data critical to this textbook. You will want to save your database files, temporary files, and other documents you develop while reading this book and working on assignments. The logical place to save information, especially while working in a university computing laboratory, is on a floppy disk. Although the capacity of a floppy is limited, it is very portable. A floppy disk is a convenient way to transport your work from your own computer to a central computer laboratory and back. So let's learn how to format a new floppy disk, just in case you purchase an unformatted disk.

You may already know that formatting a floppy disk prepares it for first-time use. Unformatted disks have no magnetic marks identifying the beginning and ending of tracks and sectors on the disk. Tracks and sectors are the "grooves" in which all data is stored. Tracks, concentric rings on a disk, hold data. The blank spaces between concentric rings separate individual tracks. Windows Explorer can format disks quickly and easily. Once formatted, a disk can be used and reused repeatedly without ever having to be formatted again. You can also format a disk after it has been used. But be aware that the formatting process erases any data that may be present on the disk. This next exercise formats a new disk so that you can use it later in the text to store data. If you have a formatted disk containing valuable data, then do not use it for this exercise if you want to keep the data. On the other hand, this is a good opportunity to format any new disks you have just purchased.

EXERCISE 1.11: FORMATTING A DISK WITH EXPLORER

1. Launch Windows Explorer, if necessary.
2. Place a floppy disk in drive A.
3. In the Folders pane of the Explorer window, right-click the drive A icon (not the Expand button). (If drive A is not visible in the Folders Pane, then slide the Folders Pane scroll button to the *top* of the scroll bar. The icon for drive A will come into view.)
4. Click the Format item in the pop-up menu.
6. Click the Start button, and click OK if a warning message appears indicating you will erase the disk's contents.
7. Click OK to close the information dialog box, and then click the Close button to close the Format dialog box.
8. Close Explorer. (You will use it soon in the next section; so, you may wish to leave it running if you will be continuing with your reading.)

Creating Folders

Folders, like their physical counterparts in filing cabinet systems, are a convenient way to store and organize your files and other folders. Folders provide a way to partition and separate one group of project files from another. For instance, you may find it convenient to keep each chapter's homework, databases, and other work in its own folder whose name clearly indicates which chapter's material is stored therein (for example, a folder named Chapter 1). The next exercise guides you through this process using Windows Explorer. To prepare for this exercise, place a floppy disk in drive A. You may want to use the disk you formatted in the previous exercise. Then complete the following exercise.

EXERCISE 1.12: CREATING A FILE FOLDER WITH EXPLORER

1. Ensure that Explorer is running and switch to it by clicking its button on the Taskbar.
2. Place a formatted floppy in drive A.
3. Click the drive A icon in the Explorer Folders pane.
4. Select File and point to New.
5. Click Folder from the cascade menu. Windows creates a folder called New Folder and displays it in the Contents pane.
6. With the folder called "New Folder" still highlighted, type the folder's new name: **Chapter 2**. Press Enter.
7. Click the Expand button on drive A to display the new folder both in the Folders and Contents panes. Figure 1.18 shows the new folder in place.
8. Click Explorer's Close button on the title bar to terminate the program.

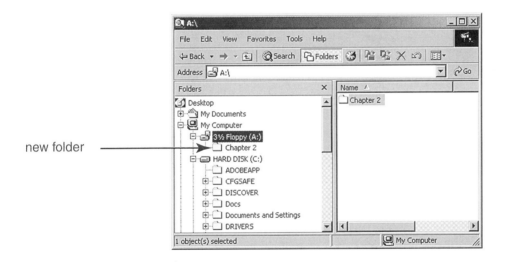

Figure 1.18 Creating a folder.

Now you know how to make new folders in which you can store files or other folders. Perhaps the most important subtlety in creating a folder is to ensure that you have selected the appropriate folder or disk *before* creating a new folder. New folders are created *below* the folder or disk currently selected in the Folders pane. That is, if you want to create a folder labeled Chapter 3 alongside the Chapter 2 folder, then first select the drive A icon. If Chapter 2 is highlighted in the Folders pane, then a new folder would be created as a *sub-folder* of Chapter 2.

Copying, Moving, Naming, and Deleting Files

The problem with opening and using Access databases that are stored on your Companion CD is that Access opens databases in a mode called read/write, whereby database records can be both read from the database and written back to it. Unless you have special software and a CD-RW drive, you cannot write data to a CD. You can read any data you wish from a CD. However, when you open a database on your CD, Access displays a warning dialog box instructing you that you cannot make any changes to your data. We have a simple solution to this dilemma.

Your Companion CD contains several databases, tables, and other objects that you will use as you read this textbook and work on the problems. In order for you to both read and write to Access databases, you have to copy files from the Companion CD to your computer's hard drive or to your floppy disk. Then, you must alter the *Read-only* file property so that the database can be both read and modified. Having done these two activities, you can operate normally on the copy of the database because it is on a standard disk and is available for both reading and writing. That's why we want you to pay especially close attention to this section where we demonstrate copying a file from the Companion CD to another disk. In the following exercise, you will copy the file *Ch02.mdb* from the CD to the folder you just created, Chapter 2, on your floppy disk. In preparation for the exercise, launch Windows Explorer, if necessary, insert the floppy disk you formatted in the preceding exercise into drive A, and insert your Companion CD into the CD drive.

EXERCISE 1.13: COPYING A FILE FROM YOUR COMPANION CD TO A DISK

1. Launch Windows Explorer, and then prepare the Folders pane display by locating the drive A icon and clicking its Expand button so that the Chapter 2 folder is displayed in the Folders pane—just as with Figure 1.18.
2. Scroll down the Folders pane display, locating the icon for your CD. Click it and click its Expand button so that the folders beginning with Ch01 are displayed.
3. Click the Ch02 folder in the Folders pane. The contents of the folder, some file names, are displayed in Explorer's Contents pane.
4. Locate the file *Ch02.mdb* in the Contents pane, click it, and then drag it from the Contents pane to the Folders pane.
5. If drive A is not visible near the top of the Folders pane, continue dragging by moving the mouse to the top of the Folders pane. It will move, revealing the floppy disk, drive A.

6. Continue dragging the file until the dimmed file name, which represents the mouse, is directly over the Chapter 2 folder in the Folders pane. The folder will be highlighted when the mouse is properly positioned.
7. Release the left mouse button, dropping the file into the folder.

When you drag and drop a file from one disk to a different disk, the default action is to *copy* the file. However, if you drag and drop a file from one folder on a disk to another folder on the *same* disk, the default action is to *move* the file. You can have more control over the action by right-clicking the selected file to drag it (we call this action right-drag for short). When you drop the file into its destination folder, a pop-up menu is displayed from which you can choose either to copy or move the file by clicking which action you'd like. Figure 1.19 shows the pop-up menu displayed when you right-drag a file.

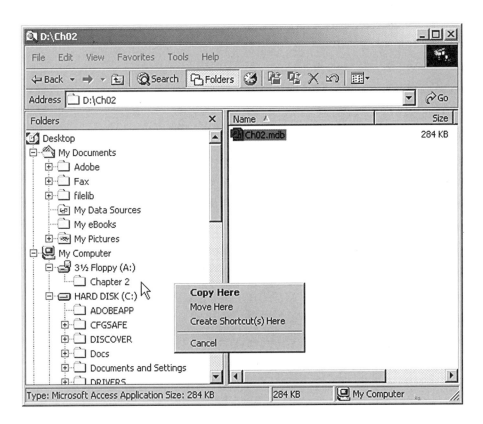

Figure 1.19   The pop-up menu displayed after right-dragging a file.

Moving a file from one place to another is a cut and paste operation. The easiest way to move a file is by right-clicking it and then dragging it from one location to another. When you release the right mouse, a pop-up menu is displayed. From the menu, you can select Move. Perhaps the fastest way to copy or move a file from one place to another is as follows:

- Locate and select (click) the file to be copied (the *source* file).

- Press Ctrl+C (to copy) or Ctrl+X (to move).

- Locate the target folder in Explorer's Folders pane and select the folder (the *target*).

- Finally, press Ctrl+V to paste the file into the target folder.

Entire files or a collection of files can be copied or moved from one folder to another using copy or cut and paste keystrokes identical to those you use when copying objects between programs and the Clipboard.

Eventually, files and folders are no longer useful to you and must be deleted. The folder and file you created on drive A—the folder called Chapter 2 and the file *Ch02.mdb*—have been used for demonstration purposes and you no longer need them. You can delete them. Deleted objects can be recovered once deleted if you act within a reasonable time. Windows places deleted files and folders in a special folder called the *Recycle Bin* where they remain until you empty the bin. Once you empty the Recycle Bin, you cannot recover them. That is, when you empty the Recycle Bin, Windows physically removes them from the disk. Let's see how to delete files and folders.

Try It

Open Windows Explorer, place your floppy disk in drive A, and select drive A in Explorer's Folders pane. Click the Expand button, if necessary, to reveal the folder called Chapter 2 in the Folders pane. Select that folder in the Folders pane. The Contents pane reveals the file (a database) named *Ch02.mdb*. With the mouse positioned over the file name, right-click the file. A pop-up menu opens containing items including Cut, Copy, Delete, and Properties. Click the Delete menu item and click Yes when the confirmation dialog box is displayed. The file is automatically placed in the Recycle Bin.

You delete folders in the same way as files. The consequences of deleting a folder can be more significant than deleting one or more files, however. When you delete a folder, you also delete any files and folders it may contain. Make sure that the folder to be deleted contains only files and folders that you are sure you want to delete. Delete a folder by selecting it in Explorer and dragging it to the Recycle Bin. (This may require you to reduce the Explorer's window so that the Recycle Bin and window are simultaneously visible.)

Restoring previously deleted files is simple. Right-click the Recycle Bin, select the file(s) to be restored, and then select Restore from the File menu. Any selected files are restored and placed in their original locations.

Whenever you feel the urge, you can empty the Recycle Bin, permanently removing all files it contains. Simply right-click the Recycle Bin and select the option titled *Empty Recycle Bin*. Then click the Yes button.

Try It

Minimize Windows Explorer and locate the Recycle Bin on the desktop. Double-click the Recycle Bin icon, and then locate and click the file *Ch02.mdb*. Select Restore from the File menu. Windows Explorer places the document back in the Chapter 2 folder on your floppy disk.

Windows provides several helpful keystroke shortcuts for selecting files. While using Windows Explorer, for example, you can press and hold Ctrl and click file names to select noncontiguous files. Hold Shift and click the first and last of a group of contiguous files (those files whose names appear in sequence next to one another) to select the whole group. Besides these tried and true methods, you can drag the mouse pointer across Explorer's Contents window, creating a rectangular dashed line. Any file names the line touches will be selected when you release the mouse pointer. Try it yourself.

You can rename a folder or file by right-clicking it and then selecting *Rename* from the pop-up menu. Then you can type the object's new name. You can cancel the pop-up menu and choose to take no action by clicking anywhere outside the menu. Another, perhaps simpler, way to rename a file or folder is to select it and then press F2. Or you can *slowly* click twice (do not double-click) a file or folder name. A vertical, blinking cursor appears at the end of the object's name. You can retype the name or use the arrow keys to move the cursor left or right to make small changes in the name. Practice clicking slowly twice to master the procedure. If you are too quick, you'll end up launching the application that is associated with the file whose name you double-clicked. Stick with one of the other renaming techniques if you have difficulty using the two-click method.

Setting File and Folder Properties

Files and folders have hidden attributes or properties that both limit actions you can take on the objects and display information about the objects. Which properties are available and can be altered depends on the type of object. Files and folders have a common set of properties that are accessible from Windows Explorer either by right-clicking the object or selecting Properties from Explorer's File menu. Some objects such as Excel spreadsheet files and Word documents have additional properties—summary information and statistics—that reveal additional details such as the date when the object was created and last altered. Four properties that all file types and folders have in common are called Archive, Read-only, Hidden, and System. Of these, only two are important to us—the properties Read-only and Hidden.

A file or folder having a Read-only property is slightly more difficult to erase. Database files, which you will use throughout this book, will not open properly if their Read-only attributes are set. (We use the term *set* to mean "has the value of yes" or "is enabled.") When you delete a file whose Read-only attribute is set, Windows displays a dialog box asking you to reaffirm your intention to delete one or more objects. Setting a file's Hidden property makes it invisible in Explorer. Hiding files is useful when you want to reduce screen clutter by eliminating some file names from displaying while using Explorer. The next exercise shows you how to clear (remove) a file's Read-only property, thus ensuring you can alter its contents and then save it back to its original file.

EXERCISE 1.14: CLEARING A FILE'S READ-ONLY PROPERTY

1. Navigate to drive A in the Folders pane and select the folder Chapter 2, which contains the file *Ch02.mdb* you copied in Exercise 1.13.
2. In Explorer's Contents pane, right-click the file *Ch02.mdb* and click Properties from the pop-up list. The Properties dialog box opens.
3. Clear the Read-only check box by clicking it if necessary (see Figure 1.20). (If the box has a check mark, clicking it will erase the check mark—clear it.) Notice that the Apply button, dimmed prior to your action, is now available.
4. Finally, click OK to affirm the change and return to Explorer.

Launching a Program from Explorer

As you become more comfortable with Windows, you will probably use Explorer as your default work surface for beginning your Access database work. Because most files are associated with an application, it is usually easiest to launch Explorer, locate the database file you want to work with, and then launch Access by double-clicking the file. This is a simple, efficient approach to starting a program *and* opening a file to work on. You have practiced this once already, in Exercise 1.7, *Launching a Program from a Data File*. In that exercise, you located a file with Find and then double-clicked the file name to launch Word-Pad. You can do the same thing in Explorer. When you locate with Explorer the database file you want to open, simply double-click its name to launch Microsoft Access. You might want to try this on your own with one of the many database files we have supplied on your Companion CD. Remember, however, to first copy the database file to your floppy disk or, better yet, to a temporary

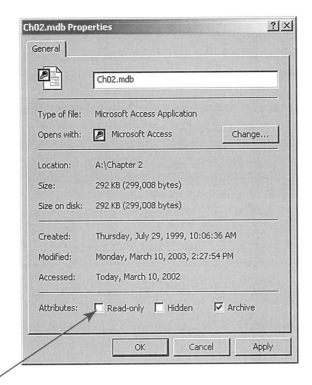

Read-only property

Figure 1.20   Clearing a file's Read-only property.

file on drive C. Then double-click the file in Explorer to run Access and open the database file.

Generally, the pattern you should follow in working with our supplied database files is to first copy the particular chapter's database file to drive C, your computer's hard drive, so that the database can be opened to both read database information as well as alter the data. This way, you will be able to make needed database modifications as you read the text and see the effects of your changes. Of course, you can open the Companion CD databases directly on the CD, but Access allows you to read the data only. You cannot post any changes to the database stored on the CD.

Exiting Explorer

Exiting Explorer is child's play. You can either choose Close from the File menu or click the Close button located in the upper right corner of the Explorer window. If you haven't closed Explorer yet, do so now using either method. The Windows desktop reappears (or another application if any are still running). Make sure all running applications are closed so that you have a clear view of the desktop.

CUSTOMIZING WINDOWS

You can customize the Windows desktop to make it more efficient for you to use and to provide the kind of detail you like. Some customization features, such as desktop shortcuts, will yield large time savings while other changes you make simply establish the desktop—your virtual office space—as uniquely yours. Windows also provides accessibility options, which make Windows easier to use for those with physical impairments. Nearly anyone can find several good reasons to customize the Windows desktop. Only those in a university computer laboratory environment will find it counterproductive to alter the appearance and functionality of the desktop because the customized desktop cannot be saved in that situation.

Different people who use a single computer may wish to customize the desktop to their liking, changing the background wallpaper, the number and types of icons on the desktop, and so forth. *User profiles* save each user's uniquely customized desktop so that no one user affects the settings of another. Which desktop environment is selected is determined by the *user name* provided. Details of how to enable tracking multiple users on a single machine are beyond the scope of this chapter.

Creating and Using Shortcuts

A *shortcut* is an icon representing a program or other object and provides a quick way to access a particular object. The Start menu items, for example, are shortcuts to programs. This can be confusing to users new to Windows, but the distinction is important. A shortcut is analogous to a telephone number found in a typical address book. The telephone number is a shortcut to the real person who (you hope) answers the phone when you call. Like a telephone number, a shortcut can be deleted without deleting the actual object—usually a program—to which it points. Shortcuts inherit the same icon as the object to which they point, thus making it sometimes difficult to distinguish between them. However, shortcut icons also contain a small arrow, which distinguishes the shortcut icon from the icon actually representing a program or other object.

The most common reason to create a desktop shortcut is to provide quick access to frequently used applications. There is practically no limit to the number of shortcuts you can create and place on the desktop, but we advise restraint. If you create too many shortcuts, the desktop can become cluttered and unreadable and you are almost back to where you started—unable to find a particular application or other object quickly. On the other hand, you may want to create shortcuts for lots of objects and then later cull the collection to the 20 percent of the shortcuts you use 80 percent of the time (the often observed "20/80" rule). In any case, it is simple enough to delete unwanted shortcuts later. Let's see how to create desktop shortcuts by creating one of your own. Bear in mind that your university computer laboratory may be set up to prevent this type of desktop customization. It can't hurt to try, though.

EXERCISE 1.15: CREATING A DESKTOP SHORTCUT

1. Close any open applications so that the desktop is clearly visible.
2. Click the Start button on the taskbar, point to Search, and click For Files or Folders.
3. Type **WordPad** in the *Search for files or folders named* text box and click the Search Now button.
4. When the search finishes, locate the file named wordpad.exe in the right panel.
5. Right-click the file name wordpad.exe in the right panel, and then click Create Shortcut, which appears in the pop-up menu (see Figure 1.21)
6. When a dialog box appears indicating that a shortcut cannot be created here, click Yes to place the shortcut on the desktop.
7. Close the Search Results dialog box. The new shortcut appears on the desktop (see Figure 1.22)

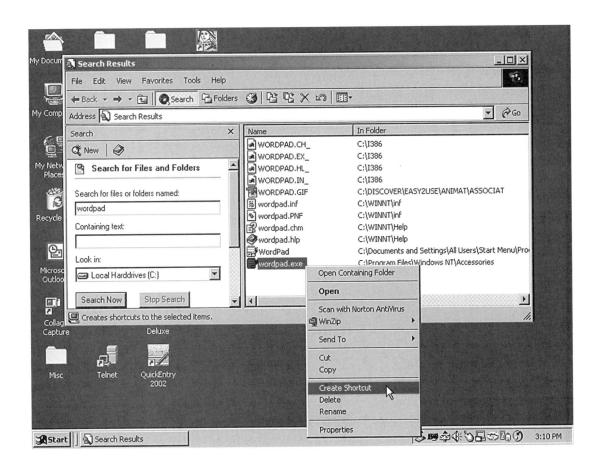

Figure 1.21   Search Results pop-up menu.

The shortcut appears on the desktop. The shortcut icon matches WordPad's icon in every respect except that an arrow appears in the lower left corner. This identifies the icon as a shortcut (see Figure 1.22).

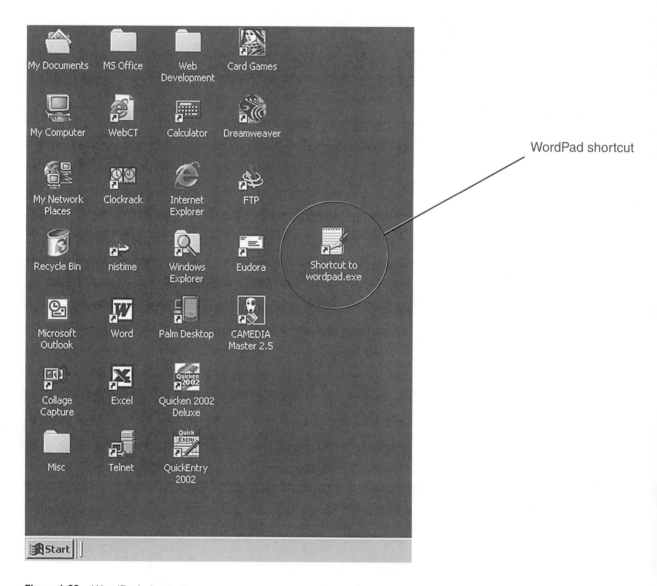

WordPad shortcut

Figure 1.22   WordPad shortcut.

Use folders on the desktop to group shortcuts if your desktop becomes too cluttered. This way, you can find a shortcut by opening the folder containing related shortcuts. Creating a desktop folder follows the same basic procedure as the first three steps of the preceding exercise. That is, right-click any blank desktop area, select New, and then select Folder. Finally, type the folder's name and press Enter to finalize the operation. The folder's name appears below the desktop folder. Then, you can drag shortcuts from the desktop and drop them into the folder. Because the desktop is both the source and destination of the operation, the shortcut is *moved* to a folder by default when you click, drag, and then drop it. To remove an object from a desktop folder and place it back on the desktop, double-click the folder to open it and then drag the object from the open folder onto the desktop. Delete a folder by selecting it and pressing the Delete key. Click Yes to confirm the delete operation.

Placing Shortcuts on the Start Menu

The Start menu can be customized like other Windows objects. One of the things that speeds up access to programs is to place on the Start menu shortcuts to the programs you use frequently. Then, when you click Start, a favorite program is immediately accessible from the menu. Plan a bit here, though. Because the real estate available on the Start menu is limited, restrict what you place there to the half dozen programs you use the most. Remember, too, if you are working in a university computing laboratory, you probably will not be able to customize the Start button. The following exercise explains how to place a shortcut to Microsoft Access on the Start menu.

Try It

Locate the Microsoft Access program file called *Msaccess.exe*. Drag the file name directly to the Start button and drop it there. The first question is how do you find the Access file object? Use the Search command on the Start menu to search for it—just like you did in the previous exercise. Click Start, point to Search, and select *For Files or Folders*. In the *Search for files or folders named* text box type **msaccess.exe** and make sure that drive *My Computer* is indicated in the Look in text box. Then, click the Search Now button. Shortly, the file name appears in the text box at the bottom of the dialog box. Select the file name in the right panel of the Search Results dialog box and drag it to the Start button. Windows creates a shortcut to Access on the Start menu. Click Start and locate the shortcut in the Start menu (see Figure 1.23).

Removing Start Menu Items

Objects including shortcuts can be removed from the Start menu. You may want to remove the Start menu shortcut to Microsoft Access you just created. Removing an item from the Start menu is simpler then adding an item to it. Perhaps the simplest way to understand this process is to actually remove a shortcut. If you followed our

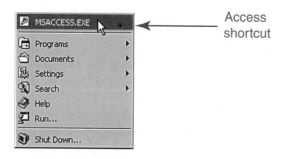

Figure 1.23   Access shortcut on the Start menu.

suggestion above and added a shortcut to the Start menu, then try the following exercise to remove the item. Otherwise, simply read the steps that follow.

EXERCISE 1.16: REMOVING A SHORTCUT FROM THE START MENU

1. Click the Start menu.
2. Right-click the msaccess.exe entry in the Start menu. A pop-up menu appears.
3. Click Delete in the pop-up menu, and click the Yes button in Confirm Shortcut Delete dialog box (see Figure 1.24).

Clearing the Start Menu Documents Window

The Documents menu displays the names of the last 25 documents that you accessed. For instance, the document *FallWashPromotion.doc* appears in the Documents window if you opened that document recently. Similarly, if you open a database, the name of that database is placed in the Documents menu. When the number of document names exceeds 25, the oldest name is removed from the bottom of the list and the newest name is placed on the top. The Document window provides a quick way to return to a document you were working with recently—whether it is a Word document, Access database, or Notepad memo. This ability reinforces the notion of a document-centric system that we introduced earlier in this chapter. For example, if you wanted to work with the *FallWashPromotion.doc* document again, the fastest way to load WordPad and the document is to locate *FallWashPromotion.doc* in the Documents menu and click the name. WordPad is launched, and the letter is opened automatically.

Take a moment to look at the Documents menu on your computer to see what names appear there: Click the Start button and then point to Documents.

Sometimes people are sensitive about document names appearing in the Documents window. For instance, suppose you had just worked on a letter named

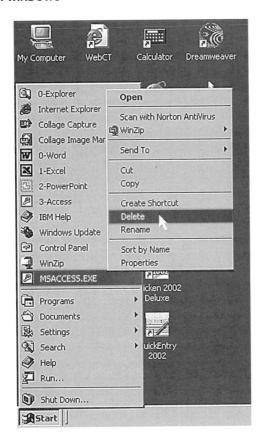

Figure 1.24 Removing a program from the Start menu.

IncomeTaxesDue.doc containing sensitive tax and income information. You certainly do not want an unauthorized person reading the document. It may be best to eliminate the name from the recently used names stored in the Documents menu. Clearing the names from that list is a matter of remembering a few keystrokes. The next exercise illustrates the required steps.

EXERCISE 1.17: CLEARING THE DOCUMENTS MENU

1. Right-click the Taskbar.
2. Click Properties from the pop-up menu.
3. Click Advanced tab (see Figure 1.25).
4. Click the Clear button. The document names are cleared from the Documents menu, and the Clear button is dimmed.
5. Click the OK button to close the dialog box.

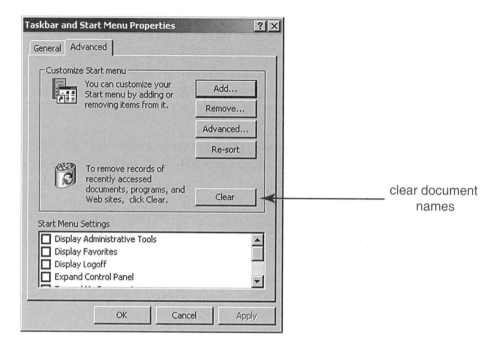

Figure 1.25   Clearing document names from the Documents menu.

Now if you examine the Start menu Documents menu items, you will see a single item indicating that the list is empty. Emptying the Documents menu does not prevent someone from accessing your documents, but it does prevent someone else from knowing what documents you accessed recently.

Customizing the Taskbar

Some people prefer to have the Taskbar out of sight until needed. Others like the Taskbar placed in a different location on the desktop. Like the Start menu, the Taskbar can be customized to suit your needs. We show you how to alter both the location and behavior of the Taskbar. However, we want to remind you to be considerate of others who may use the computer after you are done. Anyone using a public-access computer such as a college laboratory computer expects to find shortcuts and Start menu items in a familiar order. Change the Taskbar all you want, but be sure to return the computer to its original state prior to leaving the laboratory. If you hide the Taskbar, the next student who uses the computer may not know how to make the Taskbar reappear. Be sure to clear the Auto hide Taskbar property before leaving the computer.

Relocating the Taskbar or altering its size is the most obvious change you can make to it. To change the height of the Taskbar, move the pointer to the upper edge of the Taskbar. When the pointer changes to a double-headed arrow, drag the upper border towards the center of the screen to widen the Taskbar. Similarly, drag the top edge of the Taskbar towards the edge of the screen to make the Taskbar very narrow but not quite invisible. Try altering the Taskbar's size. Widen it to almost half the height of the screen, and then restore it to its standard height.

Changing the location of the Taskbar from its default position at the bottom of the screen is a straightforward procedure. Simply drag the Taskbar to one of the four edges of the screen to place it in that position.

Try It

Click any empty area of the Taskbar, and drag it to the top of the screen. Notice that the Taskbar docks itself up against the top of the display, and desktop icons automatically shift down slightly to accommodate the Taskbar. Drag the Taskbar to the right or left side of the desktop. Again, desktop shortcuts move out of the way accordingly.

Sometimes the Taskbar is unnecessary or is using up valuable screen space. You can hide the Taskbar until you need it again by setting its *Auto hide* property. To change the Taskbar's display behavior, bring up the Taskbar Properties sheet (right-click an empty area of the Taskbar and then click Properties). Click the General tab of the Taskbar and Start Menu Properties dialog box that appears. Check the Auto hide check box and click OK to set the new property (see Figure 1.26). The dialog box closes, and the Taskbar will move off the screen until you move the cursor near the Taskbar's former location. Experiment yourself. Set the Auto hide property, and then move the cursor near the edge of the screen where the Taskbar usually appears. The Taskbar reappears. When you move the pointer away from the edge of the screen, the Taskbar slips out of sight. Clearing the Auto hide property reverses this behavior. Bring the Taskbar into sight, right-click in a blank area, select Properties, and clear Auto hide on the Taskbar Options tab. Finally, click OK to establish the Taskbar characteristics.

Another property, Show clock, determines whether the time is displayed on the Taskbar. Clearing it removes the clock. Setting it displays the clock.

You probably noticed the Apply button on the Taskbar and Start Menu Properties dialog box. It serves a different function from the OK button. Clicking Apply establishes the properties you have selected but leaves the dialog box open. You can make additional Taskbar changes if you wish. Clicking OK establishes the properties you have selected and closes the dialog box, precluding further property changes until the dialog box is reopened.

RESTARTING WINDOWS

You may need to restart Windows because an error occurs that causes the keyboard to freeze, Windows indicates that an error has occurred and instructs you

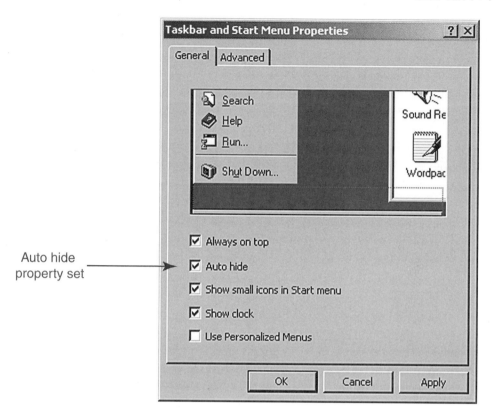

Figure 1.26   Setting the taskbar's Auto hide property.

to restart, or you may need to log off your network and reconnect as a different user. The first two cases are infrequent and require you to simply restart Windows but not necessarily reinitialize the entire machine. The latter case, logging on as a different user, is useful for several reasons. Whenever you restart Windows, you may be asked to specify your username and password. If your computer is on a network, you may also have to provide a username and password to log onto the local area network. The network and Windows usernames and passwords can be the same to simplify the task of connecting to both the network and Windows. To focus our discussion on Windows itself, let's assume for a moment that your computer is not connected to a LAN (Local Area Network). Why then are a username and password required or even useful on a standalone Windows computer? One major reason is that Windows can accommodate and keep track of multiple users' desktop preferences with usernames. This way, several people, each with a self-assigned username, can log on to a particular computer. Then, Windows restores the user's desktop icons, Start menu settings, and other work environment information for each identified user. Preserved desktop settings and environment are saved in *user profiles*. User profiles provide customized desktop configurations that allow people using the computer to work most efficiently. Forcing everyone who uses a particular computer to use a fixed set of shortcuts does not aid creativity or efficiency.

EXITING WINDOWS

If you are using a computer in a computer laboratory, chances are that you will not want to exit Windows. Doing so will require the next user to restart Windows or the computer from scratch. Avoid exiting Windows in this situation. However, you will want to occasionally take a break and turn off your computer. Always exit Windows *before* turning off your computer. Windows often has some clean-up work to do before you can safely turn off your computer. You could lose valuable data or programs if you do not follow this admonition. Shutting down or exiting Windows is straightforward. Here's how. Click the Start button on the Taskbar, and then click Shut down. The Shut Down Windows dialog box appears containing several options from which to choose. Click the list box arrow, select *Shut down*, and then click OK to initialize the shut-down process.

SUMMARY

This chapter describes the Windows environment. You have launched Windows, logged on to Windows, examined what is on the desktop, and used the mouse. You have learned how to use a typical Windows dialog box and what menu items are found in the Start menu. You understand how to launch programs directly from the Start button Programs menu item. Using the more intuitive document-centric approach, you launched applications by selecting the programs they manage. You learned how to share data between running programs by embedding a Paint graphic inside a WordPad document. You learned how easily you can switch from one program to another by using the program buttons located on the Taskbar.

After working with the Windows interface, you examined Windows Explorer. You opened disk drives, folders, and files; formatted a floppy disk for first-time use; created a folder on your floppy disk; and copied files from the Companion CD to your floppy disk. Using Explorer, you discovered how to delete and rename files, how to set selected file properties, and how to launch applications from associated data files.

You discovered that shortcuts are a very convenient and flexible Windows feature. You used existing shortcuts and learned how to create your own desktop shortcuts. You found that you could place shortcuts on the Start menu to provide quick, global access to your most often used programs. You learned that the Document menu's list of recently accessed files provided automatic and fast access to items you recently worked on. We illustrated how to clear the Document menu's list to eliminate the file names from prying eyes. Moving the Taskbar to other edges of the screen, you realized yet another way to customize the Windows desktop. Finally, you learned how to exit Windows and shut down the computer.

QUESTIONS AND PROBLEMS FOR REVIEW

MULTIPLE-CHOICE QUESTIONS

1. Using the mouse, how do you execute a program whose shortcut is displayed on the desktop?
   a. Click the program's shortcut.
   b. Double-click the program's shortcut.
   c. Right-click the program's shortcut.
   d. Select Execute from the shortcut's pop-up menu.

2. You can click the _____ button and then move to any object on the screen and click the mouse to obtain context-sensitive help about the clicked object.
   a. Help
   b. What's This?
   c. Properties
   d. Find

3. If you want to work on a file called *MyResume.doc* but have forgotten where it is filed on your computer, the fastest way to locate the file is to
   a. use Windows Explorer.
   b. select Help from the Start menu.
   c. select Locate from the Start menu.
   d. select Find from the Start menu.

4. The Settings item found on the Start menu contains several menu items including Printers, Taskbar & Start menu, and
   a. My Computer.
   b. Control Panel.
   c. Shut Down.
   d. My Network.

5. To switch between Windows programs, you can either use the Taskbar or the keystroke combination
   a. Alt+Esc.
   b. Ctrl+Alt.
   c. Alt+Tab.
   d. none of the above.

6. Using Windows Explorer, you can copy a file from one folder to another by
   a. dragging and dropping the selection to the target folder.
   b. pressing Ctrl+C to copy the source file(s), selecting the target folder, then pressing Ctrl+V.
   c. executing Copy and then Paste from the Explorer Edit menu.
   d. all of the above will work.

7. Shortcuts
   a. can be created for applications but not for documents or other files.
   b. are found only on the desktop.
   c. cause the program to be deleted when the shortcut is deleted.
   d. are frequently created to provide quick access to often-used applications.
8. Which of the following statements is true?
   a. Start menu items are permanent.
   b. The Taskbar is always visible somewhere on the screen.
   c. Only one application at a time may be running under Windows.
   d. User Profiles enable desktop settings of different users to be preserved.
9. You can minimize all open windows, revealing the desktop by
   a. clicking the Minimize button on the Taskbar.
   b. right-clicking the Taskbar and selecting Minimize All Windows.
   c. double-clicking the Taskbar.
   d. setting the Auto hide Taskbar property.
10. When you exit Windows,
    a. it performs some housekeeping chores before shutting down.
    b. you can safely turn off your computer after instructed to do so by Windows.
    c. the next user must restart Windows before logging on.
    d. all of the above are true.

DISCUSSION QUESTIONS

1. Describe in a few sentences how you would use Windows Explorer. Start by explaining the structure of the Windows Explorer panels. What types of operations can you do on files?
2. Briefly explore and describe at least five applications contained in the Accessories folder (Start, Programs, Accessories).
3. Describe two ways to create a shortcut to a program or document.
4. Describe the ways to get help on Windows in general. How would you get help with cut and paste if you were using WordPad? Describe the steps you would follow.
5. Describe some of the ways you might be able to take advantage of Windows ability to work with multiple programs and data.

PROBLEMS

1. Using WordPad, write a short, two-paragraph summary of the main points covered in one of your recent classes. For instance, write about your latest accounting information systems class lecture. Be sure to include your name on the document so you can easily identify it. After you have created a document, save it on your floppy disk. Then print the document.

2. If you have a new, unused floppy disk, use Windows Explorer to format your disk. In addition, label the new disk with your last name. Next, using either the new disk or one that already has information on it, use Windows Explorer to create two folders called *Notes* and *Homework* on your floppy disk.

3. Create a new company logo using Microsoft Paint. The logo should contain at least your company's name. Try the Airbrush, Brush, Line, and Pencil tools. Change colors. Be creative. This might be your future company's logo, after all! Choose 256 Color Bitmap in the *Save as type* list box. Save the graphic on your disk in any folder as the file *MyLogo.bmp*. Launch the WordPad program. Start the document by embedding your logo into the new document, and then write some text on the lines below your logo. Save the document as *MyLogo.wri* on your floppy disk, and print the document. Be sure your name is either in the logo or near the top of the typed material so that you can easily distinguish your output. Finally, close both Paint and WordPad.

4. Launch the following programs, one after the other: WordPad, Paint, Notepad, and Windows Explorer. Minimize all applications so they are buttons on the Taskbar. Right-click a program's Taskbar button, and select Close from the pop-up menu to stop and unload the program. Repeat the program-exiting process for all remaining programs. How many ways can you think of to exit the programs you launched?

5. Learn about Windows by consulting Help. Select Help from the Start menu, select the Index tab of Help, and type **Copying files**. Click any of the subtopics under the Copying files topic, and then click the Display button to display the first of several Windows help panels. Print any help topic of interest that you find by clicking the Options button and then clicking Print. Click the Print button in the Print dialog box to print the Help topic.

2 INTRODUCTION TO MICROSOFT ACCESS

OBJECTIVES

This chapter describes the Microsoft Access database management system in detail. You will use predefined databases to browse data, use Microsoft Access menus, and create several types of information forms. The purpose of this chapter is to bring you up to speed in using Access. If you have used Access extensively, then you can skip this chapter. Important topics covered in this chapter include:

- Starting and exiting Access.
- Understanding the Access work surface icons.
- Using the Access objects, including tables, queries, forms, and reports.
- Opening and displaying database tables.
- Retrieving information with queries.
- Modifying tables' contents with action queries.
- Creating and using forms to display and query tables and databases.
- Designing and using database reports.

We feature a small, fictitious stock brokerage firm to illustrate how organizations use databases to manipulate and store crucial business information. The brokerage firm must maintain a record of each client's portfolio of stocks, bonds, etc. Among the important information stored is client information (such as name and address) and portfolio information (such as the stock purchased, purchase date, and number of shares bought). As we work with the database package in this chapter, we will reveal various information items kept by the stock brokerage firm. More importantly, this chapter demonstrates that a relational database system can be built to track and maintain critical business information and economic events.

INTRODUCTION

Modern computer-based systems, including most accounting systems, have a database system. An accounts receivable program, for example, frequently stores its information in a special system known as a database. The information is subsequently extracted, summarized, and displayed by a program especially adept at storing, organizing, and quickly retrieving facts stored in a database. Such systems are known as *database management systems*.

What Is Access?

You will study and use one such database management system written for microcomputers, called Microsoft Access. Produced by Microsoft Corporation, Access is the most popular database management system for Windows. Once you learn the fundamentals of Microsoft Access, you will be able to create your own accounting systems with this powerful database system. (We usually use the shorthand term "Access" in this textbook rather than the longer term "Microsoft Access.")

What Is a Relational Database?

Access is a *relational* database management system. Briefly, a relational database system is founded on the rules, created and published by Dr. E. F. Codd, that collectively define a relational database management system. Of the several database management system types, the relational database management systems are the most widely accepted and easiest to use. We will uncover some of Codd's rules for relational database systems in Chapters 3 and 4 and elsewhere in the text.

The fundamental storage entity for a relational database system is easy to visualize—it is a two-dimensional object having rows and columns called a *table*. A table holds data, and each row corresponds to one instance of data. Each of a table's columns corresponds to a different characteristic, called an *attribute*. For example, consider a table holding employee information. A particular row of the table represents an individual employee. There are as many rows in an employee table as there are employees in the company, division, or department. The employee table's columns might hold data such as employees' first names, last names, hire dates, social security numbers, genders, birth dates, and so on. Each column holds only one "fact." For instance, a given column always contains employees' hire dates and nothing else; another column holds only employees' last names.

A database often is comprised of more than one table. For instance, the employee table might be only one of several tables that collectively describe a company's employees, their skills, and their complete productivity histories. Almost always, more than one table is used to store information. A collection of tables that are related and collectively describe an entity is known as a *database*. You can imagine that an accounts receivable database contains many tables that are related to one another: a customer table, a salesperson table, an inventory table (you sell goods from inventory), and so on. Although most databases contain several tables, the terms *database* and *table* frequently are used interchangeably. The term for a database consisting of only one table is *flat file*.

Most databases used in business and government are large, and they often consist of hundreds of tables. We will not subject you to such a large system in our examples or exercises. However, our databases do contain more than one table, and some of those tables have several hundred rows. Manipulating several, larger tables will give you an idea of what real corporate databases entail. The reason for using multiple tables to represent related information will become clear as you continue to read.

To better understand the concept of tables and their relationships, begin by launching Access and looking at a few tables we have prepared.

Starting Access

Your first exercise in this chapter is to launch Access. First, launch Windows if necessary. Access is usually stored with other Microsoft Office products. Locate Access, whose file name is *Msaccess.exe*, with Windows Explorer. If you have difficulty, then use Find in the Start menu and search for the file name. Once you find it, you can launch Access directly from the Find dialog box.

EXERCISE 2.1: STARTING MICROSOFT ACCESS

1. Locate the Microsoft Access program. You may wish to use Windows Explorer or the Search menu item on the Start menu and search for *msaccess.exe*. (See the Try It exercise on page 15.)
2. Access opens and displays the Task Pane (see Figure 2.1). If the Task Pane is not open, then click View on the menu bar, point to Toolbars, and click Task Pane to open it.
    The Access Startup window appears to the left of the Task Pane.

The Startup window is the principal workspace. All Access windows are opened in the Access Startup window, and they are wholly contained in it. Each type of Access window you will encounter appears in its own window. Tables are always displayed in a Table window. Forms, described in the section *Using Forms* (page 96) in this chapter, are viewed in a Form window, and so on. Each window has its own distinct commands and functions that apply only to that type of window. You will see these windows and the commands contained in them when we discuss each type of window. Take a moment to examine the Access window (see Figure 2.1 if you are not using the computer right now).

Along the top of the window are the Title bar and the Minimize, Restore, and Close buttons. Just below the Title bar is the Startup window menu bar, containing the File, Edit, View, Insert, Tools, Window, and Help menus. Below the

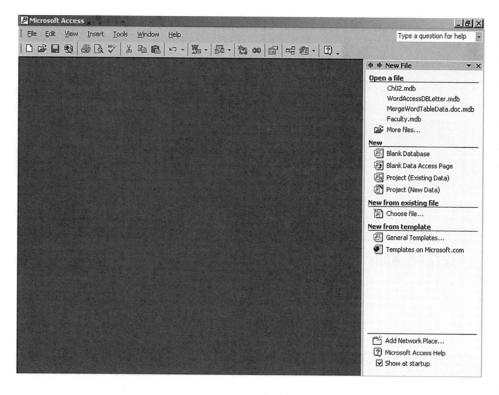

Figure 2.1　Access with the Task Pane displayed.

menu bar is the Database toolbar, displaying buttons appropriate for the current window. (They are all dim because they cannot be clicked without a database being open.) When you move the mouse over the toolbar buttons, their names appear (called Tool Tips) after a short delay.

Finding Help

It is important to know how to get help when you get stuck or would just like to know more about a particular aspect of Access. Let's see what help is available on creating forms. Make sure the Access Startup window is visible and active, and then do the following exercise.

EXERCISE 2.2: OBTAINING HELP

1. Click Help on the menu bar and then click Microsoft Access Help.
2. Maximize the Help window.
3. Click the Index tab.
4. Type **form** in the *Type keywords* text box found near the top of the dialog box and then click the Search button.

5. Click *Create a form* from the list of choices in the *Choose a topic* panel. Help about creating forms appears.
6. Click the Show All link in the upper right corner of the right panel to expand the help topics (see Figure 2.2).
7. After you have examined the help screen for a moment, close it by clicking the Close button on the Help title bar.

Print button

type **form** in this text box

help on creating a form

Create a form topic

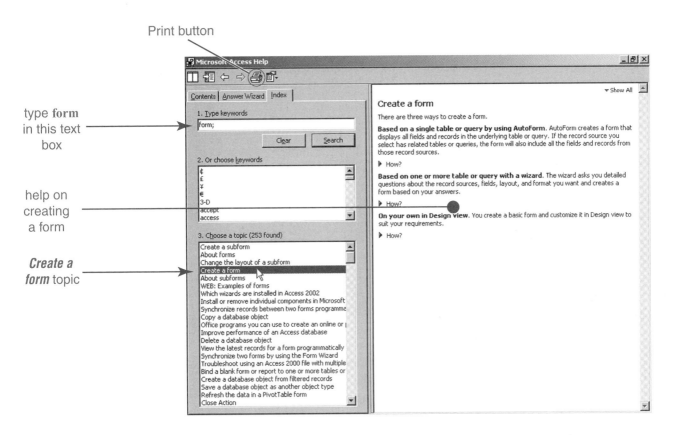

Figure 2.2 Obtaining help.

Printing Help

Occasionally, you may wish you could write down some especially important information you found in Help. You can print a help screen. By printing a few of the important help screens, you can have a handy reference within easy reach—even if you aren't near a computer. Printing help information is simple. Once you have located the help screen you want to print, click the Help page Print button (see Figure 2.2), then select the correct printer and click OK. Windows prints the help screen information. If you wish, you can continue to other screens and print them in the same way. That is all there is to it. (Print the *Create a form* help screen you located in the preceding exercise to ensure that you understand the printing process.)

Exiting Access

After completing all of your database work, you should always exit Access. This signals Access to do its housekeeping chores such as posting any changes you have made to your database on your disk, closing other information sources, and returning to Windows. If you simply press Alt+Tab, for instance, to jump to Windows—leaving Access running—you run the risk of losing important information. You exit Access by selecting Exit from the File menu found on the Access menu bar. Access quickly closes any open databases and returns to Windows.

EXAMINING THE ACCESS ENVIRONMENT

The Access Startup window's toolbar icons change as you move to other parts of Access. Toolbar buttons that are applicable in a particular window appear in color. Inapplicable buttons are dimmed.

Access Work Surface

The Startup window has menus whose names and functioning are like those of other Windows products. Through the File menu, for instance, you can open files (database files in this case) and exit Access. In addition, the File menu contains commands to create a new database and open any hidden windows. The two most popular File menu commands are New and Open. Executing New allows you to create a database, whereas executing Open makes available an existing Access database. Figure 2.3 shows the screen display after selecting the Open command. Alternatively, you can click the Blank Database link in the New panel of the Task Pane to accomplish the same result. You may find the latter method easier and more accessible.

After you either create a new database or locate and open one of the available databases, Microsoft Access displays a Database window within the Microsoft Access window. The Database window is the central control point from which all database activities are conducted. Figure 2.4, on page 58, shows the Database window for one of the databases, Ch02.mdb, found on your Companion CD.

The File menu changes once a Database window is open. Additional File menu commands become available including Get External Data, Close, Save As, Export, Print Preview, Print, Send To, and Database Properties. These important commands allow you to import data from other sources, close the current database, save the database under a new name or export it to another data type, alter database properties, and perform standard Windows print activities. You will use some of the File menu commands as you read this text and work through its examples.

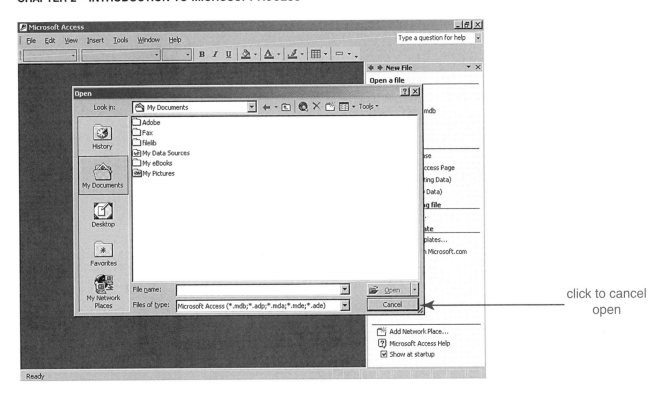

Figure 2.3   Preparing to open a database.

Other menus on the menu bar include Edit, View, Insert, Tools, and Window. The Edit menu contains familiar commands such as Cut, Copy, and Paste as well as Create Shortcut, Delete, Rename, Groups, and Add to Group. The Create Shortcut, Delete, and Rename commands allow you to create a desktop shortcut to any database object, delete an object, or rename an object, respectively.

The View menu lets you display different types of objects in the Database window. You can select Tables, Queries, Forms, Reports, Pages, Macros, or Modules from the Database Objects menu item, for instance. Or you can select those objects by clicking their names in the Objects bar on the left side of the Database window. Another group of commands—Large Icons, Small Icons, List, Details, and Arrange Icons—provides alternative views of the objects in the Database window. The Properties command displays summary information about a table or other database object. The Code command opens the Code window. You use the Toolbars command to display or hide one or more of the several special toolbars.

The Insert menu contains commands to insert tables, forms, queries, and other database objects into the current database. AutoForm and AutoReport create a new form and a new report based on the currently selected table or query. We will use these commands in this text.

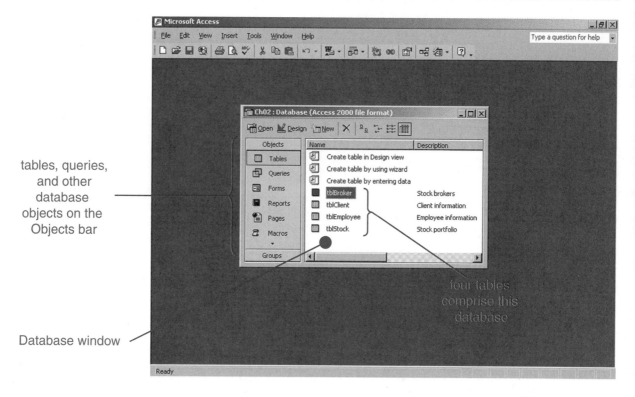

tables, queries, and other database objects on the Objects bar

Database window

Figure 2.4 The Database window.

The Tools menu contains Spelling and AutoCorrect commands; Relationships, which lets you establish relationships between tables; Security, to keep your database secure; and Options, which allows you to set database-wide default values and conditions. There are other commands in the Tools menu, but they are beyond the scope of this text.

The Window menu contains six commands. (If you see fewer than six commands, then click the double arrow at the end of the drop-down list to reveal all of them.) They are Tile Horizontally, Tile Vertically, Cascade, Arrange Icons, Hide, and Unhide. Tile Horizontally and Tile Vertically arrange all Access windows so that they do not overlap one another. The orientation depends on which of the two you choose. Cascade presents windows so that only the title bar of each open but inactive Access window is displayed. The active window is placed on top. When Access windows are reduced to icons, the Arrange Icons command lines up the icons along the bottom edge of the Access window in the same order as it found them. Finally, the Hide command hides the active window from view, whereas the Unhide command reveals a hidden window.

Figure 2.5 shows an example of several database tables. Two tables and the Database window are cascaded, and one table is reduced to an icon. It is in the

menu bar

toolbar

three cascaded
windows

minimized window
containing the
tblBroker table

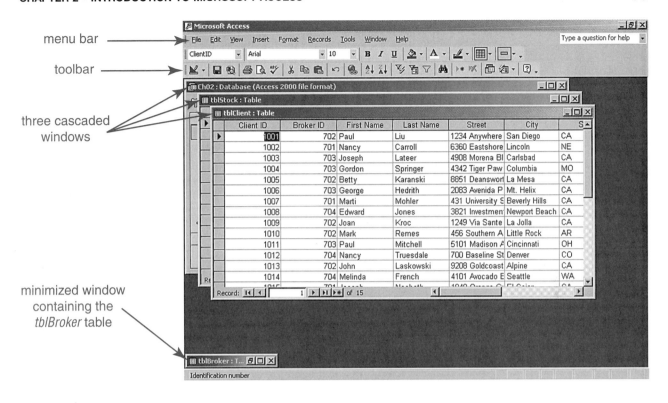

Figure 2.5 Icons and cascaded windows.

lower left corner of the Access window. (Later in this chapter you will look more closely at each of these three tables.)

Help is the rightmost menu on the Database window. Clicking Help displays a standard Help menu. We have presented an overview of the Help menu already, so we will not discuss it further.

Look at Figure 2.5 again. Notice the several toolbar icons. Those icons represent shortcuts to commands accessed from the menu bar. The toolbar buttons that are unavailable in a particular situation are dimmed. Buttons that are not dimmed may be clicked to rapidly accomplish various tasks. The buttons provide a shortcut to menu commands; they do not replace the menu commands. You will use both the buttons and menus to create and modify various database objects as you read through this text.

Access Objects

Access provides many ways to store, display, and report your data. The structures and methods you employ to store and display your data are called *objects*. Access objects include tables, queries, forms, reports, pages, macros, and modules. This text tells you how to use these objects, placing emphasis on the first four of them—

tables, queries, forms, and reports. This section presents an overview of four of these seven important types of objects and shows how each can be used in building accounting information systems. Sections that follow use tables, queries, forms, and reports we have already created to illustrate further how information is organized and retrieved with a database system located at the heart of an accounting information system. At various points in the chapter, we ask you to create some tables, queries, forms, and reports for a small system. First, let's see what these objects are that are the building blocks of a database management system that you will be using to build your accounting information systems.

TABLES. *Tables* are the fundamental storage structures for data, a company's information resource. Like spreadsheet models you have seen, tables are two-dimensional objects with columns and rows. Each row contains all available information about a particular item. (We will use the term *record* interchangeably with *row*.) All rows contain exactly the same number of columns, though not every column of every row necessarily has a value. Sometimes an entry is empty—database folks say the entry is *null*. Consider a table holding employee information. A small company having 50 employees could store employee data—name, date of birth, hire date, etc.—in a 50-row table. Each employee column would be a particular information *field*. (The terms *field* and *column* are used synonymously in this and other texts.) Each column contains one type (or category) of information. For instance, one column contains each employee's hire date, another column holds each employee's last name, and yet another column holds each employee's birth date. Figure 2.6 shows an example of a small Access table that stores employee data. The main difference between this employee table and one you are likely to see in industry is size—most employee tables contain hundreds, if not thousands, of rows. Additionally, employee data usually consists of many columns—not just five. This example is purposefully small so you can understand the principles of database tables without the added complexity of large volumes of data.

Observe that each column holds only one type of data—an important rule to keep in mind when you create your own tables. Each row contains information about an employee, and only one employee's data is stored in a given row. As you can see, several types of data can be stored in a table: text, memo, number, date/time, currency, and hyperlink. Access tables can also hold other types of data including AutoNumber (generating a unique number), Yes/No, and OLE objects.

At the top of each column is the column's name, called an *attribute*, which uniquely identifies a column. Each row corresponds to one of the employees. A row is indivisible. That is, the data in a row remains with the row, even if the rows are sorted or displayed in a different order. Though the rows are unordered, they can be organized into a more meaningful arrangement whenever necessary. This is one of the advantages of a relational database system: the order of rows in a

each column holds a
different characteristic
about the row it describes

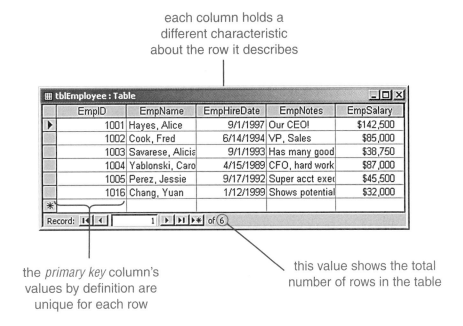

the *primary key* column's
values by definition are
unique for each row

this value shows the total
number of rows in the table

Figure 2.6 Example table containing employee data.

table is unimportant. In other words, you do not have to be worried about inputting data into a table in an orderly way. No row is more important than another.

Similarly, the columns are placed in an arbitrary order left to right. Is there some arcane rule that states columns must be arranged in a particular order? No. We have designed the Employee table so that the employee identification number is first, but no other implicit meaning or significance exists in the columns' arrangement. (Though it is not necessary to put all rows' unique identifier column first, it is customary and convenient.) You can rearrange columns so that the Salary field is second, the Notes field is last, and so on. This is another advantage of relational databases: the order of table columns is unimportant. The field *EmpID* contains mutually unique values. No two employees share the same identification number. This type of field is called a table's *primary key*. You will learn more about primary keys later.

QUERIES. There are several types of queries, but the most common query is called a selection query. A *selection query* is a question you can ask about your database. (Because selection queries are the most common, they are simply called queries.) For instance, a query is "How many employees earn more than $50,000?" or "What customers' invoices are over 60 days past due?" Queries are especially helpful for combining information from several related tables into a single, cohesive result. Also, queries provide a way to reduce the data volume by returning and displaying only the subset of table rows in which you are interested. You can use queries to summarize data, displaying only the aggregate results (for instance, the sum of all outstanding invoices in the accounts receivable file). Other types of queries can be used to insert new data into a table, delete unwanted data from a table, or change values in a table. Using Access queries, you can select which tables are the subjects of your questions, designate the columns you would like to see, and specify which table rows are to be returned.

The query result, called the *dynaset*, is displayed in a Query window. Figure 2.7 shows an example of a query's design and its dynaset, each in its own window. Notice the query design window: only the columns appearing in the *query grid* are displayed in the dynaset—the result of executing an Access query. Check marks (✔) in the query grid Show row prescribe which columns are displayed in the dynaset, and the expression **>50000**, called a *selection criterion*, filters the rows. That is, selection criteria restrict the rows that are returned to those that meet the conditions specified by the criteria—in this case, rows whose Salary field is greater than $50,000.

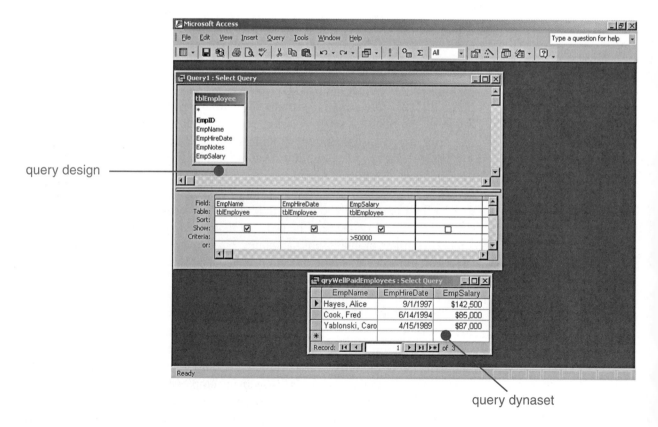

Figure 2.7   Example query and dynaset.

FORMS. Frequently, it is better to work with table data one row at a time. Tables are not an intuitive interface for many people, especially those who are not accustomed to working with databases. Access forms solve this problem. *Forms* let you see the data from a table in a format that is easier to understand. You can see one row or many rows of a table. Figure 2.8 shows an example of a form displaying the Employee table data in an attractive and intuitive layout.

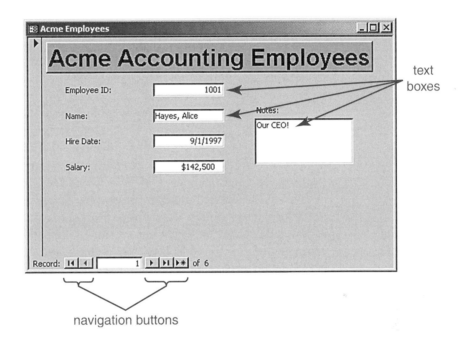

Figure 2.8   Example form displaying an Employee table row.

As you can see, a form may be an easier way to view and change data stored in your databases. One of several records is displayed. You can move to the next or the previous record, or the first or last record, by clicking the navigation buttons, which are located in the lower left corner of the window. You can move directly to a specific record by pressing F5, typing a record number, and pressing Enter. The single, right-pointing arrow button moves one record at a time, displaying the next record in the form. The right-pointing arrow button with a vertical line to its right moves directly to the last record. The opposite actions take place for the left-pointing navigation buttons.

REPORTS. Imagine showing several people in a meeting a financial statement displayed on your notebook computer's screen. That would be awkward and unprofessional. Hard copy output, a report, is a better solution. That way, the report can be distributed to an assembled group easily. Access provides a comprehensive report-producing facility.

Access reports are often the main output or result produced by a database system. While it is important to store accounts receivable information in a database and to query that database for answers, a far more important activity is to produce a printed output. For instance, you might want a list of all receivables over 60 days past due. If there are more than a few, a printed report is the most useful output. You can scan the list, marking accounts that deserve special attention. You can also make copies of a hard copy output for distribution to appropriate departments and managers.

You can use Access's report design features and tools to customize a report to look any way you would like. A report can display data from one table or from several tables that have been linked together. Figure 2.9 is an example of a simple report employing a drop shadow around the title, a graphic (a company logo), bold column headings, and sorted employee names from the Employee table. The simple report is easy to create, and the results are professional looking. An equivalent report produced using a programming language such as COBOL would require a few hundred lines of code and would require far more than the few minutes it takes to create the same report with Access.

Sections that follow describe the process of using and creating tables, queries, forms, and reports. We encourage you to participate in the exercises, because the remainder of the chapter is much more interactive. You will learn the most if you duplicate the steps we present and actually use and create the objects that we do.

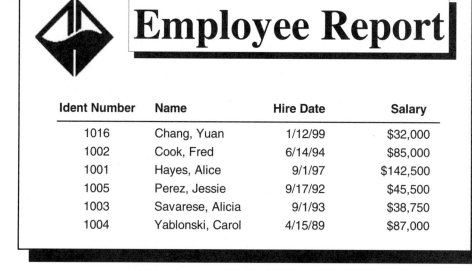

Ident Number	Name	Hire Date	Salary
1016	Chang, Yuan	1/12/99	$32,000
1002	Cook, Fred	6/14/94	$85,000
1001	Hayes, Alice	9/1/97	$142,500
1005	Perez, Jessie	9/17/92	$45,500
1003	Savarese, Alicia	9/1/93	$38,750
1004	Yablonski, Carol	4/15/89	$87,000

Figure 2.9 Example report.

To help you in this process, we have supplied many of the required tables, queries, forms, and reports so that you can try them out. In addition, you will create a few of your own.

WORKING WITH DATABASES AND TABLES

The foundation of any database system rests on its tables. Tables hold the data that is transformed into information. In this section you will learn how to use tables that we have provided, create your own tables, modify the order in which table columns are displayed, and link tables together.

Important Note: Before you work on the tables found on your Companion CD, you should first copy the database from the Companion CD to the hard disk, drive C, of the computer on which you are working (Exercise 1.13, page 32). Remember to clear the copied file's Read-only attribute (Exercise 1.14, page 36). Do these two activities *before* beginning your work session. That way, you will be able to make changes to your tables, queries, and other objects stored in the databases we supply with the textbook. You should avoid using databases directly from your Companion CD because Access limits your activities to "read-only." That means you cannot make any changes either to the structure of tables or other objects, and you cannot alter the data stored in the tables. When you have completed your work on a database, simply copy the database from your hard disk to a floppy disk. That way, you can transport your database work from one machine to another if necessary. (All database files in this textbook are designed to *individually* fit on one floppy disk.)

The only database you need to copy from the Companion CD for this chapter is found in the folder called *Ch02*. The database is called *Ch02.mdb*. Copy this file to your hard disk now, before you start working with the database. We will assume from this point on that you have copied each chapter's database(s) from the CD to drive C prior to working through a chapter. (Recall from Chapter 1 that you can use Windows Explorer to copy files from one place to another.) At the end of each work session—after you copy your database file to a floppy disk—you may want to erase the database from the hard disk. Simply locate the file on the hard disk with Explorer, select it, and press the Delete key to remove the database. You always have the original database file on your Companion CD, whose contents cannot be erased.

Before you work on your database with Access, be sure to tell Access where to find your database objects. This simple procedure is called *opening a database*. We describe this process next.

Opening a Database

Whether you are using a stand-alone computer (one not connected to a network of computers) or a computer in a laboratory on a local network, you must first open a database. A *database* is a collection of objects that are related, including tables, queries, forms, reports, macros, and modules. Access stores all the objects of a particular database within one file. Access fetches and stores information in whichever database is open, but only one database may be open at one time.

All exercises in this text refer to the *Companion CD* that comes with this text. (You used the CD-ROM in an exercise in Chapter 1.) We have segregated files of all types needed for each chapter into separate databases so that you can isolate all changes and activities by chapter. Here is how the disk directories are set up. All files needed for Chapter 2 are found in the directory Ch02 (C-h-zero-two), all files needed for Chapter 3 are found in the directory Ch03, and so on. Whenever you are working with a chapter, you can locate databases and files in the associated chapter directory on your Companion CD. The next exercise shows you how to open a database that has been copied to drive C from your Companion CD so the data is available to Microsoft Access.

EXERCISE 2.3: OPENING A DATABASE

1. Launch Access by double-clicking the Access icon (locate it, if necessary, using the Start menu Search command as you did in Chapter 1). The Microsoft Access dialog box displays.
2. Click *More files* in the Task Pane section called *Open a file*.
3. Click the Look in drop-down menu and select drive C. Folders and file names found on drive C appear in the list box (see Figure 2.10).

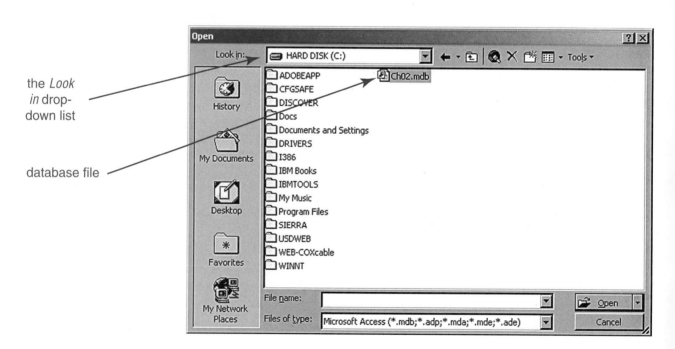

Figure 2.10   Open Database dialog box.

4. In the large list box displaying folder names and file names, select *Ch02.mdb* and click the Open button. (Alternately, you can double-click the database file name to open it.) Microsoft Access displays the Ch02 Database window (see Figure 2.11).

The Database window displays the names of all tables in the database. There are other objects held in the database including queries, forms, and reports. The names of forms in this database can be seen if you click Forms on the Objects bar. Likewise, you can see all queries by clicking Queries. If the table objects show icons or show more information, then your view setting has been changed. If your table list match doesn't match the list in Figure 2.11, select the Details command from the View menu. Now the two should look alike.

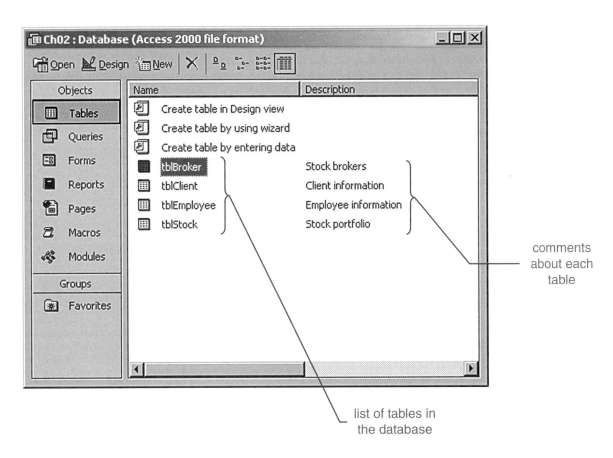

Figure 2.11 Database window.

Looking at Your Data through Different Windows

Access provides several ways to view your data. You can inspect your data in a Table window, which displays data in columns and rows called a *Datasheet view*—just like a spreadsheet's data. Or you can use a Form window to display one or more rows in a nontabular format. Forms provide an attractive way to view and change data, because they can be designed to resemble paper forms with which you are already familiar. (You can also view a form in Datasheet view.) Alternately, you can view your data in a report format with the Report window. The Report window provides a preview of a printed report so that you can review it as you would a hard copy report prior to printing it.

Because each view is found in a separate window, you can display several different windows simultaneously. Figure 2.12 shows both a Table window and a Form window of the Employee table. Because the Form window is active (notice the Form window Title bar is darker), the menu bar and toolbar are the ones used in a Form window.

One of the databases found on the Companion CD contains information about a fictitious stock brokerage firm. This small database consists of four tables, three of which are related to one another: Broker (*tblBroker*), Client (*tblClient*), and Stock (*tblStock*). We follow the object naming convention that all tables begin

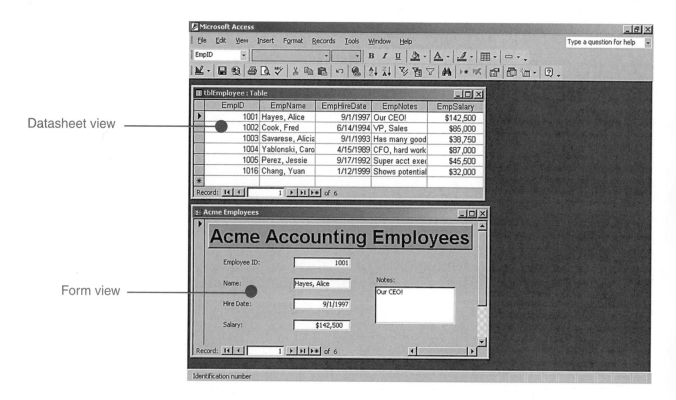

Figure 2.12   Two views of the same data.

with the prefix *tbl* followed immediately by the rest of the object name. Queries begin with *qry* and the rest of the object name, forms begin with *frm* and the rest of the object name, and reports begin with *rpt* and the remainder of the name. (For simplicity, we refer to the tables in the text without their prefixes.) The Broker table contains information about four of the brokerage firm's employees, all stockbrokers. Client contains the names, addresses, and other data about selected brokerage clients. The Stock table lists the stocks currently held by each customer whose name is in the Client list. Of course, all of these tables are smaller than corresponding tables in a real brokerage house. We want you to comprehend the *process* of extracting meaningful information from the data, not marvel at the *size* of the database. It is easier to understand database concepts if we use several small tables. Client, for instance, contains 15 rows, one for each customer. Broker contains 4 rows, which contain a few facts about the brokers. Finally, the Stock table contains 173 rows. Whenever a customer purchases an individual stock, that transaction is recorded and saved in the Stock table.

You may be interested in more details about what these three tables contain. Details about each of the brokerage firm tables are revealed as we describe fundamental Access operations and procedures in this chapter. We begin by examining the use of Access tables, the elemental building block of all database applications.

Opening a Table

The Table window is one way to view your data. When you open a table, the menu bar and toolbar change to menus and icons that are appropriate for table operations. You can better understand this process if you open an existing table and experience firsthand how some of the toolbar buttons and menus operate. In preparation for the exercise that follows, execute Access and the Ch02 database you have copied to drive C. If you forget how to open a database, review the previous exercise to refresh your memory. Now you are ready to follow the steps in the next exercise to open one of the tables on your disk.

EXERCISE 2.4: OPENING A TABLE

1. Click Tables in the Object bar to display the list of tables in the Ch02 database.
2. Double-click the table *tblClient* found in the list of tables. (Alternatively, you can select *tblClient* and click the Open button in the Database window.) Access opens the Client table in Datasheet view (see Figure 2.13).

Take a moment to examine the Client table. Notice the Datasheet navigation buttons located in the Navigation bar found at the bottom edge of the Table window. The Database window may be visible behind the table and slightly to its left. Below the Access Title bar is the Table window menu bar. The menu bar's

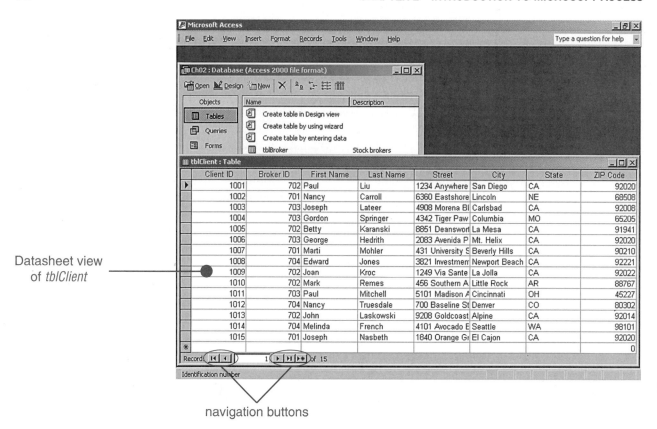

Datasheet view
of *tblClient*

navigation buttons

Figure 2.13   The Client table (*tblClient*).

contents vary depending on what type of window is active (Table, Form, etc.). Below the menu bar is the toolbar. The contents of the toolbar vary with the active window. The Table Datasheet toolbar, shown in Figure 2.14, is displayed when a Table window is active and you are viewing a Datasheet (a table). The Form Design toolbar is displayed when the Form Design window is active.

Some Datasheet toolbar buttons are familiar, because they are similar to those found in other Windows products. Familiar toolbar buttons include Print, Print Preview, Cut, Copy, and Paste, which are on the left side of the toolbar. The Print button is a familiar icon that you can click to print a table. Hover the mouse pointer over the Print button. When you hover the mouse pointer over any toolbar button, you will see text, called a *ToolTip*, appearing just below the button. The ToolTip displays the toolbar button's name.

Binoculars on the toolbar are used to search the table for particular values. Other toolbar buttons allow you to modify the table's design (Design view), sort the table into ascending or descending order, apply filter criteria to select particular records, and create forms and reports from the table. You will use some of these latter buttons later in this chapter.

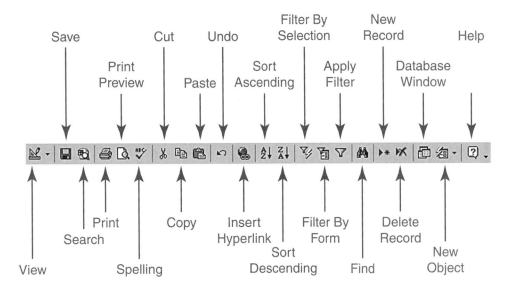

Figure 2.14 Table Datasheet toolbar.

When a horizontal scroll bar appears along the bottom of the Table window, it indicates that some table columns are out of view. The scroll bar works like any other Windows scroll bar: drag the scroll box to the right and the window pans to the right; click the scroll arrows and the window shifts for each click in the indicated direction. Vertical scroll bars appear whenever any rows of the table cannot be seen, as is frequently the case. The vertical scroll bar, located on the right side of the Table window, operates similarly to the horizontal scroll bar.

Moving Around a Table

When you open a large table, only the first few rows are displayed. There are several ways to move through a table so that its rows are displayed in the Table window. You can select one of the movement choices from the Go To selection of the Edit menu: First, Last, Next, Previous, or New Record. You can also use the keyboard: the up arrow, down arrow, PgUp, and PgDn keys move up one row, down one row, up one screen, and down one screen, respectively. Perhaps the easiest way to scroll through a table's rows is to use the navigation buttons (see Figure 2.13). Left to right, they move to the top of the table, up one row, to a specific numbered record, down one row, to the last record in the table, or add a new row to the table. The last button opens a new record, which is placed immediately following the last record in the table. The New Record button is a convenient way to add a new record to a table. Try the navigation buttons. With the Client table still displayed in a Table window, first go to the top of the database. Then click the Last Record navigation button to go to the last record (we use the term *record* interchangeably with the term *row*).

Notice that the dark *row pointer* rests in one row of the *record selector column*. The record selector column is to the left of the table's leftmost column (see Figure 2.13). As you move around the table with the navigation buttons, the record selector moves to another row. Pressing the right and left arrow keys moves the cursor to a different column in the same row.

Searching for a Value in a Column

Searching for a particular record in a table based on the value of one of its columns is straightforward. Though nearly all the data is visible in this small Client table example, most corporate tables contain thousands and hundreds of thousands of rows. Finding a particular client's record in such a large table would be extremely difficult without a database system. Let's imagine that the Client table contains many rows and you want to find a client whose name begins with the letters "Lasko" but you do not remember the exact spelling. Your task, in the next exercise, is to locate the client's record. If necessary, open the table *tblClient* in the Ch02 database.

EXERCISE 2.5: SEARCHING FOR A ROW CONTAINING A PARTICULAR VALUE

1. With the *tblClient* datasheet displayed, click the topmost name in the Last Name column. That moves the cursor to the column you will ask Access to search.
2. Click the Find button (it looks like a pair of binoculars) and type **Lask*** in the Find What text box. Be sure to include the asterisk, a wildcard, following the last letter.
3. Select Down from the Search drop-down list.
4. Click the Find Next button to start the search process. Access searches the Last Name column for a match and moves the record selector to the row containing the name *Laskowski*; the matching name is highlighted. (You may have to close the Find and Replace dialog box to see the highlighted Last Name entry.)
5. Close the Find and Replace dialog box.
6. Move the record pointer to the first record in the *tblClient* table by using the appropriate navigation button.

Try a few other search operations. For instance, locate the record whose City column contains "Seattle." What happens if there is no match? A dialog box is displayed indicating the search was unsuccessful.

Changing a Table's Display Characteristics

You can change the visual properties of any table you are viewing. For instance, you can move columns left or right in a table, alter individual column widths, and remove the grid lines that separate the rows and columns. You can change a table's display properties by selecting an entire column and then right-clicking (clicking the right mouse button) the table column selected. Even though you may change a table's display characteristics, you are *not* changing the table's structure or contents. For instance, if you move the ClientName column to the left of its current position, the underlying table, Client, is unaffected. Only the *display* characteristics of the Client table are affected. (Access gives you the opportunity to save a table's display characteristics permanently when you close the table.)

Let's change two display properties for the Client table temporarily. The next exercise moves the ClientName column to the first column, just to the right of the record selector column. You will also make one other visual change: You will optimize the widths of all columns so no data is obscured. Before starting the exercise, make sure Access is loaded, the database Ch02 is open, and the Client (*tblClient*) datasheet is displayed. Maximize the Table window so you can see more of the table.

EXERCISE 2.6: CHANGING A TABLE'S DISPLAY CHARACTERISTICS

1. Move the pointer to the First Name *field selector* (column heading). When the mouse pointer is over the column heading, it changes to a down-pointing arrow. (When the pointer is within the data column, it changes to an I-beam shape.)
2. Click and drag the mouse to the right until both the First Name and the Last Name columns darken, and then release the mouse button.
3. Click inside either darkened column's field selector and drag to the leftmost position in the table. Then, release the left mouse button. (The columns remain darkened after you release the mouse.)
4. With the columns still selected, right-click the mouse in the First Name column. A pop-up menu appears.
5. Click Column Width from the list of pop-up menu choices.
6. Click the Best Fit button. The columns resize to the smallest width that will display both the column label and the widest column entry for each column, independently.
7. Click any entry in the Client ID column to deselect the highlighted columns, and then move the mouse to the Client ID column field selector. When the mouse changes to a down-pointing arrow, click and drag it to the right, selecting the column field selectors for Client ID through ZIP Code. Release the mouse.
8. With all columns except First Name and Last Name darkened (selected), position the pointer on the right border of any darkened field selector and double-click the mouse to produce the best fit width for all the selected columns.
9. Click any data entry in the table to deselect the columns. Figure 2.15 shows the reformatted *tblClient* datasheet.

We are finished with this exercise and do not want to permanently change the Client datasheet display characteristics, so close the table by clicking its title bar Close button. A dialog box opens. It informs you that the layout for Client has changed and asks whether you want to save the new layout. Click No to discard the table display changes you have made.

two name columns moved to the leftmost position

First Name	Last Name	Client ID	Broker ID	Street	City	State	ZIP Code
Paul	Liu	1001	702	1234 Anywhere Street	San Diego	CA	92020
Nancy	Carroll	1002	701	6360 Eastshore Drive	Lincoln	NE	68508
Joseph	Lateer	1003	703	4908 Morena Blvd	Carlsbad	CA	92008
Gordon	Springer	1004	703	4342 Tiger Paw Lane	Columbia	MO	65205
Betty	Karanski	1005	702	8851 Deansworthy Street	La Mesa	CA	91941
George	Hedrith	1006	703	2083 Avenida Picante	Mt. Helix	CA	92020
Marti	Mohler	1007	701	431 University Street	Beverly Hills	CA	90210
Edward	Jones	1008	704	3821 Investments Heights Dr.	Newport Beach	CA	92221
Joan	Kroc	1009	702	1249 Via Sante Fe	La Jolla	CA	92022
Mark	Remes	1010	702	456 Southern Accent Way	Little Rock	AR	88767
Paul	Mitchell	1011	703	5101 Madison Avenue	Cincinnati	OH	45227
Nancy	Truesdale	1012	704	700 Baseline Street	Denver	CO	80302
John	Laskowski	1013	702	9208 Goldcoast Drive	Alpine	CA	92014
Melinda	French	1014	704	4101 Avocado Blvd	Seattle	WA	98101
Joseph	Nasbeth	1015	701	1840 Orange Grove	El Cajon	CA	92020
							0

each column is
resized to its
optimal width

Figure 2.15   Changing a table's display characteristics.

Sorting Table Rows

Often, you can locate a record or group of records more quickly if the table is sorted. For instance, it is somewhat difficult to scan the Client table, as small as it is, and determine quickly whether a client named Toadvine is among the last names in your client list. You can imagine how difficult searching for clients by name would be for a much longer client list containing thousands of records, especially when the records are not sorted by name. The Client table is already sorted on one of its fields, Client ID.

There are two ways to sort any table. One way is to perform a *quick sort* to organize the table on a single column. Another way is to create and apply a *filter*, which allows you to accomplish more complex, multicolumn sort operations. No matter which method you choose, the table returns to its original order once it is closed.

Some tables are automatically organized because they have *key* field(s). Client, for instance, is organized on the Client ID field because that field was designated a primary key field when the table was constructed. (Primary key fields ensure that tables contain only one record for a particular key field value.) You will sort the Client table into ascending name order in the next exercise. In preparation for the exercise, ensure that Access is still running and that the Ch02 database is open. Click Tables in the Object bar of the Database window to display the list of tables in Ch02. Then, open the Client table (*tblClient*).

EXERCISE 2.7: SORTING A TABLE

1. With the Client table displayed in Datasheet view, click anywhere in the Last Name column.
2. Click Records on the menu bar, point to Sort, and click Sort Ascending. The datasheet is sorted into ascending order by clients' last names. Do not close the table yet.

Another way to sort a table is to create an *Advanced Filter/Sort*. When you do, you can select multiple table sort columns (for instance, ascending order by State and then ascending order by City within each State). You can select column names from a list, place each sort column into a sort grid, and select either an Ascending or Descending sort order for each column. Once you create an Advanced Filter/Sort, you apply it by clicking the Apply Filter button found on the toolbar (it is the unembellished funnel). You redisplay the datasheet in its original order by selecting Remove Filter/Sort from the Records menu. Experiment a bit with these. They can do no harm, because the table's actual record order is unaffected. Only a datasheet's displayed row order is changed.

After you are done experimenting with sorting, close the Client table by clicking the Table window Close button. When the dialog box appears asking if you want to save the changes to the design of the table, click No. The Database window becomes active. Be careful not to click the Access *application* Close button, because the entire application will close and you will have to restart Access.

Printing a Table

Printing a database table could not be easier. Simply select the table (it need not be open in a window to print its contents) or display the table in a Table window and then click Print from the File menu. You can also click the toolbar Print button. However, be aware that you cannot control the number of pages or other print parameters if you use the toolbar Print button. Clicking the button starts printing the table immediately. We suggest you always select Print from the File menu to maintain greater control over the content and volume that you want printed.

When you select Print from the File menu, a Print dialog box appears (see Figure 2.16). You can choose to print all pages or a range of pages. Select a page range by entering From and To page numbers. Normally, you need only one copy of the report. However, if multiple copies are needed, simply alter the value in the Number of Copies text box. When you are ready to print the table, click the OK button. Otherwise, click the Cancel button to nullify the print process and return to the Table window.

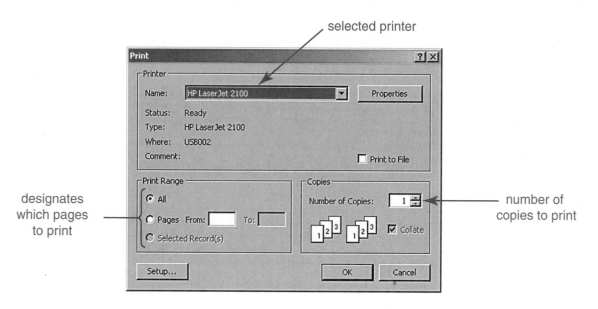

selected printer

designates which pages to print

number of copies to print

Figure 2.16 Print dialog box.

A printed table is created using a default format. The table's contents are printed in columns with horizontal and vertical table grid lines. Today's date appears in the upper right corner of the report, and the table's name appears centered above the table. At the bottom center of the page is a page number. Additional pages are printed whenever a table's columns are wider than can be printed on a single page.

The table report is functional but far from beautiful. Access provides tools for producing boardroom-quality reports replete with fonts, specialty features such as underlining and boldface, etc. Later in this chapter we describe how to create and use Access reports. Table printouts are quick and easy to produce and allow you to quickly check values in various columns.

Printing information about the *structure* and *definition* of any table is a bit more complicated. Click Tools, point to Analyze, and then select Documentor. Check the box corresponding to the name of the object(s), *tblClient*, for instance (see Figure 2.17). Click OK. Then, select Print from the File menu to print detailed information such as properties, relationships, permissions, data names, data types, and sizes. A printed copy of a table's definition provides good system documentation.

QUERYING A DATABASE

One of the real power capabilities of relational databases is the ability to ask questions that return interesting and meaningful answers derived from a database. Relational database systems make asking questions particularly easy, and Access is no exception. A *query*, the usual name for a question, can be simple or complex

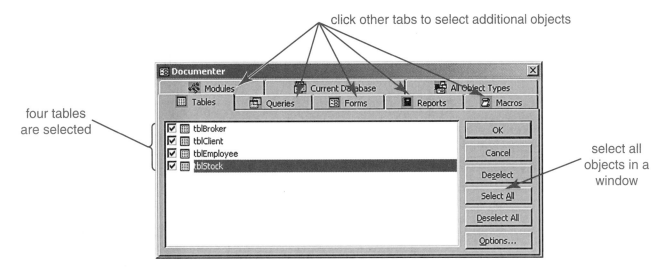

click other tabs to select additional objects

four tables
are selected

select all
objects in a
window

Figure 2.17   Using Documentor to print table structure information.

and can involve only one table, dozens of tables, or even hundreds of tables. In a query, you specify which tables are involved in the data retrieval operation, which columns are to be retrieved, which records are to be returned, how to sort the returned rows, and what calculations should be performed. The result is also a table. Relational database systems are *closed* systems, because queries use tables as input and return tables as answers. Simply stated, you put tables in and get tables out. A very important distinction between tables and queries, though both appear similar, is that tables are the only database objects that actually hold data. Queries *do not* hold data. They are merely stored definitions that extract and display data from tables when they are run.

The most frequently used type of queries are called *selection queries*, because they *retrieve* rows from tables. There are other types of queries that do not retrieve answers. Instead, they alter tables—insert new records into a table, delete existing records from a table, update data in one or more columns of a table, or create new table columns. All of the examples and discussion in this section illustrate selection queries. The section called *Creating Action Queries* describes the other types of queries that alter table data.

What are examples of the kinds of information you could retrieve with a query and why not simply print a table? Consider a larger version of the Client table. Suppose it contained information on over 14,000 clients and your supervisor wants to know how many clients are located in California. Or perhaps another manager wants to know how many clients are served by broker number 701. You probably would not print a 14,000-row client table and then manually look for the answers. That could take hours and be fraught with error and frustration. To compound the problem of sifting through data, the File Print command does not allow you to regulate which rows or which columns are printed.

Queries allow you flexibility in deciding which rows and columns of a table should be printed and provide an easy way to sift through large volumes of data. That is, queries provide a simple way to ask questions that return subsets of table rows, columns, or both. Access uses a query method called *Query by Example*, or *QBE*. Queries are formulated by giving Access an example of the result you want, and Access uses that model to return a result in a special, table-like structure called a *dynaset*. Let's look at an example.

Using a Query

Suppose you are a stockbroker and you want a list of all your California clients. Furthermore, you want the list sorted by city. Because you are planning to mail literature to those customers, you want to see the clients' name and address fields (including zip code). However, you do not need to see the clients' identification numbers nor their assigned brokers' numbers. To extract the needed information, you would create the query by opening a Query window and showing Access an example of what you want. Figure 2.18 shows both a Query window and the resulting dynaset.

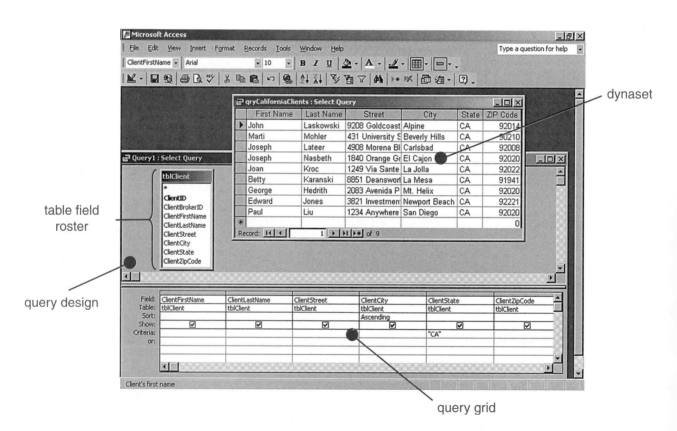

Figure 2.18   A query design and resulting dynaset.

Let's try running the preceding query just to see how the question formation process works. The query shown in the Query window of Figure 2.18 has been saved in the Ch02 database under the name *qryCaliforniaClients*. By using the *qry* prefix on all query names[1], we can easily distinguish queries from other database objects.

With that in mind, we show you how to use an existing query. In the next section we will build a new query from scratch. Set the scene before doing the next exercise: launch Access, if necessary, and ensure that database Ch02 is open. Then complete the following exercise to open and run a query.

EXERCISE 2.8: RUNNING A QUERY

1. Click Queries in the Objects bar of the Database window to display a list of the queries stored in the Chapter 2 database, *Ch02.mdb*.
2. Double-click the query *qryCaliforniaClients*. (Double-clicking a database object's name is a fast way to open it in nondesign view. Alternatively, you can click the query name and then click the Open button.) Shortly, a dynaset appears displaying the query's result.
3. After you have examined the results, click the Query window Close button.

The preceding dynaset displays clients living in California, sorted by city. Candidate rows are drawn from a table called *tblClient*. If you are a bit curious about how the query is structured, you can click the toolbar Design View button. It is the leftmost icon on the toolbar and displays a ruler and a triangle.

Creating a One-Table Query

You create new queries using the Query By Example (QBE) method. For instance, suppose you want to see a list of all customer invoices that are over 60 days past due. Printing or displaying the Invoice table would not be the answer, since all invoices would be printed. What you want is to sift through all the invoices and display only those whose invoice date is older than 59 days.

You create a query by clicking Queries in the Object bar of the Database window and then clicking the New button. When the query grid is displayed, you write a query that tells Access to search through the Invoice table for all invoices more than 59 days old. Rows that satisfy the age condition will be displayed.

---

[1]*A note about naming objects:* We follow the convention that query names have the prefix *qry* followed by the query name. No object name contains embedded blanks. Blanks in names can be troublesome and should be avoided. For instance, the name *qryNewCustomers* is preferred to the name *qry New Customers*, with blanks between the words. Squash the separate words together and distinguish them by using initial capital letters for each word (except the prefix).

Queries that restrict which rows are returned (by using some criteria) use a relational database operation called *selection*. (You specify which rows to *select*.)

Let's go through the process of creating a simple selection query that searches the *tblStock* table, returning a portion of the rows. In the exercise that follows, we will create a query that lists all stock transaction information for the client whose number is 1015. One table holds all the information we want: *tblStock*. Prepare for the exercise by closing all open windows except the Ch02 Database window. Then, complete the exercise.

EXERCISE 2.9: CREATING A ONE-TABLE QUERY

1. Click Queries in the Database window to display the list of queries.
2. Click the New button in the Database window. The New Query dialog box opens.
3. Select Design View, if necessary, from the list and then click OK. The Show Table dialog box appears (see Figure 2.19).

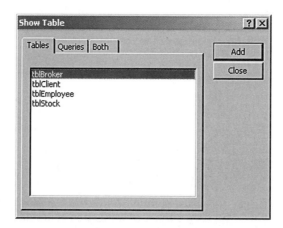

Figure 2.19   Show Table dialog box.

4. Click the Stock table (*tblStock*), and then click the Add button. Microsoft Access adds the Stock table to the query.
5. Click the Close button to indicate that no more tables are to be part of the query definition. The Show Table dialog box closes. Now you can select the fields (columns) that the query displays.
6. Drag the asterisk (*) field from the *tblStock* field list to the first cell in the Field row of the Query By Example (QBE) grid. (The asterisk stands for all fields in the table.) Dragging the asterisk saves time; you avoid dragging individual fields to the QBE grid, but you lose control over the left-to-right placement of fields.

7. Drag the ClientID field from the *tblStock* field list to the second cell in the Field row of the QBE grid. (A shortcut is to double-click the field name in the list of fields to place it in the next available Field row cell of the QBE grid.) Notice that the check boxes in the Show row are checked, which means the data for that column will appear in the dynaset.

8. Click the Show row check box under the ClientID column to clear (erase) it. There's no need for ClientID to be displayed twice, but we want to select only rows containing a particular value for ClientID. Therefore we include, but do not display, a separate column to hold selection criteria.

    Next, we limit the search for records to those that satisfy our criteria: rows whose ClientID is 1015. That is, we want only client 1015's rows displayed in the dynaset, not all rows. We limit rows by entering the example value 1015 in the Criteria row of the ClientID column in the QBE grid.

9. Point to the cell in the Criteria row that is under the ClientID column, click the cell, and type **1015** (see Figure 2.20).

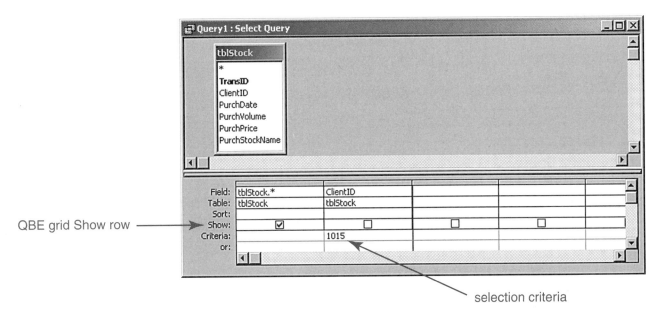

QBE grid Show row

selection criteria

Figure 2.20   One-table query, Design view.

10. Click the Datasheet View button on the toolbar (it is the grid-looking icon left-most in the toolbar). The dynaset displays the results of this query (see Figure 2.21).

You will be creating more queries, so you can leave the Query window open. Or you can close the database and continue at another time.

TransID	ClientID	Date	Volume	Price	Name
20210	1015	12/17/2001	100	$124.25	America Online
20471	1015	3/11/2002	75	$27.87	Walt Disney Co
20476	1015	3/18/2002	125	$24.25	Quantum Corp.
20575	1015	4/1/2002	150	$71.44	Fannie Mae
20725	1015	5/10/2002	150	$16.38	Computer Task
20748	1015	5/21/2002	150	$43.69	Unisys
20787	1015	6/8/2002	250	$3.59	ZI Corp
20792	1015	6/8/2002	125	$26.83	Compaq Compu
20941	1015	8/4/2002	250	$72.81	Ameritech
21093	1015	9/9/2002	150	$94.00	Microsoft
21134	1015	9/20/2002	250	$17.25	Sequent Compu
21234	1015	10/15/2002	150	$146.32	Texas Instrumei
21626	1015	8/5/2003	125	$24.13	Comdisco
21770	1015	11/1/2003	250	$14.56	Ducommun

Record: 1 of 14

only rows with *1015* in the ClientID
column appear in the dynaset

Figure 2.21   One-table query dynaset.

Saving a Query

You can execute queries periodically to produce current lists of clients, spare parts, invoices over 60 past days due, etc. Always save queries so that you do not have to recreate them. By saving a query, you can later rerun it to obtain accurate, timely information about changing data. Note that you cannot save the dynaset because it is not an object. It merely displays data from the underlying table that pass the criteria test. (You can create a special query, called a Make-Table query, which can save the dynaset as a table. We explore this and other special query types later in this chapter.)

Try It

You save a new query by selecting either Save or Save As from the File menu and then entering a name in the Query Name text box. Click OK and the query is saved. Let's check it out by saving the current query. Select the Save command from the File menu. The Save As dialog box appears. Type the name **qryClient1015** in the Query Name text box. Click OK. The query is saved in the Ch02 database in the Queries window with the name *qryClient1015*. We have saved the query in your database under the name *qryClient1015Stock* on your Companion CD in case you choose not to save your query.

For any existing query you may have altered, the procedure to save it is almost the same. Simply select Save from the File menu, and the query will be saved under the existing name in your database. Keep in mind that if there are several query windows open simultaneously, only the *active query*—the one whose window is active—is saved.

Sorting the Results

Normally, Access displays a dynaset—the result of a selection query—in order by the primary key of the underlying table. (For instance, the *tblClient* table's key column is ClientID.) If the table searched by the query has no primary key, then the dynaset's rows display in no particular order. However, you can specify your own sort requirements so that dynaset rows will be in a more meaningful order. You select a sort order by selecting either Ascending or Descending beneath the appropriate column(s) in the QBE grid Sort row.

Try It

Display in Design view the query *qryCaliforniaClients* and click in the Sort row beneath the first column. Select either Ascending or Descending from the drop-down list. Continue, if necessary, selecting other columns to the right in the QBE grid. You can select Ascending or Descending for any number of columns, but the leftmost column having the Sort row cell filled is the *primary* sort column. The significance of other sort columns are determined by their *relative position* in the QBE sort grid, left to right. You may wish to drag one or more columns to the left to enhance their influence on the final sort order. Better yet, you can add columns to the right specifying sort orders for each column. Clear the Show check box of any duplicate columns so they are used to sort, but are not displayed, in the dynaset.

Using More Complex Selection Criteria

Suppose the manager of the stock brokerage firm wants to know the number of stock transactions and the volume of each purchase that occurred in her office during the month of January. She is considering sending most of her brokers on vacation for January if activity is sufficiently low during that month. Let's see how we could answer that question with a query.

To answer the preceding request, a query is formulated that returns all Stock table rows for which the value in the Date column is greater than 12/31 of the previous year *and* less than 2/1 of the current year. The criteria clearly involves two conditions—two different dates. Furthermore, both conditions must be true for a row to be returned in the Answer table. For situations like this, the criteria must use an *AND* operator. In fact, you can use the AND operator in the criteria whenever you select rows based on a range of values for a single column of a table. Let's create a new query to select all rows representing January 2002 stock purchases.

For this query we need not list all columns of the Stock table, because the manager is interested only in gross numbers of transactions, their volume, and the price of each trade. It is sufficient to list only the client identification number (ClientID), the purchase date (Date), number of shares purchased (Volume), and the purchase price (Price) columns. We are using the projection operation. A *projection* operation is one in which a subset of a table's columns is displayed. In this example, we include a subset of the Stock table's columns in the dynaset returned by the query. Projection is one of the important operations available with relational database systems such as Access. Close all windows except the Database window in preparation for the next exercise.

EXERCISE 2.10: WRITING SELECTION CRITERIA USING AN "AND" OPERATOR

1. Click Queries in the Objects bar of the Database window and then click the New button.
2. Select Design View in the New Query dialog box and click OK.
3. Double-click the *tblStock* table from the list shown in the Show Table dialog box and click the Close button. (Double-clicking a table's name is a fast way to add it to a query.)
4. Click ClientID in the *tblStock* table field roster and then hold down the Ctrl key and click, in turn, the following fields: PurchDate, PurchVolume, and PurchPrice. Release the Ctrl key.
5. Click inside any of the selected fields in the table field roster and drag the list to the first cell in the Field row.
6. Release the mouse. When you release the mouse, the four fields are placed in separate Field row cells in the QBE grid.
7. Click the Criteria cell below the PurchDate column and enter the following selection criteria: >#12/31/01# And <#2/1/02#. Be sure to include the > and < symbols and to surround the date constants with the # symbols.
8. Click the Datasheet View button to see the results of your query (see Figure 2.22).
9. When you are finished, click the Query window Close button to close it.
10. Click No when you are asked if you want to save the newly created query. The query is already saved as *qryJanuaryStockPurchases* on your Companion CD in the Ch02 database.

Look carefully at the expression in the QBE grid in Figure 2.22 in the Criteria row of the Date column. That expression is used to filter rows, selecting only those rows whose Date value falls within the specified range.

Three new symbols and a logical operator are introduced in the criteria. The *And* separates two expressions. This indicates that the conditions to its left and right must be met simultaneously. In other words, rows are displayed only if the

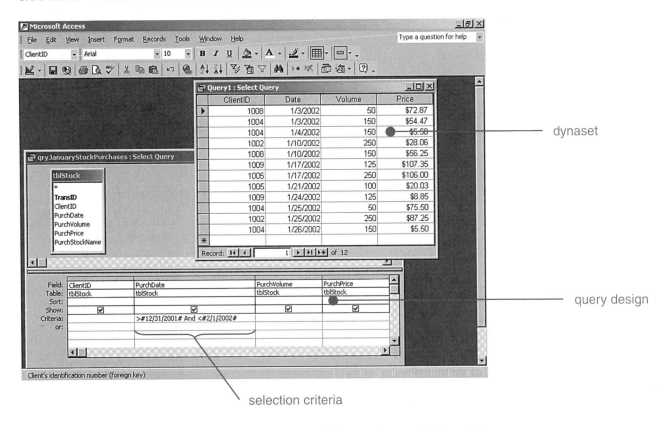

Figure 2.22 Selection and projection operations with an AND operator used in the criteria.

Date value is later than December 31, 2001 *and* before February 1, 2002. Pound signs (#) enclose each date value. Embedding dates in # symbols ensures that Access recognizes the enclosed values as dates rather than arithmetic expressions. An alternate way to write an expression having the same effect is the criterion: Between **#1/1/02# And #1/31/02#**. Most people prefer to use this form instead.

You probably are already familiar with the greater than (>) and less than (<) symbols. These are just two of the *comparison* operators that bracket the date range. A complete list of comparison operators is given in Figure 2.23. Among the *logical* operators is "And." The list of logical operators is given in Figure 2.24.

When you want to use criteria on two or more fields simultaneously, you place those conditions under the respective column names in the query image. For instance, suppose you want to list all stock purchases made by a particular client in a particular month of a given year, which involves a combination of queries similar to those you created in previous exercises.

Operator	Meaning
<	Less than
>	Greater than
=	Equal to
<=	Less than or equal to
>=	Greater than or equal to
<>	Not equal to

Figure 2.23   Comparison operators.

Operator	Meaning
And	Conditions on both sides must be true for the statement to be true. Otherwise, the statement is false.
Or	The statement is true if a condition on either side is true or if both conditions are true. Otherwise, the statement is false.
Not	A unary operator, it negates the logic it precedes.

Figure 2.24   Logical operators.

Try It

Modify the preceding query—*qryJanuaryStockPurchases*—to answer your new question. Click the Criteria row in the ClientID column and type 1008. Running the new query returns rows whose ClientID value equals 1008 *and* whose Date column value is any day in January 2002. The value 1008 is an *exact match* criterion, whereas the Date criterion is a *value range* criterion. What you have learned is that AND queries involving different fields of a table are created by entering all of the criteria in the same Criteria row of the QBE grid.

Creating Selection Criteria Using the OR Operator

You are likely to encounter queries similar to the following: "Which clients have purchased either item A or item B? Locate those purchase transactions and list them." Another example is this one: "List all client records whose stock purchase price is less than $3.50 or whose stock name is *Microsoft*, regardless of purchase price." Both of the preceding questions involve two conditions, either of which is reason enough to list the record. That is, the criteria are called OR conditions. Unlike AND conditions in which *all* conditions must be true to select and return a row to the dynaset, only *one* of the conditions must be true for a row to be returned.

How do you form a query involving OR conditions? Let's examine the latter example in the previous paragraph and see exactly what is needed to form a query.

Two independent criteria are involved. There are two basic ways to formulate OR criteria, depending on whether the criteria concern one field or different fields. If two different fields are involved (stock price and stock name, in our example), then you create a query containing two Criteria rows—one row for each condition. If a criterion involves only one field, then you can place alternate acceptable values in one field, separating them with the word *Or*.

The next exercise uses the first method, since two different fields are involved. Close any open Access windows, but leave the Ch02 Database window open.

EXERCISE 2.11: FORMING AN "OR" QUERY

1. Click Queries in the Objects bar to ensure you are about to create a query, not a table, form, or some other object.
2. Click the New button.
3. Select Design View in the New Query dialog box and click OK.
4. Double-click the *tblStock* table in the Show Table dialog box, and then click the Close button to close the Show Table dialog box.
5. Drag the asterisk (*) from the *tblStock* field list to the first cell in the Field row of the QBE grid.
6. Drag the PurchPrice and PurchStockName fields from the field list to the second and third cells in the Field row.
7. Clear the check boxes under the PurchPrice and PurchStockName columns so Access does not display values in those columns. (They will be displayed anyway because you dragged all fields to the Field row when you placed the asterisk in the first cell.)
8. Click the Criteria row under the PurchPrice column in the QBE grid, press Shift+F2 to enlarge the Criteria cell (this action is called "invoking the Zoom window"), and type the criterion **<3.5**
9. Click the OK button to close the Zoom window.
10. Click the *second* Criteria row under the PurchStockName column. Type the expression **Microsoft** (either lower- or uppercase is fine). Access will automatically surround the text criterion with double quotation marks when you click another cell in the QBE grid. (Access ignores capitalization when searching for matches.)

    Now each Criteria row specifies an independent selection criterion. Each will return a table row whenever its criterion is satisfied. Thus, both criteria contribute to the dynaset. However, when a row satisfies both criteria, only one copy is inserted into the dynaset.
11. Click the Datasheet View button to see the query results.

The dynaset, whose rows are in TransID order (because TransID is the queried table's primary key), is shown. Figure 2.25 shows both the query and the returned dynaset. (Normally, you can see either the query or the dynaset, since they are opposite sides of the same "coin." We have created a second query so you can see both at once.)

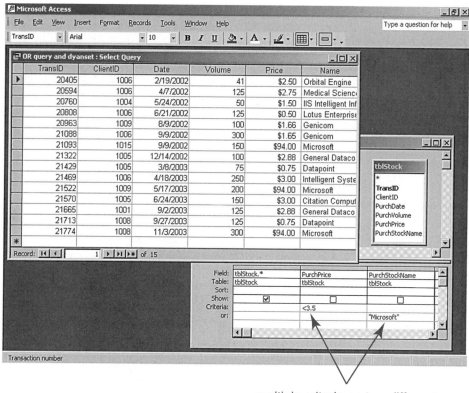

multiple criteria on two different
criteria rows implements an OR
between the criteria

Figure 2.25   OR query and dynaset.

Notice that to form an OR query you have as many Criteria rows in the query grid as there are independent selection criteria. Each row contains characters, a value, or an expression below a single column. When OR conditions involve only one field, there is an alternate way to write the criteria. For instance, suppose you want to display Stock table rows for anyone who has purchased either Microsoft or Biogen stock. Because both criteria involve the same field, StockName, you can write both criteria in one query image row, separating the criteria with the reserved word *OR* (either uppercase or lowercase):

"Microsoft" Or Like "Biogen*"

Normally, when dealing with character fields in a table, capitalization is significant. However, Access ignores capitalization and locates matching rows based on spelling alone. Character matching rules vary from one database product to another, however. Be sure to experiment with it first. *BIOGEN* in a query may not match *Biogen* in the database if you are not using Microsoft Access.

The asterisk following the word *Biogen* is one of the *wildcard* characters, which can stand for none or for any number of letters. This allows a match on a string such as *Biogen, Inc.*, *BIOGEN LTD.*, and so on. The asterisk can be used on either or both ends of any query string. Whenever you use a wildcard with a character string, Access automatically inserts the word *Like* ahead of it. Of course, the order of the strings separated by OR does not matter.

What would happen if you formed a query with only one row and placed the expression <3.5 beneath PurchPrice and placed MICROSOFT beneath PurchStockName? No rows would be returned in the dynaset because no table rows satisfy both criteria *simultaneously*. The latter query is an example of specifying AND criteria. Simply stated, each Criteria row states conditions that must all be satisfied before any rows are selected by that particular criteria for inclusion in the dynaset. Of course, if there are other Criteria rows, they too may select rows to be retrieved. You should try the AND criteria as described above with Price and StockName values. Verify that no rows are returned for the data we have supplied.

Including Expressions in a Query

For most applications, it is useful to calculate values that are not stored in the database. Accounting applications are a good example. For instance, brokers keep a watchful eye on their larger accounts. One measure of a client's account size is the total purchase price of each stock a client owns. However, the Stock database does not record that value. There are two approaches to solving this problem; one is correct and the other is wholly incorrect.

An incorrect solution would be to create a new *tblStock* table column that holds the total purchase price of a stock. While this might be an acceptable solution when using a spreadsheet product, doing this with a database can lead to inconsistencies in the database and trouble later on. Why? Suppose that the total purchase price is calculated as the product of the PurchPrice and PurchVolume columns (that is, purchase price is the product of price per share and the number of shares purchased). Suppose further that a mistake is discovered in transcribing the volume purchased for a particular transaction. Instead of recording 200 shares, someone recorded the transaction as 100 shares. Later the error is discovered and rectified.

Even though the PurchVolume value is corrected in the database record for a particular errant transaction, there is a danger that the total purchase price is not. Unlike a spreadsheet, a field value in a database row does not change automatically when other values on which it depends are changed. Here's an important rule covering this situation: *Never store in a table any value (field) that is functionally dependent on two or more fields in the record.* That's a simplification of a rule that will be described in Chapter 3, but it merely states you shouldn't store in a database a value you can calculate or derive from the database.

So, what is the correct way to arrive at the total purchase price for each stock for every customer? The correct way is to include an *expression* in the query QBE grid to calculate the desired value dynamically—each time the query is executed. Instead of having you go through the process of creating such a query, we have provided an example for you to simply execute. You will find a query containing a calculation stored as *qryStockValue* in your Ch02 database on the Companion CD.

Try It

Click Queries in the Objects bar of the Database window. Then double-click the query *qryStockValue*. The query displays rows from the *tblStock* table as well as each transaction's total value. Examine the query in Figure 2.26 as well as the dynaset showing the retrieved and calculated results.

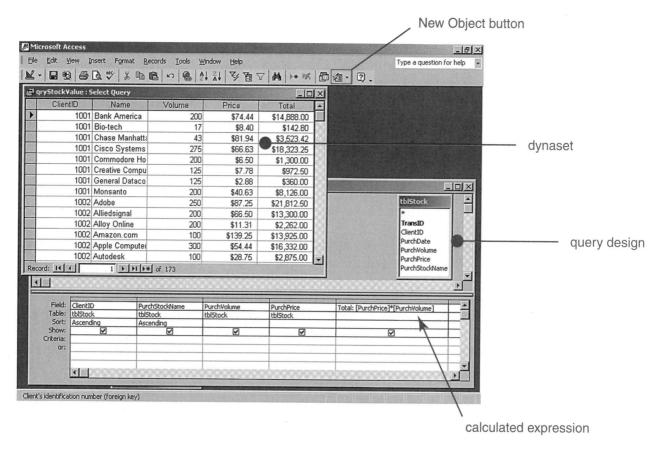

Figure 2.26   A query calculating a value with an expression.

Click the Design View button and examine the query. Pay particular attention to the expression in the Field row. (You may have to click the horizontal scroll bar to bring the field into view.) The expression *Total: [PurchPrice]*[PurchVolume]* is placed in the Field row. The expression computes total stock purchase price for each row in turn and creates a new column in the dynaset. The word *Total* followed by a colon and a space designates the name (also called an *alias*) for the column that appears in the dynaset (otherwise, the expression is the column label). The expression variables *[PurchPrice]* and *[PurchVolume]* reference table field names and get their values from the columns Price and Volume, respectively.

Printing Dynasets

To print a query's resulting dynaset, first display the dynaset (click the Datasheet View button if necessary). Before printing, always check the dynaset to make sure it contains the results you expected. Occasionally, you may pose a query that is too broad and encompasses too many database records. Or perhaps you inadvertently omitted a needed column. Always preview the query's result first. Print it only when you are satisfied.

Print the dynaset by choosing Print from the File menu. The familiar Print dialog box, shown earlier in Figure 2.16, appears. Make any selections necessary, perhaps limiting the range of pages to print, and then click OK to proceed. That's all there is to printing the results of a query—you simply print the dynaset.

Printing Query Definitions

You can document an object—a table, query, and so on—by printing its definition. It is very helpful to print the definitions of all your queries, because these serve as documentation for your evolving system. You might want to keep a notebook with a special section devoted to all query definitions for each database.

Printing a query's definition is a little tricky. Here's a brief overview of the steps to print the documentation for the *qryStockValue* query. Open the Query window by clicking Queries in the Object bar of the Database window. Select the Tools menu. Then, point to Analyze and click Documentor. The Documentor dialog box opens. Click the Queries tab. All of the query names appear along with their check boxes. Click the *qryStockValue* check box and any other queries whose definition you want to print (Figure 2.27). Finally, click OK to preview the definition report. If you are satisfied with the report preview, select Print from the File menu to print the query definition report.

CREATING ACTION QUERIES

Besides selection queries, you can create another type of Access query called an *action query*. Action queries provide a powerful means to make changes to a database's tables. Action queries can create a new table, remove records from an existing table, update one or more fields of an existing table, and add new records to an existing table. Action queries resemble selection queries such as those discussed in the previous section. The major difference is that they *alter* the database in some way, not merely display results from the database. Action queries include make-table, update, delete, append, and crosstab.

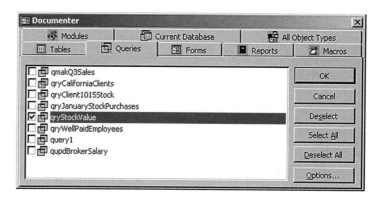

Figure 2.27   Preparing to print a query's definition.

With a make-table query, you can retrieve a subset of rows from one or more tables and save the dynaset as a table. Perhaps you want to concentrate on the smaller table, or you want to export the smaller table to Excel to analyze it further. Update queries allow you to change existing database information. You can create or run an update query to increase all programmers' hourly pay rates by 8 percent, for instance. A delete query selects and removes records from one or more tables. You could run a delete query to purge records of clients who have not contacted your office in over two years. With an append query, you can add new records to an existing table. Finally, a crosstab query summarizes and combines data from more than one source to present a compact, spreadsheet-like result. You might use a crosstab query to sum stock sales by broker for the first quarter of 2003—a statistic that is not apparent by observing tables alone. We present a concise description of how to create and run four of these action query types next.

Make-Table Query

You can create a new table from existing tables by using a make-table query. Suppose you want to create a new table containing only third quarter 2003 stock sales transactions from the *tblStock* table. The new table has the same structure, but contains only July, August, and September transactions. You could create a make-table query to deliver the information in two steps. First, create a selection query based on the *tblStock* table that retrieves all columns but only those rows whose transaction date falls between 7/1/03 and 9/30/03. Then, turn the selection query into a make-table query and run it to create the desired table.

Try It

Click Queries in the Object bar of the Database window and click the New button to create a new query. Select Design View and click OK when the New Query dialog box is displayed. Add the table *tblStock* and then close the Show Table dialog box. Drag all fields from the *tblStock* field roster to the Field row of the QBE grid. Drag another copy of the PurchDate field to the QBE grid. Clear the Show box corresponding to the second copy of PurchDate. In the Criteria row beneath the second copy of PurchDate, enter the selection criteria **Between #7/1/03# And #9/30/03#** and select Datasheet from the View menu to preview the new table. Select Design from the View menu to return to the Design view window. Now, for the new part! In the Design view window, select Make-Table Query from the Query menu. The Make-Table dialog box is displayed. Enter a new table name—the name of the table you will be creating—**tblThirdQuarterSales**—and click OK. You can save the make-table query and run it later, or you can run it now. (We have included this query on your Companion CD as *qmakQ3Sales*.) Save the query first: select Save from the File menu and name the query *qmakThirdQuarterSales*. (The prefix *qmak* indicates the query is a make-table query.) Finally, you can run the query to create a new table. In Design view, select Run from the Query menu. A warning is displayed indicating "You are about to run a make-table query that will modify data in your table." Click Yes to approve creating the new table. If you run the make-table query, you will find a new table when you click Tables in the Object bar of the Database window. Of course, you can delete the table (you may want to save the query, however) by selecting the table, choosing Delete from the Edit menu, and clicking Yes when asked to confirm the deletion. You can also right-click the table and select Delete from the pop-up menu.

Update Query

With update queries, you can make changes to many records in a table. You can update one field, or you can simultaneously update several. Update queries alter individual table fields, replacing them with new values. For instance, suppose we are sensitive to gender equity and want to make a mid-year adjustment to female brokers' salaries. We determine that they should receive a 5 percent raise. (Their male counterparts will have to wait an additional six months to qualify for a raise.) An update query is what's needed to make mass changes to the table containing brokers' salaries. Of course, our table is small, but this is an example of the kind of database change that would be laborious if it were done manually, one record at a time. The following activity leads you through making an update query. You can choose to actually create and run the query, or you can simply run the one we have created called *qupdBrokerSalary*.

Try It

Create a selection query of the records to be updated, placing in the QBE grid only the fields to be updated or used for criteria. In this case, place only the *tblBroker* fields BrokerSalary and BrokerGender in the QBE grid. (Salary will be updated, but Gender is used to select which rows' salary values are updated.) In the Criteria row, type **F** below the QBE BrokerGender column. Before proceeding, view the affected records to ensure your selection criteria are in good shape. Select the Datasheet View button to view the selected records. Switch back to Design view and continue. Select the Update Query command from the Query menu. Notice that the QBE grid changes. A new "Update To" row is added. In the Update To row beneath the BrokerSalary column type the expression **[BrokerSalary]*1.05** (be sure to enclose BrokerSalary in square brackets). Figure 2.28 shows the completed update query prior to execution. You can run the query to update the BrokerSalaries fields of the *tblBroker* table by selecting Run from the Query menu or by clicking the Run button on the Query Design toolbar.

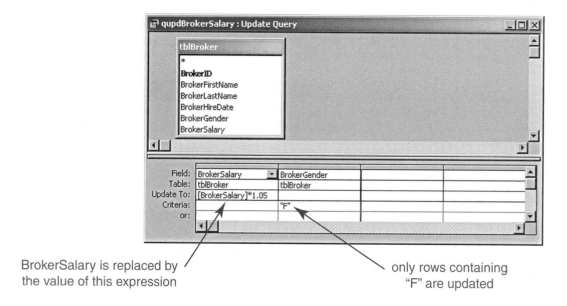

BrokerSalary is replaced by
the value of this expression

only rows containing
"F" are updated

Figure 2.28   An update query example.

Bear in mind one extremely important fact about updating database tables. An update operation *cannot be reversed with an Undo command—there is no undo*. You can undo some update operations by formulating a new update query to restore updated values, but many update operations are irreversible. For instance, suppose you choose to update the location field of an employee's work address to "New York" for all employees whose city is currently Indianapolis. This will effectively move all Indianapolis employees to New York. However, you cannot easily reverse the change if other employees already are listed as living in New York. That is, it is not a matter of changing the City field of New

York back to Indianapolis, because some are New Yorkers who were never located in Indianapolis in the first place! Always select Datasheet View before running an update query to check the scope of your changes.

Delete Query

A delete query is used to delete records from tables. It is *not* used to delete entire tables. To delete an entire table, not just the records it contains, you click Tables in the Database window, select the table, and press the Delete key. The entire table, plus data, is removed from the database. Deleting records is a much subtler activity. Suppose, for instance, that you want to remove from the *tblStock* table all transactions that occurred on or before December 31, 2002. In other words, you want to "clear the books" for a new year, 2003. A delete query with the proper selection criteria will do the trick. First, create a selection query and then examine its Datasheet view to ensure that proper records will be deleted when the query is transformed to a delete query. To create a delete query from a selection query, ensure the query is displayed in Design view and then select Delete Query from the Query menu.

Once you have properly defined a delete query, simply run it to delete the targeted records. Figure 2.29 shows an example of a delete query that removes from the table *tblStock* all stock transactions that occurred before 2003. The delete query, called *qdelOldTransactions*, is stored in your database, Ch02. Notice that the only fields that are needed in the QBE grid are those that are being used for criteria. In this example, only the PurchDate field is required, because that is the sole criterion—the purchase transaction date. Remember, though, that the entire record will be deleted.

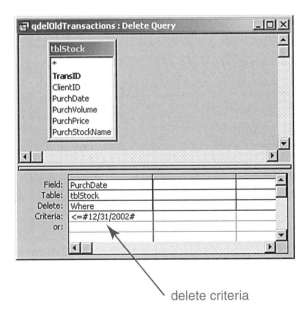

delete criteria

Figure 2.29 A delete query example.

Append Query

You use an append query to add records from a table or query to the end of another table. For instance, you would use an append query to create a comprehensive employee table containing all employees in all divisions. The table *tblEmployee*, for instance, represents only one division of a larger company. By creating an append query, you can add other divisions' employee records to the *tblEmployee* table.

To create an append query, simply create a selection query including fields from the source tables that are in the target (destination) table *and* any fields that are used as criteria. In the Criteria row of the query, establish the conditions that are used to select records from the other table to append to the current table (for instance, only division 1 and division 2 employees). View the potential new records by clicking the Datasheet View button. Then, switch back to Design view and select Append Query from the Query menu to turn the selection query into an append query. When prompted for the target table name by the Append dialog box, enter the target table's name or select it from the Table Name drop-down list. Click OK to complete the query definition. Figure 2.30 shows an example in which a fictitious division's employee records are to be appended to the *tblEmployee* table.

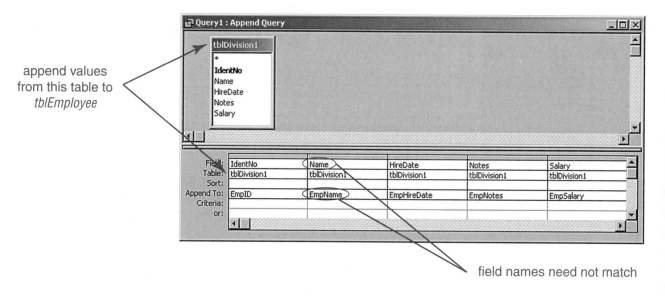

append values from this table to *tblEmployee*

field names need not match

Figure 2.30   An append query example.

USING FORMS

A form provides a convenient, less cluttered work surface through which you can enter or alter information in your tables. A form can display information from one or more tables. Additionally, a form can display information from a query (that is, the query's dynaset).

One of the advantages of using a form to enter or change data is that the form can look like a paper form with which you or your clients are already familiar. When the form on the screen mimics a paper form, those using the form will intuitively know what information goes where, and they usually feel more comfortable with a familiar interface. Entering data directly into a table can be more confusing and error-prone, especially for anyone not familiar with databases in general or Access in particular. Another advantage of a form is that you can enforce a medley of validation checks on values that are entered in a table through a form.

Viewing a Table through a Form

To help you understand a form better, we have created one that displays information from the Client table (*tblClient*), which is shown in Figures 2.13 and 2.15. The form is found on your Companion CD and is called *frmClient*. (All forms on the Companion CD have the prefix *frm*.) Work through the next exercise to open a Form view of the *tblClient* table.

EXERCISE 2.12: OPENING AND USING A FORM

1. Close all open windows except the Database window. (This isn't necessary, but it reduces screen clutter.)
2. Click Forms in the Objects bar of the Database window to display all forms in the Ch02 database.
3. Double-click the form *frmClient*. The Client form appears (see Figure 2.31).

All fields from the Client table (Figure 2.13) appear in a pleasant arrangement in the form in Figure 2.31. Familiar navigation buttons appear along the bottom edge of the Form window. Those buttons perform the usual actions: move to the top of the table, move up one row, and so forth. Look at the 15 records one at a time by clicking the Next Record button at the bottom of the Form view window. After you have moved to the last record, click the First Record navigation button to display the first record. Notice that the form displays records in order by ClientID. The form is built from the *tblClient* table whose primary key, ClientID, maintains the table (and thus the form) rows in order by the ClientID field. If you want rows displayed in the form in name order, you could create a query that returns rows sorted on ClientLastName (specify Ascending in the QBE grid under ClientLastName). Then you can build a form based on the query. We illustrate a query-based form in the next section.

Several interesting design elements have been employed in the Client form so that it is at once intuitive and attractive. Along the top is a simple title, in Arial typeface, identifying the form. Each form field is labeled and arranged on the form in a logical order. In the upper left part of the form is the client's identification

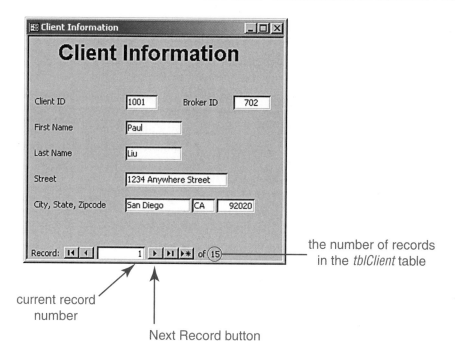

Figure 2.31   A client form.

number. It is entered first. Below it are the client's name and address. Notice that wherever information is supplied from the table—data to be changed or viewed—it is contained in a box frame that appears sunken. (You can change that, of course.) This helps the user visually separate labels from data.

Viewing a Query through a Form

You can create forms from queries as well as tables. It makes no difference whether the form displays a table's contents or a query's contents. Figure 2.32 shows a form that displays a subset of the fields from the *qryStockValue* query, which is shown in Figure 2.26. Unlike the previous form, this one has no Minimize or Restore buttons available in the form's Title bar. Notice that the Form window status line displays the current record and the total number of records. In this case, the total number of records depends on how many rows are selected by the query upon which the form is built. It is likely that you will create and use many forms based on queries. The form shown in Figure 2.32 is stored on your Companion CD in the Ch02 database as *frmStockValue*. Try it out yourself.

Creating a Form Quickly

When you want to enter data into a table one record at a time, your best work surface may be a form. We illustrate how easy it is to create a functional and

no Minimize or Maximize
button is available

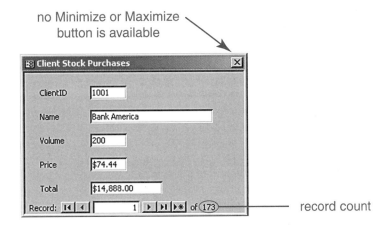

record count

Figure 2.32 Form based on the query, *qryStockValue*.

attractive form by simply choosing a table and clicking a button. Let's create a simple form for the *tblBroker* table through which we can observe or alter information. First, switch to the Database window (the fastest way is to click the Database Window button on the toolbar). Then, create an *AutoForm* by completing the steps in the following activity.

Try It

Click Tables in the Object bar of the Database window to display a list of the Ch02 table names. Highlight the table name *tblBroker* in the list of tables. Click the New Object button list arrow (see Figure 2.26) on the toolbar and then select AutoForm from the drop-down list. (Clicking the New Object button instead of the list arrow is a shortcut to create an AutoForm.) A Form window appears containing your newly created form (see Figure 2.33). The Form window Title bar contains the table name by default. You can change it later if you want. Leave the Form window open, because you will save the form in a few moments. That's all there is to creating a form from a table. You probably agree with us that the form is attractive and functional. We show you how to modify and enhance a form in Chapter 5. For now, simply save the new form on your copy of the database.

Saving a Form

You can save a form design either by executing Save or Save As from the File menu. Then you supply the form's name. Let's save the form in your hard-drive copy of the database.

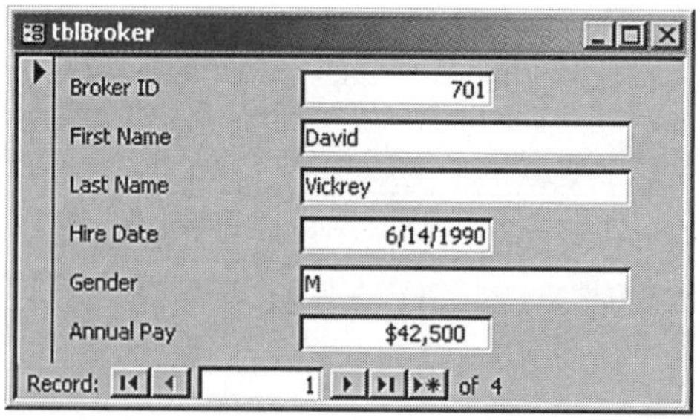

Figure 2.33 Broker form.

Try It

With the newly created Broker form still displayed, select Save in the File menu. Type the name **frmBrokerAutoForm** in the Form Name: text box of the Save As dialog box. Click OK to complete the form save operation. Click the form's Title bar Close button to close the form.

The form is saved in your C drive copy of the current database, Ch02. We have also saved the form in the Ch02 database on your Companion CD. It is called *frmBroker*.

Editing Data with a Form

It is often easier to alter data in a table using a form. Because only one table row is usually displayed on the form, you are less likely to make mistakes. Editing table data through a form is simple. While looking at a form in Form view (not Design view), you click the field that you want to change and make any needed changes. Let's try editing a record in the Broker table with the form. In preparation, make sure the Broker form is displayed in the Form view window. Then, complete the following exercise.

EXERCISE 2.13: EDITING DATA WITH A FORM

1. Move to the record for David Vickrey (press PgUp or PgDn or use the navigation buttons if necessary).
2. Press Tab to move to the Hire Date field. (The entire value is highlighted if you use Tab or the arrow keys to move to the selected fields.)
3. Type the correct hire date, 7/5/88
4. Click the Form window's Close button to close the form.

Changes to a particular record are not posted (saved) to the table until you move to another record or close the database. Simply click one of the navigation buttons on the form to store the changed record in the table. Go back to the record you changed to verify that the new hire date value has been saved. Keep in mind that the form merely displays table data. The form itself is not changed. Only the table data is actually changed. Changed data is automatically saved for you, and you need not save a form again unless you change the form's design.

Querying a Database with a Form

When you are looking for a particular record in a table containing many records, there's no better way to locate it than by using a form. You can load a form and then use the command *Filter By Form* or *Filter By Selection*. Additionally, you can create a more complex search using the *Advanced Filter/Sort* tool. To illustrate this process, let's use the Filter By Form command to locate all the stocks purchased by client 1013. You can imagine the daunting task this would be if you had to visually examine every row in the *tblStock* table looking for all a given client's transactions. Naturally, you wouldn't do it that way. Instead, you would request Access to apply a *filter*—another term for applying selection criteria so that only a subset of records is displayed—and retrieve only records of interest. Let's try it. In preparation, open your copy of the Ch02 database, if necessary.

EXERCISE 2.14: FILTERING DATA THROUGH A FORM

1. Click Forms in the Object bar of the Database window to display the existing form names.
2. Double-click *frmStockValue* to open that form.
3. Select the Records menu, point to the Filter menu item, and then select Filter By Form. Notice that a down-pointing arrow appears on the ClientID data field and that the menu has changed. The ClientID has changed into a drop-down list box from which you can choose one of the unique ClientID values retrieved from the *tblStock* table ClientID column.
4. Click the ClientID drop-down list box arrow to reveal the collection of ClientID values (see Figure 2.34).
5. Choose 1013 from the list. The ClientID field displays the value 1013.
6. Select Apply Filter/Sort from the Filter menu found on the menu bar. The first of several client 1013 records is displayed in the form. Notice that the indicator (filtered) appears just to the right of the navigation buttons. This indicates the form is displaying a subset of the underlying table (a filtered view), not all the records.
7. Use the navigation buttons to scroll through a few of the records.
8. When you are done, select Remove Filter/Sort from the Records menu or click the Remove Filter button (the funnel in Figure 2.34) found on the toolbar. The Remove Filter toolbar button is renamed Apply Filter when not engaged. You can toggle the filter on and off by clicking the button on and off.
9. Close the form.

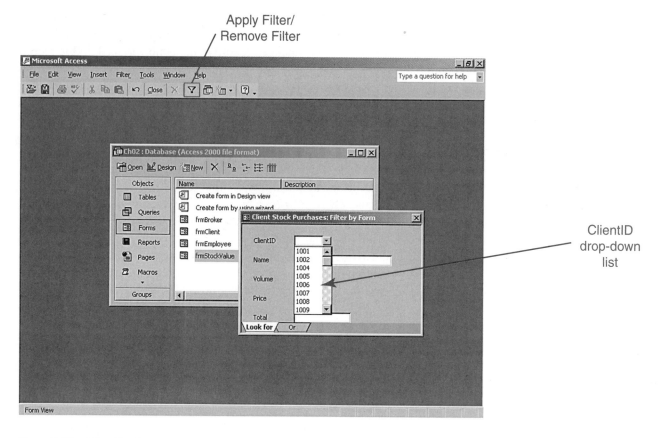

Figure 2.34 Filter By Form example.

You can filter by any form field. Repeat steps 1 through 3 and select the field by which you want to filter. Then, clear the other fields; otherwise, other field values will further restrict the records that are retrieved. Try it yourself. See if you can display in the *frmStock* form information about clients who own Microsoft stock.

Using Filter By Selection works almost the same way. When you choose Filter By Selection, it filters records shown in the form based on the currently selected data. To Filter By Selection, select a field or part of a field in a form and then click Filter By Selection. Only records matching the selected value are displayed in the form.

Printing a Form

Though forms are best suited for onscreen work, you can print them too. To print one record, open the form, locate the record, and click the File menu Print command. (If you click the toolbar Print button, *all* forms begin printing—something you probably do not want to do.) When the Print dialog box appears, click the

Selected Record(s) option button, and then click OK. You will notice that neither the form's Title bar or its navigation buttons appears on the printout.

Printing a range of records is an equally straightforward process. Select Print from the File menu, click the Pages option button, enter the beginning and ending page numbers in the two page range boxes, and click OK. Access prints table rows in the format of the displayed form. However, you probably will not want to print more than a few records this way. There is a better way to print larger amounts of information from tables. An Access report is the most efficient way to design and produce tabular output of the records in a table or a query result. Access reports are introduced next.

DESIGNING REPORTS

Producing reports could not be much easier than the click of a button or two. Frequently, you will want either to preview a report onscreen or to produce a printed report, which you can pass around at a meeting or keep as a permanent record. Access reports are just that—reports. You cannot enter data or edit data in a report. Reports range from simple, utilitarian designs to professional-looking reports replete with attractive typefaces, drop shadows, and graphics.

Previewing a Report

Reports typically display information from a table, a collection of related tables, or a query. We have created a report from the query you examined earlier (Figure 2.26). Though a lot can be gained from looking at the query's results onscreen, it is even more useful to have a printed report. The report you are about to preview and then print has some added features that make the information delivered by the query *qryStockValue* (Figure 2.26) more understandable and useful. First, let's learn how to open a stored report definition and preview the report prior to actually printing it. Switch to the Database window (click the Database Window button on the toolbar). Then, complete the following exercise to display a report.

EXERCISE 2.15: LOADING AND PREVIEWING A REPORT

1. Click Reports in the Objects bar of the Database window. A list of available reports appears.
2. Click the report named *rptClientStocks* and click the Preview button. A preview of the report appears in the Print Preview window.
3. Click the Maximize button to display the whole window and use the scroll bars to pan the report. Click the mouse to zoom out and zoom in. Figure 2.35 shows the report preview.
4. Close the report if you wish, or continue examining the report by following the directions in the paragraph that follows.

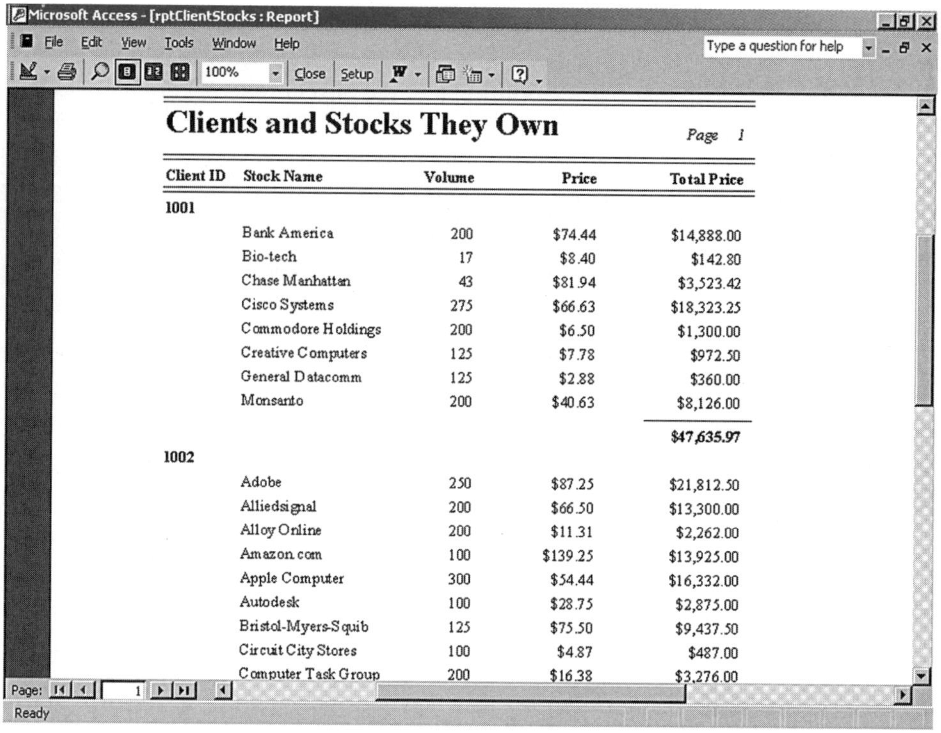

Clients and Stocks They Own

Page 1

Client ID	Stock Name	Volume	Price	Total Price
1001				
	Bank America	200	$74.44	$14,888.00
	Bio-tech	17	$8.40	$142.80
	Chase Manhattan	43	$81.94	$3,523.42
	Cisco Systems	275	$66.63	$18,323.25
	Commodore Holdings	200	$6.50	$1,300.00
	Creative Computers	125	$7.78	$972.50
	General Datacomm	125	$2.88	$360.00
	Monsanto	200	$40.63	$8,126.00
				$47,635.97
1002				
	Adobe	250	$87.25	$21,812.50
	Alliedsignal	200	$66.50	$13,300.00
	Alloy Online	200	$11.31	$2,262.00
	Amazon.com	100	$139.25	$13,925.00
	Apple Computer	300	$54.44	$16,332.00
	Autodesk	100	$28.75	$2,875.00
	Bristol-Myers-Squib	125	$75.50	$9,437.50
	Circuit City Stores	100	$4.87	$487.00
	Computer Task Group	200	$16.38	$3,276.00

Figure 2.35 Previewing a report.

Use the Report window's scroll bars to move around the displayed page. To move to another page, use the navigation buttons in the lower left corner of the Print Preview window. You can also use the arrow keys and the PgUp and PgDn keys to move around the report. Take a few moments to try out the page navigation buttons. Go to the last report page, and then go back to the first. There is a brief pause as Access moves to a particular page and repaints the Print Preview window. Experiment with printing a report page. Select Print from the File menu, click the Pages option, enter a page range to print, and click OK to start the printing process. Close the report by clicking the Close button in the upper right corner of the Print Preview window. The Database window for Ch02 is redisplayed.

Now that you have seen an example of a report based on a query and how to preview and print it, let's create a simple report. It is based on the *tblClient* table.

Creating a Report Quickly

Creating a report from a table is similar to creating a form from a table. You select a table name in the Database window, click the New Object toolbar button, and select AutoReport from the drop-down list. A default-format report appears. In the following exercise you will create an AutoReport based on the Client table.

EXERCISE 2.16: CREATING A REPORT QUICKLY

1. Click Tables in the Object bar of the Ch02 Database window.
2. Click *tblClient* in the list of tables (highlight its name, but do not open the table).
3. Click Insert on the menu bar and then click AutoReport. The default style report is displayed in a Print Preview window (see Figure 2.36).

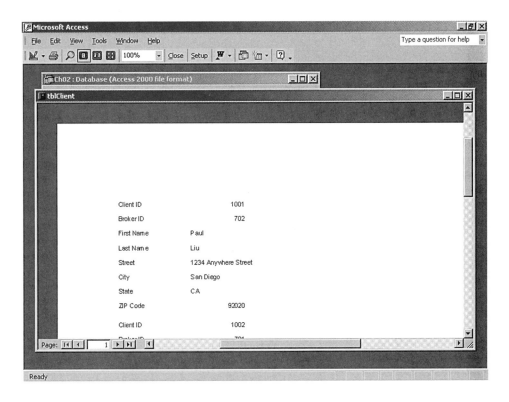

Figure 2.36 Typical AutoReport-style report.

By default, an AutoReport-generated report contains each table field arranged vertically, one above the other, with the numeric data fields right aligned and the character fields left aligned. You can easily change any of these elements or remove them. However, you must display the report in Design view to make structural changes to any report.

Click the Close button located on the Print Preview toolbar (or select Design View from the View menu). The report's design is displayed in the Design view window. Figure 2.37 shows the Client report's design.

In the Design window, you can change a report in many ways. For instance, you can remove a report field by selecting it with the mouse and then pressing

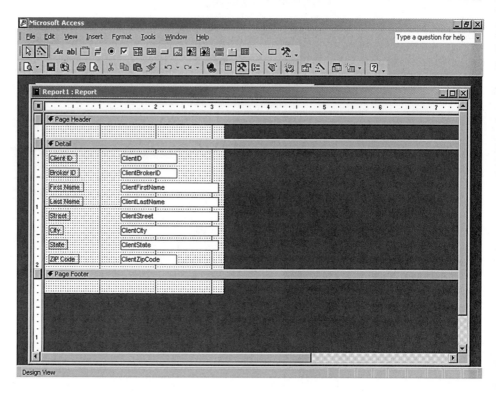

Figure 2.37 Report design.

the Delete key after the square selection handles appear surrounding the field. If you make a mistake, remember you can use the Undo command (Undo Delete in this case) in the Edit menu.

Saving a Report

Reports are saved like any other objects described in this text—by selecting the Save or Save As command from the File menu.

EXERCISE 2.17: SAVING A REPORT

1. Select the Save As command from the File menu. The Save As dialog box appears.
2. Type **rptClientTest** in the upper text box, labeled *Save Report 'Report1' To:* That label is the report's name, and it is listed along with the other Report objects in the database.
3. Click OK to complete the save operation.
4. Click the Close button on the Report window title bar to close the report.
5. Click File on the Access menu bar, and then click Exit to close the database.

SUMMARY

You have learned a great deal about database systems in general and the Access database system in particular. You understand what a relational database is and why it is the best choice for dealing with related sets of information. Tables are the building blocks of a database system and consist of columns and rows.

You can manipulate tables in several ways to produce the result you want. Access maintains table rows in order when a table has a primary key. The navigation buttons in the Table window facilitate moving to various rows in a table. You can move a column in a table to another position by dragging its heading left or right. This alters the table's display characteristics but does not actually alter a column's position in the stored table.

In addition to tables, Access contains other objects including queries, forms, and reports. Queries, or questions, use the Query by Example method to pose questions about the data stored in one or more tables. Able to retrieve a subset of rows or columns, queries narrow the search for relevant information to just those elements of interest. You learned how to create queries using simple criteria as well as more complex expressions involving comparison operators. You created AND criteria in which two or more conditions must be simultaneously true. You saw that OR criteria are created by placing conditions on two or more rows of the query model. Besides selection queries, you learned how to create a variety of action queries, which alter the database's tables.

Forms provide a simpler interface to tables, because only one row at a time is displayed. You used a form and created a quick form from a table. Forms can be made to look like paper forms encountered in a business. When a form resembles an existing paper—one already in use—the computer form is rather intuitive and easy to use. You learned that by merely clicking a form entry and typing, you can change a table's data. When you move to a new record, the change is then posted to the table. And you learned that you can filter data through a table, thereby restricting which table rows are shown in a form.

Finally, you got a brief look at the hard copy output facility of Access: the report. First, you previewed an existing report. Then, you created an AutoReport for a table. Reports provide a way to print and summarize information from one or more tables in a pleasant-looking format. Reports are output only. You cannot change a table's contents with a report.

This chapter has given you the fundamental tools to begin using Access to build systems. In Chapter 3, we introduce more formal foundations of relational database management systems. In that chapter you will learn about some rules and techniques that will help you design and build accounting information systems using tables, which are well-suited for the purpose.

QUESTIONS AND PROBLEMS FOR REVIEW

MULTIPLE-CHOICE QUESTIONS

1. Access is a(n) _____ database management system.
   a. algebraic
   b. flat file
   c. strictly Windows-based
   d. relational

2. Access help screens
   a. are only available when no Access table windows are open.
   b. can be printed for handy reference.
   c. only give information about Windows in general.
   d. are for advanced uses beyond the scope of this text.

3. The structure holding the result of a query is called the
   a. primary key.
   b. open query.
   c. dynaset.
   d. relational operator.

4. _____ are the fundamental storage structures for data.
   a. Forms
   b. Spreadsheets
   c. Tables
   d. Queries

5. A _____ is a question you can ask about your data in tables.
   a. help command
   b. query
   c. form
   d. request

6. You can examine your data in which of the following structures?
   a. table
   b. form
   c. report
   d. all of the above

7. A query can involve
   a. one table.
   b. two tables.
   c. three tables.
   d. all of the above.

8. An example of a logical operator that can be placed in a selection criteria of a query when you want two conditions to be true at once is
   a. but.
   b. nor.
   c. and.
   d. none of the above.
9. _____ provide a convenient, less cluttered work surface through which you can enter or alter table information.
   a. Forms
   b. Reports
   c. Conditional operators
   d. All of the above
10. Reports
    a. are output only—no table data can be altered with a report.
    b. can be used to change a table's information.
    c. can only be printed.
    d. all of the above.

DISCUSSION QUESTIONS

1. Describe the Access work surface icons, discuss their uses, and tell how they differ from the menu commands.
2. Discuss when it is advantageous to view your data in a Table window and when a Form window is better. Explain your reasons.
3. List the steps necessary to open and display database tables.
4. Discuss why you would use database queries to retrieve information.
5. Describe the different ways to design a database report, and discuss the possible situations where you might use these different designs.

PROBLEMS

Note: Before doing any of the following exercises, first copy *Ch02.mdb* from your Companion CD to the hard drive of the computer on which you are working. Then, clear the copied database's Read-only file attribute (see Chapter 1, Exercise 1.14, *Clearing a File's Read-Only Property*). Having done that you can complete each exercise using the copy of the Companion CD database.

1. Sort the *tblClient* table on the ClientState and ClientCity fields so that the rows are in order first by state (A to Z) and then city (A to Z) within each state. Print the sorted table directly from the Table window.
2. Create and execute a query based on the *tblClient* table that displays which clients are assigned broker 702. Display only the columns ClientFirstName, ClientLastName, ClientID, and ClientBrokerID (in that order, left to right).

The query should sort the rows into descending order by the clients' names (like a telephone book listing does). Print the resulting dynaset.

3. Run the query *qryClient1015Stock* found in the query list for the Ch02 database. It produces a list of client 1015's stock purchases in ascending order by transaction identification number. Change the sort order of the rows so that the query returns rows in Price order (low to high). Print the dynaset. Then modify the sort order so that the dynaset is sorted in descending order (high to low) by the Volume column. Print the dynaset. Can you combine these sort criteria so that the dynaset is sorted first in descending order by Volume and then in ascending order by Price within matching volumes? Try it. Print the third dynaset. Remember to write your name on all three printed dynasets.

4. You can create an AutoForm from a query in exactly the same way you do from a table. Create an AutoForm for the query called *qryStockValue* in the query list for the database Ch02. Begin by selecting the query from the list. Click the AutoForm button. When you are done, save the form design under the name *frmAutoForm*. Turn in a printed copy of the first two pages of the form. Remember to write your name on the output.

5. Create an AutoReport report for the *tblStock* table found in the Ch02 database. Print only the first two pages of the report. Print your name on the report. If you feel adventuresome, try adding a label containing your name in the report in either the report header or the page header.

3 DATABASES AND ACCOUNTING SYSTEMS

OBJECTIVES

This chapter introduces database accounting systems and compares them to the double-entry bookkeeping systems with which you are already familiar. It also explains how accountants break down business activities into transaction cycles and how database accounting systems use those transaction cycles as organizing themes. This chapter covers the theoretical foundations for database accounting systems and contains practical examples of applying database theory. You will learn about the connection between accounting systems and database systems, why a relational database system is the best choice for capturing accounting information, and some of the theory and history of relational database management systems. Just enough theory is provided to aid you in creating efficient, optimal database objects, but the discussion avoids presenting more database theory than you need. In this chapter, you will learn about:

- Differences between double-entry bookkeeping and database accounting systems.
- Advantages and disadvantages of database accounting systems.
- Business activity classifications.
- Transaction cycles.
- The relationship between accounting systems and database systems.
- A brief history leading to the development of database management systems.
- Functions of database management systems.
- Theory and application of relational database management systems.
- The structure of database objects that store accounting events.
- The importance of normalizing tables.
- Performing database selections, projections, and joins.

This chapter will help you understand the differences between double-entry book-keeping and database accounting. The information about business activity classifications and transaction cycles will provide a framework that will help you apply your knowledge of Microsoft Access to the task of building accounting database components.

This chapter uses an accounting application, processing and maintaining invoice data, to illustrate the use of databases in accounting. The company used in our example, a coffee bean and tea wholesaler called The Coffee Merchant, purchases whole-bean coffees and teas at international auctions and sells the coffees and teas to a variety of coffee roasters. To begin, we will briefly examine the connection between accounting and database systems and explore how accounting came to use relational database management systems.

INTRODUCTION

Most accounting students learn the mechanics of accounting for economic transactions using the tools of manual double-entry bookkeeping such as journals and ledgers. This chapter begins with a discussion of the differences between database accounting systems and manual double-entry bookkeeping systems. We then explain the advantages and disadvantages of using a database approach to building accounting systems.

The chapter's discussion of business activity classifications then introduces three levels of complexity that accountants use to classify firms. These classifications will help you understand when to incorporate particular database features into your accounting database system designs. Finally, the chapter describes transaction cycles, which provide a way for accountants and others to classify economic events into related categories.

Many students have learned how to use Microsoft Access as a software application but have not learned much of the database theory that is essential for creating complex applications such as accounting systems. Chapters 4 and 5 describe how to use database software to build accounting system elements for a specific transaction cycle. In these chapters, you will learn how to create forms, queries, and reports to accomplish accounting tasks in all of the major transaction cycles.

DATABASE ACCOUNTING SYSTEMS

Much of the current interest in using databases for accounting systems arose as businesses saw the advantages of relational databases such as Microsoft Access for all their information processing needs. Rather than maintain separate files and programs for each business function, firms are trying to consolidate their data and data-handling operations. Some firms have created enterprise-wide databases that store all of the firm's information in one system.

Events-Based Theories of Accounting

Over the past forty years, accounting researchers such as William McCarthy, Eric Denna, and George Sorter have developed and refined various events-based approaches to accounting theory. Their work provides a solid theoretical underpinning for accountants' increasing use of relational databases to perform accounting tasks. These events-based approaches argue that accountants should strive to store all relevant attributes of economic events in a readily accessible form. Relational database software products, such as Microsoft Access, provide tools that accountants can use to accomplish that objective.

Double-Entry Bookkeeping vs. Database Accounting

For many years, double-entry bookkeeping provided an excellent method for recording transactions. It satisfied accountants' need to capture the essence of each transaction. When double-entry bookkeeping was first developed over five hundred years ago, the costs of gathering and storing information were very high. Recording transactions with pen and paper was a time-consuming task. Double-entry bookkeeping gave accountants a valuable tool that quickly identified essential elements of transactions. Therefore, double-entry bookkeeping let businesspersons capture and store key attributes of transactions in a highly aggregated form. This helped keep the cost of information gathering and storage at affordable levels. Also, the debit-credit balancing check provided an important internal control feature in manual accounting systems.

Try It

If you would like to see how far we have come in replacing manual accounting systems with database systems, go to your local office supplies store and try to find a pad of two-column accounting paper. If you have trouble finding it, ask a salesperson for help. He or she will probably look up the product's location—in the store's computerized inventory database.

Computerized transaction processing has released accountants from the limitations and drudgery of manual accounting systems. Using computers, we can now capture a wide variety of information about each transaction quite easily. For example, supermarkets and other retail stores routinely read bar codes at checkout stations to capture the date and time of purchase, the identity of the item purchased, the store location, the checkout station number, and the cashier number. Even more important is that they obtain all of this information with one quick swipe!

Technologies such as bar code readers and optical scanners have played a major role in reducing the cost of acquiring and storing multiple attributes of each economic event. To see more clearly how double-entry bookkeeping and database accounting differ, let's consider a simple sales transaction. Most sales transactions begin when a customer sends a purchase order. If the firm receiving the purchase order has the goods in stock and finds the customer's credit to be acceptable, the firm ships the ordered goods and invoices the customer. A double-entry bookkeeping system would record this transaction for the selling firm with the following journal entry:

Date	**Account**	**Debit**	**Credit**
Date	*Accounts Receivable*	*Amount*	
	Sales		*Amount*
	Explanation		

Note that this journal entry includes five items of information:

- Transaction date.
- Names of the accounts debited.
- Names of the accounts credited.
- Transaction amount.
- Explanation of the transaction.

In a general journal entry such as the one shown above, the explanation might contain the name of the customer. Firms that use specialized journals and subsidiary ledgers can store one additional information item, the customer's name or account code. For example, if the above journal entry had been posted to a subsidiary ledger, the record keeping process would store the customer's name or account code in the subsidiary ledger. If the sale had been recorded in a specialized sales journal instead of in a general journal as shown above, the format would differ. For example, the account names might be implied by the transaction appearing in the sales journal rather than being explicitly stated; the information recorded would be the same in both cases. To summarize, a double-entry bookkeeping system records five or six transaction attributes and records one of them, the amount, twice.

Now, consider how a relational database accounting system might handle the same transaction. A database accounting system would record the transaction in a set of database tables similar to those that appear in Figure 3.1.

The database system shown in Figure 3.1 stores some attributes of the sales transaction in the Sales table, which appears in the figure as *tblSales*. We use the "tbl" prefix in this book to indicate that the Access object is a table. We use similar prefixes for other Access objects, including "frm" for forms, "rpt" for reports, and "qry" for queries.

Note, however, that many other attributes of the sales transaction are stored in the eight other tables that appear in Figure 3.1. A database accounting system can store many more attributes of the sales transaction than a journal entry can store. Note that this database accounting system for sales information stores these

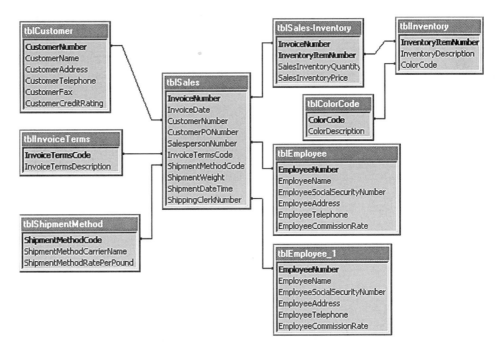

Figure 3.1 Sales transactions stored in a database accounting system.

attributes in an atomic form, scattered throughout the tables. In Chapter 2 you learned a number of rules for designing effective database tables that store information attributes in multiple tables, yet allow the information to be pulled back together when needed. One of these rules requires you to establish a primary key for each table. The primary key consists of one or more fields in each table that provides a unique identifier for each row in the table. The primary key fields of the tables in Figure 3.1 are shown in bold type.

The database system shown in Figure 3.1 stores 10 transaction attributes in the *tblSales* table and a virtually unlimited number of attributes in the other tables. For example, if the invoice included 20 items, the *tblSales-Inventory* table would store 40 attributes (20 item quantities and 20 item prices) for the transaction. Contrast this with the information stored in the double-entry bookkeeping journal entry. The journal entry does not even tell you how many items were on the invoice, much less tell you anything about those items.

Not only does the database accounting system store many more attributes than the double-entry bookkeeping system, it stores them more efficiently. A key feature of relational database software such as Microsoft Access is that it allows table designs that reduce or eliminate the storage of redundant information. For the sales information database in Figure 3.1, let's examine what is stored in each table, how the tables are linked, and how we might extract information from this sales system.

The primary key of *tblSales* is the InvoiceNumber field. The other attributes of the sale that are stored exclusively in this table include the invoice date, the customer's purchase order number, the shipping weight of the items sold, and a shipping date-time stamp. The other five fields in *tblSales* are foreign key fields. Access, like many other relational database software packages, uses links between primary key fields and corresponding foreign key fields in other tables to maintain the connections among information attributes. The foreign keys in Figure 3.1 show the links from *tblSales* to other tables that contain information about sales.

Foreign key links help accountants avoid recording information more than once. For example, the first foreign key field in *tblSales* is CustomerNumber, which links *tblSales* to *tblCustomer*. Instead of storing customers' names, addresses, and other information in *tblSales* repeatedly for every invoice, this database design lets you store customer information once for each customer and link it to individual sales by including just one field, the CustomerNumber field, in *tblSales*.

The other foreign keys in *tblSales* are SalespersonNumber, InvoiceTermsCode, ShipmentMethodCode, and ShippingClerkNumber. The InvoiceTermsCode links each sale to a table of invoice terms, such as cash, 2/10 net 30, 1/15 net 30, or net 30. If these terms were entered directly in *tblSales*, each input clerk might enter them differently and corrupt the sales database. The ShipmentMethodCode performs a similar error-control function.

Try It

With several other members of your class, see how many different logical ways you can record the names of the shipping firms with which you are familiar. You might be surprised at how many variations you can create.

The SalespersonNumber and the ShippingClerkNumber foreign key fields contain the identification numbers for these two employee participants in sales transactions. Although Figure 3.1 shows *tblEmployee* twice to accommodate these two links, the firm has only one Employee table.

The primary key of *tblSales*, InvoiceNumber, participates in a link to *tblInventory* as part of the primary key in *tblSales-Inventory*. Since this primary key includes two fields, it is called a composite primary key. As you may know from your previous work with Microsoft Access, the only way to link two tables that have a many-to-many relationship is through a relationship table. In a sales transaction, each invoice can have many inventory items. Also, each inventory item can appear on many different invoices. In this sales system, *tblSales-Inventory* is the relationship table that models the many-to-many relationship between *tblSales* and *tblInventory*. Its composite primary key includes two fields that link to the primary keys of the two tables that participate in the relationship.

Note that the database system directly records only some of the items that the double-entry bookkeeping system records. The database system records directly the date of the sale, the customer number, and the nature of the transaction as a sale. The database system does not record directly the transaction as an element of accounts receivable. Since sales transactions constitute the left side of the accounts receivable account, storing information about sales in the tables that appear in Figure 3.1 is sufficient in a database accounting system.

To calculate the amount of a particular invoice—the amount that the double-entry bookkeeping system recorded twice in the journal entry—an accountant using a database system would run a query that links *tblSales* with *tblSales-Inventory* and *tblShipmentMethod*. The query would obtain the SalesInventoryQuantity and SalesInventoryPrice for each InventoryItemNumber in *tblSales-Inventory* for the InvoiceNumber. The query would also obtain the ShipmentMethodRatePerPound from *tblShipmentMethod* and the ShipmentWeight from *tblSales*. The query would then multiply the SalesInventoryQuantity by the SalesInventoryPrice for each InventoryItemNumber and multiply the invoice's ShipmentWeight by the ShipmentMethodRatePerPound for the ShipmentMethodCode on the invoice. Finally, the query would sum these products to determine the amount of the invoice.

Although database theory argues against storing calculated fields in relational databases, accounting databases sometimes store intermediate calculation results such as this invoice amount calculation. Accountants violate the strict database rules intentionally to increase processing efficiency in databases that store large amounts of transaction data. However, accountants do this reluctantly and avoid storing calculated fields when possible.

Accounting systems that use the database approach can do everything that double-entry bookkeeping does and more. Accountants can use the database tables in Figure 3.1 to calculate invoice amounts and generate the same accounts receivable records and financial statement amounts provided by journals and ledgers. However, the real power of using relational databases to store accounting information arises when managers need specific information that they did not know they would need when the system was created. For example, if a manager wanted to know how many green-colored inventory items were sold during March of last year, the journals and ledgers of double-entry bookkeeping would be virtually useless. Using a database accounting system for sales, however, accountants could quickly provide the manager with an answer that includes number of items and sales in dollars. The database system could even generate subtotals by customer or geographic location for both number of items and sales in dollars.

Try It

Examine Figure 3.1 carefully. Identify interesting facts about the firm's sales and sales-related activities that you might find or calculate by searching the database tables and combining the information attributes they contain.

As you can see, relational databases record far more information for each transaction than a traditional double-entry bookkeeping system can record. A database accounting system also provides a flexible web of information relating a firm's economic events to each other. In the next two sections, we discuss some of the advantages and disadvantages of using database management systems in accounting applications.

Advantages of Database Accounting Systems

Manual double-entry bookkeeping systems can be very efficient; however, computer implementations of double-entry bookkeeping use a flat file processing design. In manual systems, the dual nature of the accounting debit and credit model provides a built-in error correction mechanism. In automated systems, this same duality is inefficient and serves no real control purpose.

Database accounting systems store data only once. This feature leads to a number of advantages over flat file double-entry accounting systems. A database accounting system can:

- Reduce data storage costs.

- Eliminate data redundancy.

- Eliminate data inconsistencies.

- Avoid duplicate processing.

- Ease add, delete, and update data maintenance tasks.

- Make data independent of applications.

- Centralize data management.

- Centralize data security.

Database accounting systems offer greater flexibility in extracting data than flat file double-entry accounting systems. This flexibility leads to other advantages. For example, a database accounting system can:

- Ease report modifications and updates.

- Provide *ad hoc* query capabilities.

- Facilitate cross-functional data analysis.

- Permit multiple users simultaneous data access.

Database accounting systems also provide data entry and integrity controls as part of the database management system. Accounting systems designers can embed these controls into the structure of the tables as they create them, which eliminates the need to program controls into every application that uses the tables' data.

Because a database stores data only once, the storage costs will be lower than for a flat file system that requires redundant storage. By avoiding the need to store data in multiple locations throughout the system, a database accounting system prevents users from creating data inconsistencies. For example, when a customer address changes, a database accounting system needs to make the change only once, in the Customer table. Every application that uses customer addresses—which may include invoicing, billing, sales promotions, marketing surveys, and sales summaries—automatically begins using the updated address from the Customer table as soon as it is entered. Data inconsistencies can be a source of many potentially embarrassing problems for businesses. Since data is entered only once, the tasks of adding, deleting, and updating records can be accomplished more efficiently. By avoiding data redundancy, a database approach also ensures that the data items used in accounting applications will have the same field names, field lengths, and data types as other applications.

Centralizing data management and security lets businesses fix responsibility for these functions on one person or group. By concentrating this activity, a database approach enables the person or persons responsible for data management and security to develop valuable expertise in this function. When a firm adopts a database approach to manage its data, it usually hires a database administrator. The database administrator holds ultimate responsibility for the specifications and structure of all database tables in the information system. The database administrator is also responsible for enforcing security, making backups, and coordinating contingency plans for emergency situations.

Having the best collection of data in the world will not do managers any good if they cannot access it. A major advantage of database accounting systems is that they facilitate users' access to accounting data. By providing intuitive, graphically based report generators, database management software such as Microsoft Access allows accountants to easily change the structure and format of their reports.

One of the most difficult challenges of designing any accounting system has always been the task of creating reports. Designers found it very hard to anticipate every report that accountants and managers using the system might ever want because they had to do it before the system even existed. The powerful query languages built into Access and other database management systems make this task much easier. Queries let users ask database accounting systems for information by combining data tables and performing calculations in ways the systems' designers never imagined. Further, these user-designed queries and reports can access more than accounting data. For example, tables containing marketing and production information can be combined with accounting information tables to create truly cross-functional reports. This *ad hoc* querying and report-generating capability is one of the key advantages of using an accounting system built with relational database software.

Finally, database accounting systems implement many important data input and data integrity controls at the database level. In Chapter 4 you will learn how to include some of these controls in accounting data tables. By implementing these controls as part of the database, you avoid the need to include the controls in every application that uses the data.

Disadvantages of Database Accounting Systems

Despite the long list of advantages outlined in the previous section, database accounting systems do have some disadvantages. The increased functionality of a database system does not come free—the higher price tag for a database system can include costs for items such as:

- Greater hardware requirements.

- The database software itself.

- Employing a database administrator.

Although centralizing management and security control functions in a firm can be advantageous, such centralization can create drawbacks such as:

- The system operation becomes critical.

- Incorrect data entry corrupts many users' work.

- Territorial disputes over data ownership may arise.

One last disadvantage that accountants occasionally note—a disadvantage that is more psychological than real—is accountants' distrust of single-entry accounting systems in general. Double-entry bookkeeping is so pervasive in accounting education and practice that most accountants automatically question and fear anything else.

The increased cost of a database accounting system is often offset by reduced needs for data storage and reduced programming costs. The elimination of data redundancy in a database system reduces the data storage capacity required. Since the data table structures can include many data entry and integrity controls, application programming is simplified—and simpler programming takes less time and costs less money.

The centralization of data and security control is a double-edged sword. Centralization puts all of a firm's information eggs in one basket, and that increases risk. However, it also allows a focusing of resources on contingency planning, security, backup, and recovery that can actually reduce risk levels.

Many firms have decided that the advantages offered by database accounting systems outweigh the disadvantages. Most new accounting system implementations are built using relational database systems. We expect this trend to continue as database management software becomes less expensive, more capable, and easier to use.

BUSINESS ACTIVITY CLASSIFICATIONS

Different businesses require different kinds of accounting information systems. The size of a business determines part of its accounting information requirements. Larger businesses process more transactions and require greater computing capacity than smaller businesses. However, dollar volume alone is not always a good indicator of the kind of information systems a firm needs. The complexity of a firm's business activities also has a significant effect on its accounting system design. Accountants classify the complexity of firms' business activities using three broad categories: service, merchandising, and manufacturing. Not all businesses fit neatly into one of these categories, but the categories provide a good beginning reference point when considering accounting information system options.

Service Firms

Service firms comprise the simplest form of business activity. They provide their customers or clients a service for which they charge a fee. Service firms' accounting information systems track revenues and expenses only; they do not need to track inventory information because service firms do not have inventory. Examples of service firms include:

- Accounting firms.
- Advertising agencies.
- Barbershops.
- Entertainers.
- Interior decorators.
- Law firms.
- Management consulting firms.
- Physicians.
- Realtors.
- Trucking companies.

You can see the simplicity of service firm accounting system requirements by examining the income statement in Figure 3.2.

This income statement shows revenues and expenses. The expenses are shown in one list; they are not broken down into categories of expenses. The most important information that most service firms must track is information about revenues. Some service firms also need detailed information about their expenses, including salaries paid to employees.

Example Service Firm
Income Statement
Year Ended December 31, 2003

Revenue		$ 353,150
Expenses:		
Advertising	$ 42,170	
Depreciation	27,640	
Insurance	9,420	
Salaries	94,210	
Rent	106,400	
Other	62,180	342,020
Net income		$ 11,130

Figure 3.2   Example Service Firm income statement.

Merchandising Firms

Merchandising firms are the next step up in complexity from service firms. The goal of merchandising firms is to buy goods at a low enough cost and sell those goods at a high enough price to earn a margin that will cover other expenses and provide a profit. Examples of merchandising firms include:

• Computer stores.

• Department stores.

• Discount merchandise chains.

• Food markets.

• Hardware stores.

• Health food stores.

• Mail-order merchandisers.

• Office supply stores.

• Shoe stores.

• Wholesalers.

Merchandising firms' accounting information systems must track revenues and expenses, just like service firms' systems. However, the single largest expense for merchandising firms is the cost of goods that they have sold. A merchandising firm's income statement devotes a separate section to the cost of goods sold calculation. Because firms often buy goods in one period and sell those goods in the next period, their accounting systems must also track inventory. Figure 3.3 contains an example of a merchandising firm's income statement.

Example Merchandising Firm
Income Statement
Year Ended December 31, 2003

Sales		$ 822,370
Cost of goods sold:		
Beginning finished goods inventory	$ 59,530	
Purchases	472,930	
Less: Ending finished goods inventory	(63,240)	469,220
Gross profit		$ 353,150
Selling and adminstrative expenses:		
Advertising	$ 42,170	
Depreciation	27,640	
Insurance	9,420	
Salaries	94,210	
Rent	106,400	
Other	62,180	342,020
Net income		$ 11,130

Figure 3.3   Example Merchandising Firm income statement.

Note how the merchandising firm's income statement uses beginning and ending inventory in the cost of goods sold calculation. You should recall from your earlier accounting courses that the purchases amount shown on this income statement is net of purchase returns and allowances and includes freight on incoming inventory shipments. Merchandising firms track detailed information about their sales and expenses. Many merchandising firms maintain comprehensive records of which products were sold along with the locations and dates of the sales. Some merchandising firms even record the times at which products were ordered and shipped.

Manufacturing Firms

The most structurally complex type of firm is the manufacturing firm. In addition to the activities that merchandising firms undertake, manufacturing firms produce the goods that they sell. Examples of manufacturing firms include:

- Automobile manufacturers.
- Canneries.
- Construction firms.
- Farmers.
- Machine tool manufacturers.
- Meat packers.
- Oil refineries.
- Pharmaceutical firms.
- Restaurants.
- Steel mills.

All manufacturing firms engage in similar types of activities even though they create and sell a wide variety of products. Manufacturing firms must engage in activities such as:

- Purchasing raw materials and labor.
- Incurring other manufacturing costs.
- Processing the raw materials, labor, and other manufacturing costs into finished goods.
- Selling the finished goods.

A manufacturing firm's accounting information system must track information about all four of these activities. Therefore, a manufacturing firm's system must track the service and merchandising firm activities of purchasing and selling and must bear the additional burden of tracking acquisition costs through the production activity. Figure 3.4 contains an example of a manufacturing firm's income statement.

The manufacturing firm's income statement reflects the increased complexity of its activities. The merchandising firm's *Cost of goods sold* section has expanded to include the three manufacturing costs: direct materials, direct labor, and manufacturing overhead. These costs, adjusted by beginning and ending work-in-process inventories, are shown on the income statement in Figure 3.4 as the *Cost of goods manufactured*. The cost of goods manufactured was $472,930. The cost of goods manufactured is analogous to purchases on a merchandising firm's income statement.

Example Manufacturing Firm
Income Statement
Year Ended December 31, 2003

Sales				$ 822,370
Cost of goods sold:				
Beginning finished goods inventory			$ 59,530	
Cost of goods manufactured:				
Beginning work-in-process inventory		$ 44,900		
Direct materials:				
Beginning inventory	$ 26,270			
Purchases	98,910			
Less: Ending inventory	(28,360)	96,820		
Direct labor		153,460		
Manufacturing overhead		210,600		
Less: Ending work-in-process inventory		(32,850)	472,930	
Less: Ending finished goods inventory			(63,240)	469,220
Gross profit				$ 353,150
Selling and adminstrative expenses:				
Advertising			$ 42,170	
Depreciation			27,640	
Insurance			9,420	
Salaries			94,210	
Rent			106,400	
Other			62,180	342,020
Net income				$ 11,130

Figure 3.4 Example Manufacturing Firm income statement.

Manufacturing firms are not the only firms using manufacturing accounting systems today. Many service and merchandising firms now use accounting systems based on the manufacturing systems model. For example, many law firms now use a manufacturing-style job-order cost accounting system that treats each case as a separate job. Service firms have found it useful to track details about key business processes using accounting systems that were originally designed for manufacturing applications.

Now that we have seen how the different levels of complexity in the three business activity categories affect a firm's income statements and cost-accumulation procedures, we can discuss accounting information system requirements for each category. These accounting information system requirements are often expressed in terms of transaction cycles.

TRANSACTION CYCLES

Most accounting information systems and auditing textbooks are organized around business cycles. Some authors refer to these cycles as transaction cycles or accounting cycles. This framework, in which accounting systems are viewed in terms of cycles rather than financial statement accounts, is consistent with a database approach to accounting systems. A diagram of commonly used transaction cycles appears in Figure 3.5.

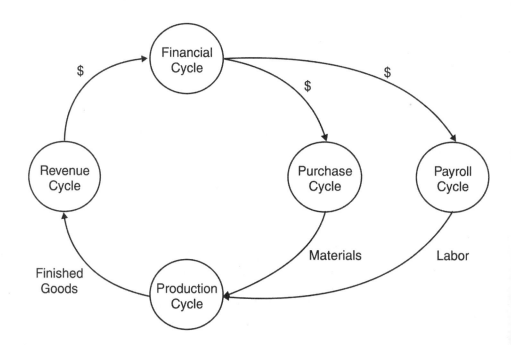

Figure 3.5 Transaction cycles.

You can see how the transaction cycles relate to each other in Figure 3.5. In the revenue cycle, firms sell finished goods for cash or the promise to pay cash. This cash enters the financial cycle. In the financial cycle, firms obtain cash by issuing equity and debt securities. They also pay dividends on the equity securities and the interest and principal repayments on debt securities in the financial cycle. Cash flows out of the financial cycle and into the purchase and payroll cycles. In the purchase cycle, the firm exchanges cash for materials, supplies, and other expenses related to providing products or services to its customers. In the payroll cycle, the firm exchanges cash for salaries and related labor costs. The production cycle converts materials, labor, and other acquired resources into finished goods, completing the cycle.

Although most accountants use the cycle definitions shown in Figure 3.5, these exact definitions are not universally accepted. Some accountants and systems designers include payroll activities in the purchase cycle since both payroll and purchase cycles culminate in writing a check. However, most accounting information systems texts treat payroll separately because payroll transaction processing is more complex and requires tables and calculations that the purchase cycle does not require. You may also see the revenue cycle divided into separate sales and cash receipts cycles. Similarly, the purchase cycle can be divided into separate purchase and cash disbursement cycles.

A firm may not have all of the transaction cycles depicted in Figure 3.5. For example, service and merchandising firms usually do not have a production cycle. The purchase cycle in a merchandising firm acquires finished goods for resale; the purchase cycle in a manufacturing firm acquires raw materials and other resources for production. In many service firms, the purchase cycle is relatively unimportant, since the dollar amounts of materials and supplies purchased are small.

Most accounting information systems courses avoid extensive treatment of the transactions specific to the financial cycle because these transactions are few in number. However, auditing classes do spend significant time on financial cycle transactions because they are unusual and often involve large dollar amounts. The transactions that occur only in the financial cycle, such as stock issuances and large borrowings, are interesting but do not require highly complex information processing systems in most firms because of their infrequent occurrence.

Some accounting systems books describe a general ledger or financial reporting transaction cycle. When a firm uses database accounting, its financial reporting activities do not require it to record a separate set of transactions. Accountants can accomplish these reporting activities by querying and summarizing the data that the firm stores as it conducts its revenue, purchase, payroll, and production activities. Therefore, we do not treat financial reporting as a separate cycle in this book. The remainder of this chapter provides a brief introduction to the revenue, purchase, payroll, and production cycles.

Revenue Cycle

The revenue cycle includes all sales and cash collection activities. The three main transactions that we must record in the revenue cycle are customer orders, sales, and customer payments. We must also record the shipment of goods if it occurs separately from the sales transaction. The revenue cycle accounting system must be able to generate documents and reports that include:

- Sales order reports.

- Invoices.

- Shipping documents.

- Remittance advices.

- Cash receipts summaries.

- Sales analyses.

- Balances owed by customers.

Manufacturing, merchandising, and service firms all have similar revenue cycles. They all sell goods or services to customers, and they all expect customers to pay them. A typical revenue cycle database would include the following data tables:

- Cash receipt.

- Customer.

- Finished goods inventory.

- Sales.

- Sales order.

- Salesperson.

The database design should also include relationship tables, such as a Sales-Finished Goods Inventory table.

Purchase Cycle

A manufacturing firm's purchase cycle includes all activities related to ordering raw materials from vendors, receiving the materials ordered, and paying for the materials. A merchandising firm's purchase cycle includes the activities related to ordering, receiving, and paying for goods acquired for resale. If a service firm has a purchase cycle system, it will record the purchase of materials incidental to providing services, such as office supplies. The main transactions that we must record in the purchase cycle are purchase orders, receipt of goods ordered, and payments to vendors. The purchase cycle accounting system must generate documents and reports that include:

- Purchase orders.

- Receiving reports.

- Checks.

- Backorder reports.

- Purchase summaries.

- Goods received summaries.

- Balances owed to vendors.

The details included in the purchase cycle tables will vary depending on whether the firm is service, merchandising, or manufacturing; a typical purchase cycle database would include the following data tables:

- Cash disbursement.

- Purchase order.

- Raw materials inventory.

- Raw materials inventory receipt.

- Vendor.

The database design would also include necessary relationship tables, such as a Purchase Order-Raw Materials Inventory table.

Payroll Cycle

The payroll cycle includes the system elements needed to calculate employees' gross pay, deductions, and net pay. The payroll cycle must comply with a complex set of government regulations. The payroll cycle is closely related to the human resources management system in all firms—many firms have even integrated the two systems. The main transactions that occur in the payroll cycle are employees earn pay, the employer makes payments to employees, and the employer makes payments of payroll taxes and taxes withheld from employees' pay to various governmental entities. The payroll cycle must generate documents and reports that include:

- Employee time reports.

- Employee commission reports.

- Checks.

- Payroll registers.

- Employee earnings records.

Manufacturing, merchandising, and service firms all have similar payroll cycles since they all have employees. A typical payroll cycle database would include the following data tables:

- Cash disbursement.

- Employee.

- Time worked.

Production Cycle

A manufacturing firm's production cycle converts raw materials and labor into finished goods. The production cycle accounting database must record the use of materials and labor in production and record the allocation of manufacturing overhead costs to units produced. Merchandising and service firms do not usually have a production cycle. The production cycle's main transactions are all internal cost flows and include:

• Materials inventory costs flow into production.

• Labor costs flow into production.

• Overhead costs are allocated to production.

• Total production costs flow into finished goods inventory.

The production cycle accounting system must generate documents and reports that include, for example, bills of materials and job cost reports. A typical production cycle database for a job-order manufacturing system might include the following data tables:

• Finished goods inventory.

• Job.

• Raw materials inventory.

• Time worked.

ACCOUNTING INFORMATION SYSTEMS AND DATABASE SYSTEMS

Historically, accounting information has been captured in ledgers and journals. Information about credit sales, for instance, would be recorded in a sales journal. Each month, accountants would create financial statements such as income statements and balance sheets from the information in the ledgers. If a manager needed information about the firm's activities in the middle of the month, that manager had to wait until the books were closed at the end of the next month to obtain that information. In today's fast-paced and highly competitive business world, however, managers need more than the standard periodic accounting reports. Some information cannot be obtained easily, if at all, using traditional double-entry accounting software. For example, it would be difficult for a manufacturing manager to obtain data about total monthly inventory spoilage from a traditional accounting system. Other valuable aggregations of data that provide pictures of a company's current financial or labor situation are hard to obtain from traditional accounting systems. Conventional aggregation methods provided by accounting systems have buried valuable information.

Today's accounting systems use a different approach. Customized reports based on database queries are increasingly replacing traditional accounting reports. The advent of both inexpensive and widely available computer hardware and database management software has accelerated the move toward capturing accounting information in database systems. *Events accounting* consists of storing data about an economic event, such as a cash sale or receipt of a purchase order, in one or more database tables. Events accounting goes beyond merely recording the aggregate numbers associated with the event. Information recorded about an economic event can include who was involved (e.g., the customer's name), why the event occurred, when the event occurred, and what resources were affected by the event.

Events-based accounting systems are not bound by accountants' assumptions about how the information captured is to be aggregated, output, or used. Rather, the managers who will be making decisions based on the information are empowered to extract that information from the accounting events database. An inventory manager, for example, can create (or request the creation of) a report to display current stock levels and the percentage change in stock levels from the previous month.

This is a significant change from accounting information systems that made use of the debit and credit method of recording transactions in a highly aggregated form. If managers need information from the accounting system to help make crucial decisions, they simply request the data they need and then review the resultant report. Managers and other decision makers need no longer rely exclusively on the standard financial statements and other reports produced by traditional accounting systems. Although some of the standard financial statements can help managers make enterprise-wide decisions, much information is lost during the aggregation that takes place in traditional accounting systems when those systems generate financial statements.

In this book, you are learning about accounting information systems implemented using database management systems. Because database management systems can store anything an organization wants to record, they provide a wealth of information. Much useful business information can be generated from the data stored in a database's tables. As an emerging accounting information systems expert, you are on the leading edge of this significant shift to more useful accounting systems.

Next, you will learn about the evolution of database management systems and some advantages and disadvantages of using database systems. We begin with a brief look at what software business tools were available before the advent of database systems.

DATABASE MANAGEMENT SYSTEMS

Database management systems (DBMSs) are valuable to business enterprises because they provide a way to store, retrieve, and modify crucial business data. DBMSs can be very cost effective, even though the software can be quite expensive. The next section briefly describes data management and reporting before the advent of database management systems. Subsequent sections describe the general capabilities of database management systems—what core services they typically provide—and the advantages and disadvantages of using database management systems.

Pre-DBMS Data Acquisition and Reporting

Before the availability of modern database management systems, corporate data acquisition and reporting were far different from today. Assume that it is the late 1960s and you are responsible for maintaining customer information for The Coffee Merchant, a small coffee wholesaler, on its medium-sized minicomputer. The data processing department has a staff of computer programmers and support personnel to supply all the company's data processing needs.

Flat files are data files containing information that is not explicitly linked to other information files. Flat files were an important part of business information processing in the early days of computerization. For instance, the accounts receivable department kept customer names and addresses in one file. When purchase orders were received, someone entered the coffee and tea order information into other flat files kept on disk. An orders file contained purchase order data such as the items ordered, quantity requested of each item, and whether the purchase was subject to tax—goods acquired for resale are not taxable until they are sold to a retail customer. Accounts payable kept its own set of files, which contained the names and addresses of vendors to which they owed money, invoice numbers, purchase order numbers, and similar information items.

Standard, frequently requested reports were readily available. These reports summarized data held in the files. When a manager wanted to see the latest sales figures for the previous month, he could place a request with the data processing department. The requested report would be on his desk by the next morning. Finding the current stock levels on all coffees and teas was a typical request that could be easily satisfied. Again, the data processing department would process the management request, run a program that accessed the appropriate files, and produce the report. This was typically how reports were generated for standard, traditional requests.

Requests for custom or unusual reports were a different matter. Although standard reports could be produced by scheduling and running programs written for that purpose, unusual report requests had to be custom-designed and written. For example, suppose the purchasing manager wanted to compare the inventory levels of the 20 most popular coffees and teas with the same period in the previous year. Such a report would require programmers to design and write a custom program. When a special request was received, a system analyst determined what files contained the information used in the report. The analyst would also provide a program design. After the design was approved by the user(s), one or more programmers wrote the program that would read the files, manipulate and summarize the data, and print a report. It was not unusual for a requested custom report to take several weeks before it was delivered to the requesting manager! Keeping a large pool of systems analysts and programmers on staff to supply the data processing needs of the company was expensive. Time is money, and managers could ill afford to wait weeks for critical reports.

Other problems existed in pre-DBMS days. Those problems included the creation of outdated and redundant data. Many departments and individuals created and maintained their own computer files, which resulted in the entry and storage of duplicated information. They would do this so they could access and examine data with their own programs quickly, rather than waiting for the overworked data processing department to respond to their requests. Duplicate data files led to occurrences of data redundancy and data inconsistency.

In many firms, the marketing department kept its own files of information about large customers so they could send out advertising and promotional mailings. The marketing department hired a bright young programmer to maintain the files and write programs to produce mailing labels from them. Problems occurred when the independently maintained customer list fell out of date. Although the master list of customers was kept current by the data processing department using purchase orders received from customers each month, the marketing department did not have access to the updated data. As existing customers moved and new customers were added, the marketing department's customer list became outdated and, eventually, became useless.

You can begin to see the types of problems that arose when businesses used separate information systems. A wall existed between the information consumers and the information itself. That wall was the data processing department, a necessary element in the information request and receipt cycle. Departments coped with unresponsive data processing departments by spawning separate islands of information that were independently maintained. These separate information islands created data redundancy and data inconsistency. In short, much time and money was expended to store and retrieve business data on computers before the arrival of database management systems and accounting information systems based on them.

Functions of a Database Management System

A database management system is a file management system that can store and manage different types of records within one integrated system. Using a database management system's tools, a database administrator can create a sophisticated system that maintains company records, generates invoices, and in general keeps track of all a company's transactions. A *database* is the physical implementation of a particular set of records, and the database management system controls access to those records. A *relational* database management system, one of three classical models of database management systems, consists of tables containing data whose contents are related to one another through the data content of the tables. The capabilities that a database management system provides in development of an information system are the following:

- Efficient data maintenance: storage, update, and retrieval.

- User-accessible catalog.

- Concurrency control.

- Transaction support.

- Recovery services.
- Security and authorization services.
- Integrity facilities.

One of the most important abilities of a database management system is its capacity to store, update, and retrieve data. Unlike a flat file system, you need not write and run a special program to store new data in a database. Likewise, when you want to extract information from various data files that are maintained by the DBMS, you can formulate a relatively simple report request in the database system's language. You need not enlist the support of a programmer to write lengthy and complicated programs to extract information. Besides, the DBMS hides all the file storage details from the user. Instead, the user is presented with an uncomplicated view of the data that the DBMS maintains.

Advantages of Database Management Systems

Some of the advantages that a database management system provides should be clear from the preceding material. DBMSs have other advantages over the old file and programmatic access methods. Many larger database systems provide each user with an individual view of the database. Also known as a *subschema*, a view appears to the user to be the real table. It is a definition stored in the database that can extract information from one or more tables and exclude selected rows and columns from being displayed. For instance, a manager might have a view of the database that displays employee data for the employees who report to the requesting manager, but no others. Views are implemented by database systems and provide a measure of security.

Data independence is another advantage of a database management system. The term *data independence* refers to a database management system's ability to hide the details of the physical storage of information from application programs that use the data. To extract information from a database, you merely request information by name and supply conditions that limit which rows are selected. The database system is responsible for translating the information request into data access statements that the database system can understand.

Changes to the structure of a database can be made transparently to the users. This is important because table designs can change over time and it becomes necessary to make changes to the internal structure of one or more tables. Frequently, table structure changes are made to provide significantly shorter database access times. When structure changes occur, using database views can mask those changes since database *views* restrict what various users can retrieve from the database. The views mimic users' old perceptions of the affected tables' contents, and the database structure change causes no changes to users' access techniques or methods. On the other hand, imagine the degree to which programs would be affected in a flat file system if just a few changes were made to the structure of the files they access. Programmers would have to spend a great deal of time changing all the programs that reference the files whose structure was changed. In large systems it can be very difficult to find all programs that reference a particular file or set of files.

Finally, database systems help users share data with each other. Because corporate data is centrally stored, everyone has access to the same information and that information is always current and consistent, because there is only one copy of it. There are no duplicate versions of inconsistent data, as was often the case in the years prior to the advent of database management systems.

Disadvantages of Database Management Systems

The main disadvantage of a database management system is that it can occupy a large amount of expensive disk storage space. You should consider the cost of disk storage when determining whether a database system is cost effective. Though database systems can occupy more than ten times the space required to hold the same data in flat files, DBMSs can still be a good value. Disk storage costs are much lower than the cost of maintaining data in flat files. Programming costs have gone up rapidly in the last 15 years, but prices of hardware such as disk drives have dropped sharply.

Large database systems often require additional people such as a database administrator to keep the system running smoothly. Other database experts may be hired to handle the information needs of the company. With few exceptions, these added costs are far less than the cost of not using a database management system. Of course, smaller businesses using PC-based database management packages such as Microsoft Access can often avoid these additional personnel costs. In such cases, only the additional disk space cost is a factor in the decision.

RELATIONAL DATABASE MANAGEMENT SYSTEMS

Database management systems can be implemented by following one of three data models in widespread use today. A *data model* is an abstract representation of a database system providing a description of the data and methods for accessing the data managed by the database. The three models in use are the *hierarchical* model, the *network* model, and the *relational* model. Throughout most of the late 1960s and early 1970s, most databases used the hierarchical or network model. IBM's IMS database system, which was widely used in the 1970s, is one example of a hierarchical database management system. Cullinet's IDMS/R is a database built on the network model that was also popular in the 1970s. However, things changed rapidly during that decade. E. F. Codd, working in an IBM research laboratory, developed the relational model for database systems. Since that time, the relational model has evolved and the number of database systems based on the relational model has exploded. Today, the relational model is the overwhelming choice for database systems running on all kinds and sizes of computers.

The relational model provides several significant advantages over the hierarchical and network models. In the relational model, the logical and physical characteristics of the database are distinct; this provides users with a more intuitive view of the data. Using the relational model requires very little training. The relational model includes more powerful retrieval and update operators that allow complex operations to be executed with concise commands. Perhaps most importantly, the relational model provides powerful tools to let analysts know when a database has inherent design flaws.

The advantages of the relational model overwhelm the disadvantages of using database systems. From this point on in the text, when we refer to a database management system, we specifically mean a *relational database management system*, or *RDBMS*.

Database Objects

The relational model is based in mathematical set theory, the theory of relations, and first-order predicate logic. The model defines the conceptual view that the user has all of the objects contained by the database system. Both the data objects and the relationships between them are represented as a collection of tables. All data in a relational database, including the database table definitions and information about database objects such as forms and reports, exists only in tables. This provides a simple and consistent view of the database.

A relational database is a collection of relations. The primary structure in a relational model database is a relation. A table is an example of a relation. For that reason, you will often see the terms *relation* and *table* used interchangeably. A table, or relation, consists of rows and columns, similar to a matrix or spreadsheet. The formal term for row is *tuple*, but most database experts use the less formal term *row*. The formal term for column is *attribute*, but most database experts use the term *column*. Alternative common terms used for relation, tuple, and attribute are file, record, and field, respectively. Figure 3.6 summarizes these three sets of terms.

Formal Term	Common Term	Alternative Common Term
relation	table	file
tuple	row	record
attribute	column	field

Figure 3.6　Three sets of database terms.

You may have used spreadsheet software in some of your other accounting courses. A spreadsheet page resembles a database table in several ways. For example, a spreadsheet page has columns and rows. The columns in a spreadsheet page often have titles that describe the content of the columns. You might want to think of database tables as a special form of spreadsheet pages. The difference is that database tables must comply with very strict rules about what can be included in each row and column. The most important properties of database tables include the following:

• The entries in each column of any row must be single valued.

• Each attribute (column) in a table has a distinct name, called the attribute name.

• Every entry in a column contains a value for that column only, and the values are of the same data type.

• The order of the rows is unimportant.

• The order (position) of the columns in relation to each other is unimportant.

• Each row is unique; it differs from all other rows in the table.

The preceding table properties are very important. Later in this chapter, you will learn about each of these properties in detail. Figure 3.7 shows an example relation that is one of the tables included in the The Coffee Merchant's database. Only the first 25 rows and the first six columns are shown in the figure.

The Customer table contains hundreds of rows, in no particular order, one for each of The Coffee Merchant's customers. Because the row order is unimportant in a RDBMS, there is no implied meaning that one customer is more important than another. All you can tell from the row order is that the identification

	CustomerID	CompanyName	Contact	Address	City	State
	30121	Fairfield Communities Inc.	Best, F. Stanley	2800 Cantrell R	Little Rock	AR
	30125	Alamo Group Inc.	Maul, Duane A.	1502 East Walr	Seguin	TX
	30129	Kiwi International Air Lines Inc.	Rigas, Alan J.	Demishphere C	Newark	NJ
	30132	Republic Bancorp Inc.	Murray, T. Peter	1070 East Main	Owosso	MI
	30136	Browne Bottling Co.	Shelton, Carl E.	411 First Avenu	Oklahoma City	OK
	30139	Cavco Industries Inc.	Golkin, David	422 Wards Corr	Phoenix	AZ
	30142	Bucyrus Erie Co.	Kostantaras, Jack R. Jr.	1100 Milwaukee	South Milwauke	WI
	30144	U S Office Products Co.	Gerson, Terrence	2155 Monroe Dr	Washington	DC
	30147	Ciatti S Inc.	Townes, Patrick J.	5555 West 78Tl	Edina	MN
	30148	Tab Products Co.	Montrone, Frank A.	1400 Page Mill	Palo Alto	CA
	30149	Diversicare Inc.		105 Reynolds D	Franklin	TN
	30153	Audiovox Corp.	Choate, Robert	150 Marcus Bor	Hauppauge	NY
	30155	Twin Disc Inc.	Crist, Dennis P.	1328 Racine Str	Racine	WI
	30158	Bay State Gas Co.	Huff, Richard E.	300 Firebug Par	Westborough	MA
	30159	Fort Wayne National Corp.		110 West Berry	Fort Wayne	IN
	30163	Medusa Corp.	Hart, John M.	3008 Monticello	Cleveland Heigh	OH
	30164	Stv Group Inc.	Hill, Alex W.	11 Robinson Str	Pottstown	PA
	30168	Commercial Federal Corp.	McMeel, John D.	2120 South 72N	Omaha	NE
	30170	Ketema Inc.	Crosley, Lynn H.	1000 East Main	Denver	CO
	30174	Thomas Nelson Inc.	Harber, L. H.	Nelson Place A	Nashville	TN
	30177	Public Service Co. of North Carolina	Bauer, Roger A.	400 Cox Road	Gastonia	NC
	30181	Heartland Express Inc.		2777 Heartland	Coralville	IA
	30183	Roanoke Electric Steel Corp.	Garcia, James D.	102 Westside E	North West Roa	VA
	30186	Borland International Inc.	Graf, Robert R.	100 Borland Wa	Scotts Valley	CA
	30190	Bugaboo Creek Steak House Inc.	Tobin, Clifford M.	1275 Wampano	East Providence	RI

Record: 14 ◀ | 1 ▶ ▶I ▶* of 1789

Figure 3.7 The Customer relation, *tblCustomer*.

number field, called CustomerID, is in ascending order. In relational databases, a row's identity is determined by its content, not by its location within a table.

Primary and Foreign Key Attributes

The table that appears in Figure 3.7 contains ten columns. Six of these attributes appear in Figure 3.7: CustomerID, CompanyName, Contact, Address, City, and State. However, there is no theoretical reason to list the columns in that order. We have chosen to place the primary key column, CustomerID, as the first table column. Although Access does not require the primary key column to be first, most database designers follow this convention. We could, for example, place the Contact column in the second column, followed by the State and City columns.

Within each column you can see the attribute values for each row. For instance, the row identified as CustomerID 30121 contains "Fairfield Communities Inc." in its CompanyName value and "Best, F. Stanley" in its Contact value. Each row may store a different value for each attribute. In particular, the CustomerID value is unique for each row. This satisfies the rule that each row must be unique. A row is unique if any one of its columns is unique.

Every relation must have a primary key that uniquely identifies each row in the table. The primary key can include one or more columns. When the primary key includes more than one column, the individual column values need not be unique, but the combined column values must be unique.

Every row in a RDBMS must be distinct from all other rows in that table, or else it cannot be retrieved easily. This is one of the fundamental rules of a relational database management system. To ensure uniqueness, a primary key is designated for a table. A primary key, as mentioned previously, is a column (or group of columns) that uniquely identifies a given row. Therefore, the system can distinguish one record (row) of a table from another. In the *tblCustomer* table, for instance, the CustomerID column—the customer's identification number—uniquely identifies a row. Thus, CustomerID is the primary key for the *tblCustomer* table.

Another important table field is a foreign key. A *foreign key* is an attribute in one table that matches the primary key field of another table. Figure 3.8 shows two of The Coffee Merchant tables used to retrieve invoice data from the set of tables constituting the database. Many database designers use the same field name for related primary key and foreign key columns to indicate the two columns tie together two tables. For example, the foreign key CustomerID in the table *tblInvoice* is related to the identically named field in the table *tblCustomer*. Although many database designers do follow this naming practice, Microsoft Access and other database management software packages do not require it.

The CustomerID column in the Invoice (*tblInvoice*) table is a foreign key, because it references a primary key found in one row of the *tblCustomer* table. The associations between foreign keys and primary keys are important because relational databases use them to establish connections between related tables.

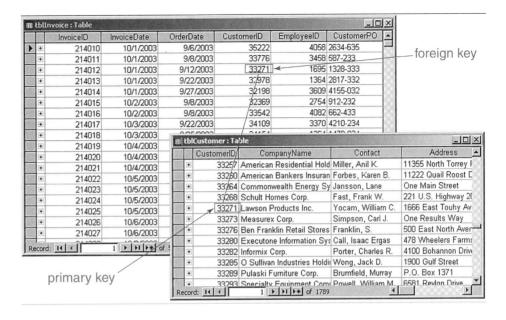

Figure 3.8 Primary key and foreign key relationship.

Schema of a Relation

The *schema* of a relation is a set of information that includes the name of a relation and its attributes. Some database designers also call this set of information a *table structure*. A compact representation of the schema for the *tblCustomer* table, using the reduced number of columns in this illustration, is:

Customer(<u>CustomerID</u>, CompanyName, Contact, Address, City, State)

The table's attributes are enclosed in parentheses following the table name. In this notation, an underline indicates the primary key column(s). This is not the only way to write this schema, but it is one you will find in common use in many books on database design and in many accounting information systems textbooks. Though not shown here, a double underline or a line appearing over one or more fields indicates the field is a foreign key. Another common notation system uses bold type to indicate a primary key and italics to indicate a foreign key.

Data Dictionary

Relational database systems have a data dictionary. A data dictionary is a collection of tables containing the definition, characteristics, structure, and description of all data maintained by the RDBMS.

In addition to table descriptions, the data dictionary can store view definitions, database object owner names, database login names, and passwords. Fields in the data dictionary are automatically changed whenever an object's structure is changed. For example, if you delete a column from a table and rename another table, both operations cause changes to the data dictionary entries. A row in a table holding other tables' column names is deleted when you delete a column, and a row containing table names is updated when you rename a table. Having a data dictionary makes the job of the database management system and the database administrator easier, because all information needed about the system is contained in one place.

Unfortunately, Microsoft Access does not include a facility that automatically creates a data dictionary. You can create a data dictionary in a separate Access file, but it will not automatically update itself when you change the elements of the database.

The Coffee Merchant Tables

To understand how accounting information can be organized in a database system, let's look at an example. Several of the tables contained in the *Ch03.mdb* database, which is stored in the Ch03 folder on your Companion CD, include invoice data for customers of The Coffee Merchant. Figure 3.9 shows schema for each table used in the invoicing subsystem of The Coffee Merchant's database.

tblCountryName	(CountryID, CountryName, ExportCoffeeBags, ExportTeaPounds)
tblCustomer	(CustomerID, CompanyName, Contact, Address, City, State, ZipCode, PhoneNumber, FaxNumber, CreditLimit)
tblEmployee	(EmployeeID, EmployeeFirstName, EmployeeLastName, EmployeeWorkPhone, EmployeeTitleID, EmployeeCommRate, EmployeeHireDate, EmployeeDOB, EmployeeGender, EmployeeNotes)
tblEmployeeTitle	(TitleID, Title)
tblInventory	(InventoryID, ItemID, Caffeinated, Price, OnHand)
tblInventoryDescription	(ItemID, Name, BeverageType, Flavored, CountryID, Comments)
tblInvoice	(InvoiceID, InvoiceDate, OrderDate, CustomerID, EmployeeID, CustomerPO)
tblInvoiceLine	(InvoiceID, InventoryID, Quantity, UnitPrice, Discount)
tblSalesTaxRate	(StateAbbreviation, StateName, TaxRate, Population, LandArea)

Figure 3.9   Schemas of tables in the invoicing system.

When bits of data from each of these tables are combined in the proper way, you can build and print an invoice. The *tblCustomer* table contains information about each customer. Each customer is assigned a primary key—a sequence of integers beginning with any number is sufficient—so that a customer can be uniquely identified. The Invoice table, *tblInvoice*, contains a history of invoices sent out by The Coffee Merchant. Each row is identified by the primary key, InvoiceID, and it holds each customer's invoice date (InvoiceDate), order date (OrderDate), customer identification number (CustomerID), identification number of the associated salesperson (EmployeeID), and the customer's original purchase order number (CustomerPO). Of course, an invoice shows more details than these held in the Invoice table *tblInvoice*, but those additional details (such as the customer's address) are contained in *tblCustomer*, which is linked to the Invoice table on the CustomerID attribute—the primary key in *tblCustomer* and a foreign key in *tblInvoice*. Figure 3.10 shows a Datasheet view of some *tblInvoice* rows.

primary key   foreign keys

InvoiceID	InvoiceDate	OrderDate	CustomerID	EmployeeID	CustomerPO
214010	10/1/2003	9/6/2003	35222	4058	2634-635
214011	10/1/2003	9/8/2003	33776	3458	587-233
214012	10/1/2003	9/12/2003	33271	1695	1328-333
214013	10/1/2003	9/22/2003	32978	1364	2817-332
214014	10/1/2003	9/27/2003	32198	3609	4155-032
214015	10/2/2003	9/8/2003	32369	2754	912-232
214016	10/2/2003	9/8/2003	33542	4082	662-433
214017	10/3/2003	9/22/2003	34109	3370	4210-234
214018	10/3/2003	9/25/2003	34154	1364	1470-034
214019	10/4/2003	9/5/2003	31183	3370	3464-131

Record: 1 of 500

500 records in this table

Figure 3.10   Example rows in the Invoice table, *tblInvoice*.

Order lines contain details about individual items ordered by the customer and included on the current invoice such as quantity ordered, unit price, and discount. These order line details are not stored in the Invoice table. Instead, those details are stored in three other tables: *tblInvoiceLine*, *tblInventory*, and *tblInventoryDescription*. Figures 3.11, 3.12, and 3.13 show sample rows from each of these tables. The *tblInvoiceLine* table may appear to be a bit unusual at first glance. It contains only five attributes: two fields that make up its composite primary key and three other fields that contain information about the items on each invoice. These information items include the quantity ordered, the quoted unit price (which can vary for a given product depending on the customer), and the discount percentage for each item on each invoice. A composite primary key consists of more than one attribute. In this table, InvoiceID and InventoryID combine to form the composite primary key. These two attributes identify the invoice and each inventory item number that will appear on a line of that invoice. The *tblInventory* and *tblInventoryDescription* tables store information about the coffees and teas available from The Coffee Merchant. Only a few of the over 100 items stored in the inventory tables appear in Figure 3.12. InventoryID identifies each inventory item uniquely, and other characteristics about the inventory item are stored in the *tblInventory* and *tblInventoryDescription* tables.

primary key foreign key

tblInvoiceLine : Table

InvoiceID	InventoryID	Quantity	UnitPrice	Discount
214010	1184	18	$6.90	5%
214010	1192	17	$13.30	10%
214010	1195	17	$3.90	0%
214010	1209	14	$6.20	15%
214010	1237	17	$10.90	5%
214011	1104	19	$5.30	5%
214011	1133	8	$7.90	0%
214011	1137	15	$7.00	15%
214011	1197	2	$7.10	0%
214011	1211	10	$14.70	15%

Record: 20 of 2192

Figure 3.11 Example rows in the Invoice Line table, *tblInvoiceLine*.

primary key foreign key

tblInventory : Table

InventoryID	ItemID	Caffeinated	Price	OnHand
1101	116	☑	$8.10	512
1102	422	☐	$5.30	3,190
1103	440	☐	$7.70	-130
1104	455	☐	$5.30	3,380
1105	449	☐	$7.60	3,300
1106	224	☑	$7.40	1,130
1107	113	☑	$8.80	315
1108	134	☑	$10.30	443
1109	275	☑	$8.00	354
1110	353	☐	$13.70	354

Record: 20 of 154

Figure 3.12 Example rows in the primary Inventory table, *tblInventory*.

These tables do not store the extended price, subtotal, and other information that normally appears on an invoice. The way to obtain these information items is to have Access calculate them when it prints invoices. Calculated values need not be stored in tables because they can be obtained by multiplying each invoice line's quantity and price attributes. It is undesirable to store values in a table that can be calculated from other table fields. Thus, the data in these four tables plus the Customer table, *tblCustomer*, contain all of the information needed to produce invoices for The Coffee Merchant.

primary key

foreign key

ItemID	Name	BeverageType	Flavored	CountryID	
305	Fujian Oolong Ti Kuan Yin	t	☐	90	China oolong tea tends to be rough in comparison
308	Orange Blossom Oolong	t	☐	41	China oolong tea tends to be rough in comparison
311	Ethiopia Yergacheffe	c	☐	61	Piquant and having a sweet, fruity taste. Full toa
314	Mocha Java	c	☐	83	Powerful, bold, and exotic. World's oldest and m
317	Kenya AA	c	☐	93	Rich bourbon-like, bright, sweet with hints of bla
320	Yukon Blend	c	☐	0	Robust and earthy; lingering richness.
323	Sulawesi Peaberry	c	☐	83	Smooth, buttery, refined, and a true treasure. Th
326	Java	c	☐	83	Spicy sweetness and strong to heavy bodied an
329	Sumatra Boengie	c	☐	83	Sumatra arabicas have a concentrated flavor, pu
332	Celebes Kalossi	c	☐	83	Sweet and fruity aroma; smooth and full bodied;
335	Brazil Sul De Minas Cerra	c	☐	28	Sweet flavor; most varieties are relatively non-dis
338	Italian Roast	c	☐	0	Sweet, dark, spirited; rich caramel-like taste.
341	Haiti Strictly High Grown W	c	☐	78	Sweet, mellow, fair-bodied coffee with a rich flavo
344	Brazil Bourbon Santos	c	☐	28	Sweet, neutral flavor; most varieties are relatively
347	Tanzania Moshi	c	☐	171	Tanzanian coffees are known for their sharp, win
350	Chanchamayo	c	☐	138	The Chanchamayos are often as good as the be

Record: 20 of 132

Figure 3.13   Example rows in the secondary Inventory table, *tblInventoryDescription*.

Now that you understand the details of The Coffee Merchant's database tables, you can learn about normalization. We will use The Coffee Merchant tables to illustrate the reasons for and the definitions of normalized tables.

Normalization

In a relational table design, it is important to think carefully about where individual pieces of data are stored. The process of determining the correct location for each attribute is called *normalization*. Another way of thinking about normalization is this: normalizing a database is storing data where it uniquely belongs. Unnormalized databases can lead to redundant, inconsistent, or incorrect information being stored in tables.

There are many ways to arrange the invoice system attributes in sets of tables. Some arrangements are better than others. A particular subset of the ways that attributes can be organized into tables is called a *normal form*, and the basis of this arrangement is called normalization theory.

Database theorists have identified seven normal forms. Like layers of an onion, each normal form includes compliance with the rules of all lower normal forms. For example, a table that is in third normal form is automatically in first and second normal forms and complies with the rules for those three normal forms. The rules applied to achieve each normal form are successively more stringent. The least restrictive is called the *first normal form*, which is abbreviated as 1NF. Following that form are the *second*, *third*, *Boyce-Codd*, *fourth*, *fifth*, and *Domain-Key* normal forms. Most accounting systems require use of only the first three normal forms. Tables in third normal form are better than tables in second normal form. Likewise, tables in second normal form are better than tables in first normal form. The goal of the normalization process is to start with a collection of tables (or relations), apply normalization, and arrive at an equivalent collection of tables in a higher normal form. The process is repeated until all tables are in third normal form (3NF).

FIRST NORMAL FORM. A table that contains a repeating group is called an *unnormalized* table. The relational model requires that all tables be in first normal form. To achieve this, repeating data must be removed from the table and stored elsewhere. For example, suppose that an invoice table held each invoice line for all invoices in the arrangement shown in Figure 3.14.

InvoiceID	InvoiceDate	CustomerID	InventoryID	Quantity	UnitPrice	Discount
214010	10/1/2003	35222	1184	18	$6.90	5%
			1192	17	$13.30	10%
			1195	17	$3.90	0%
			1209	14	$6.20	15%
			1237	17	$10.90	5%
214011	10/1/2003	33776	1104	19	$5.30	5%
			1133	8	$7.90	0%
			1137	15	$7.00	15%
			1197	2	$7.10	0%
			1211	10	$14.70	15%
214012	10/1/2003	33271	1127	17	$4.50	0%
			1129	5	$8.40	0%
			1189	14	$5.30	15%
			1203	12	$8.10	15%
			1249	2	$11.90	0%
214013	10/1/2003	32978	1139	10	$5.30	15%
			1198	17	$8.10	5%
			1208	14	$4.50	15%
			1216	19	$7.20	5%
			1229	5	$12.90	0%
			1249	5	$11.90	0%
214014	10/1/2003	32198	1170	6	$44.50	10%

Figure 3.14 Example table containing repeating groups.

Notice that for each invoice in the Invoice table, there are several inventory item numbers, quantities, unit prices, and discounts. For instance, invoice number 214010 contains five items; each item corresponds to an invoice detail item on a printed invoice. The schema for this table is:

tblInvoice (<u>InvoiceID</u>, InvoiceDate, CustomerID,
InventoryID, Quantity, UnitPrice, Discount,
InventoryID, Quantity, UnitPrice, Discount, . . .)

where the ellipsis indicates that InventoryID, Quantity, UnitPrice, and Discount can repeat any number of times—as many times as there are items listed on a single invoice.

To be in first normal form, a table cannot store repeating groups (multiple values) in one table column, nor can it store a variable number of {InventoryID, Quantity, UnitPrice, Discount} sets in each row. To convert the table shown in Figure 3.14 into first normal form, you can remove the repeating groups from the existing Invoice table and place them into a new table. However, you must add an additional column to the new table linking the rows of the newly formed table with the original Invoice table. An example of the structure of the two tables conforming to first normal form is this:

> tblInvoice(<u>InvoiceID</u>, InvoiceDate, OrderDate, CustomerID, EmployeeID, CustomerPO)
> tblInvoiceLine(<u>InvoiceID</u>, <u>InventoryID</u>, Quantity, UnitPrice, Discount)

The new table, *tblInvoiceLine*, contains five columns. The first two columns, InvoiceID and InventoryID, combine to form the new table's primary key. This is a *composite primary key* because the primary key includes two attributes.

SECOND NORMAL FORM. Tables in first normal form can be placed into a relational database system, but in many cases first normal form is not sufficient to prevent problems. For example, Figure 3.15 shows an example of some rows of a customer table in first normal form. The schema for this table is:

> tblCustomer(<u>CustomerID</u>, CompanyName, PhoneNumber, Contact, <u>InvoiceID</u>, Total)

The customer table contains customer information including the customer identification number, company name, telephone, and contact person. The last two

CustomerID	CompanyName	PhoneNumber	Contact	InvoiceID	Total
30125	Alamo Group Inc.	(210) 555-1483	Maul, Duane A.	214480	306.80
30139	Cavco Industries Inc.	(602) 555-6141	Golkin, David	214123	225.11
30139	Cavco Industries Inc.	(602) 555-6141	Golkin, David	214460	315.10
30174	Thomas Nelson Inc.	(615) 555-9079	Harber, L. H.	214390	491.96
30174	Thomas Nelson Inc.	(615) 555-9079	Harber, L. H.	214418	185.95
30206	Matlack Systems Inc.	(302) 555-2760	Gordon, W. Phil	214334	218.39
30212	Lilly Industries Inc.	(317) 555-6762	Choong, Jerry	214117	152.20
30221	Mcdonald & Co. Investments Inc.	(216) 555-2368	Bianco, Andrew R.	214249	297.34
30225	Krause S Furniture Inc.	(510) 555-6208	Woltz, Neil G.	214087	260.15
30228	F N B Corp. Pa	(412) 555-6028	Fancher, William R.	214284	98.35
30231	Everest & Jennings Internation	(314) 555-7041	Gray, Robert R.	214036	270.60
30231	Everest & Jennings Internation	(314) 555-7041	Gray, Robert R.	214256	165.96
30258	Lcs Industries Inc.	(201) 555-5666	Lebuhn, Eugene	214230	895.25

Figure 3.15 Example rows of the Customer table in first normal form (1NF).

columns indicate the customer's invoice number and amount. The two table columns, CustomerID and InvoiceID, form the table's primary key. Both are needed to access a row.

Several potential problems exist with the proposed 1NF customer table. Suppose that the customer table is the only place in which customer information such as address or name is stored. Further, suppose that a new customer has paid for an order in advance. The design would not allow such a customer to be added because the InvoiceID value would be empty. When an attribute is empty, or has no value, it is *null*. The InvoiceID attribute cannot be null, because the primary key cannot be null or include a null attribute if it is a composite primary key. The inability to add a record is called an *insertion anomaly*.

Consider this scenario. Cavco Industries pays for its two invoices, numbers 214123 and 214460 (see Figure 3.15, second and third rows), bringing its amount due to zero. The two rows corresponding to Cavco Industries are removed from *tblCustomer*. Not only are the two invoices removed, but the customer's identification number, name, phone, and contact person are deleted as well. So the deletion has a wider effect than desired; you lose knowledge of the customer entirely. Your mailing list is being destroyed! This predicament is known as a *deletion anomaly*.

Finally, the *tblCustomer* table shown in Figure 3.15 contains much redundant information. For instance, the company identification number, name, phone number, and contact person are repeated for each new invoice that is issued for a particular customer. The customer name *Cavco Industries Inc.* is entered twice, as is *Golkin, David*, the contact person. It is pure luck that both the company name and contact person's name have been spelled correctly both times. To change the company name you must find all occurrences of the name in the database and change each one. What a time-consuming task that could be! This small example illustrates that tables in first normal form can contain redundant data.

Altering a table's structure and changing it into second normal form can prevent these anomalies. A table (relation) is in *second normal form* (2NF) if it is in first normal form and none of the nonkey attributes depend on only one portion of the primary key. That is, second normal form requires that each nonkey attribute depend on the entire primary key, not just part of it. This rule applies only when you have a composite primary key—one consisting of more than one table column.

The attribute Total in the customer table in Figure 3.15 violates the 2NF definition. The value of Total is determined by the partial primary key InvoiceID. We say that Total is *functionally dependent* on InvoiceID, because a particular value of InvoiceID determines a single value of Total. On the other hand, Total does not depend on the attribute and partial primary key CustomerID, because the total invoice amount varies from invoice to invoice; no relationship exists between Total and a particular customer. On the other hand, the attributes CompanyName, PhoneNumber, and Contact each functionally depend on the partial primary key CustomerID. These two sets of functional dependencies are shown in Figure 3.16.

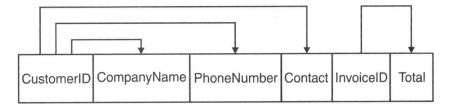

Figure 3.16   Functional dependencies in the Customer table.

The arrows lead from a primary key to another attribute. For instance, the arrow leading from CustomerID to CompanyName means that CustomerID *determines* CompanyName (or CustomerID is a *determinant* of CompanyName). It is clear that we can correct this problem by breaking *tblCustomer* into two tables. Of course, we must note the relationship between these two tables by including an extra attribute—a foreign key—that links both tables on the CustomerID key. You can restructure *tblCustomer* and the related table *tblInvoice* so they are in second normal form by using a design such as this:

   tblCustomer(<u>CustomerID</u>, CompanyName, PhoneNumber, Contact)
   tblInvoice(<u>InvoiceID</u>, <u>CustomerID</u>, Total)

In this design, the CustomerID field in *tblInvoice* is a foreign key to *tblCustomer*. The double underline below CustomerID in *tblInvoice* indicates that it is a foreign key.

THIRD NORMAL FORM. The design goal for relational databases is to create tables that are in third normal form. A table is in *third normal form* (3NF) if it is in second normal form and all transitive dependencies have been eliminated. A *transitive dependency* exists in a table if attribute B determines attribute C, and attribute C determines attribute D.

You have probably heard an expression that can help you understand and remember the difference between 2NF and 3NF. Part of the phrase used to swear in witnesses who are about to take the stand in a trial is: "... to tell the truth, the whole truth, and nothing but the truth." The second normal form is analogous to "the whole truth" part of the phrase—each attribute depends on the *whole* primary key. Similarly, the third normal form is analogous to "and nothing but the truth." Each attribute depends *only* on the primary key and on no other attribute in the relation. For example, consider the Invoice table shown in Figure 3.17.

The Invoice table's primary key is InvoiceID. Because only one customer may be assigned a particular invoice number (the value in the InvoiceID field), the invoice number uniquely determines the invoice date, order date, customer identification number, employee identification number, and company contact

InvoiceID	InvoiceDate	OrderDate	CustomerID	EmployeeID	Contact
214010	10/1/2003	9/6/2003	35222	4058	Shaffer, Shaun P.
214011	10/1/2003	9/8/2003	33776	3458	Olbrych, Fred H.
214012	10/1/2003	9/12/2003	33271	1695	Yocam, William C.
214013	10/1/2003	9/22/2003	32978	1364	Swift, Scott C.
214014	10/1/2003	9/27/2003	32198	3609	
214015	10/2/2003	9/8/2003	32369	2754	Gosa, Myron E.
214016	10/2/2003	9/8/2003	33542	4082	Henderson, L. Keith
214017	10/3/2003	9/22/2003	34109	3370	Pirie, Thomas R.
214018	10/3/2003	9/25/2003	34154	1364	Ammerman, Donnie I
214019	10/4/2003	9/5/2003	31183	3370	Dykstra, Bruce A.

Figure 3.17   Invoice table in second normal form (2NF).

person. There are no repeating groups in the table. Therefore, it is in first normal form. Furthermore, it is in second normal form because all attributes depend on the single-attribute primary key. However, it is not in third normal form because all attributes are not functionally dependent on only the InvoiceID attribute. There is a transitive dependency in this design. The InvoiceID determines the CustomerID value and CustomerID, in turn, determines the Contact column. Figure 3.18 shows the dependency in the Invoice table.

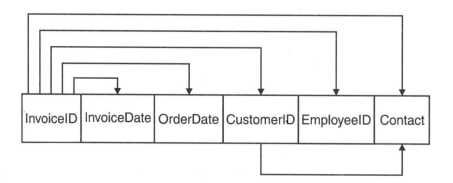

Figure 3.18   Transitive dependencies in the Invoice table shown in Figure 3.17.

The arrows above the attribute boxes show the dependencies that exist between attributes and the table's primary key. Those relationships are fine. However, the arrow below the boxes shows a transitive dependency between CustomerID (the determinant attribute) and Contact. The easiest way to remove the transitive dependency is to create another table containing at least the determinant attribute and all attributes that are dependent on that determinant attribute. Once the transitive dependency is removed, the table will be in 3NF. The CustomerID field becomes a foreign key to link the invoice to individual customer information. The new tables could be structured as follows to bring them into compliance with 3NF:

tblInvoice(<u>InvoiceID</u>, InvoiceDate, OrderDate, <u>CustomerID</u>, <u>EmployeeID</u>)

tblCustomer(<u>CustomerID</u>, Contact)

Third normal form enforces an informal rule stating that a table should store one fact and one fact only. Prior to decomposing *tblInvoice* into two separate tables, it housed two facts: one fact about invoices (InvoiceDate, OrderDate, etc.) and one fact about customers (Contact). After two tables are created from a single table, each new table's structure (shown previously) holds only one fact.

TABLE RELATIONSHIPS. You have learned that the process of normalizing a database's tables usually produces several additional tables. Yet, the relationships between associated tables is maintained by the foreign key to primary key links. There are three fundamental types of relationships between related tables: one-to-one (1—1), one-to-many (1—M), and many-to-many (M—M). The capital letter *M* indicates *many* records. Knowing about these three is important in understanding how to reconstruct information from data stored in constituent tables. Recall that rows from two tables are joined when the foreign key in one table's row matches the primary key in another table.

One-to-one relationships usually indicate unnecessary tables in the database design. You can usually combine tables with a one-to-one relationship into one table. Exceptions to this general rule can occur. For instance, the Customer table could have a one-to-one relationship with *tblCustomerNotes*, which might hold supplementary information about a few of The Coffee Merchant's customers. Because only a few customers have notes in the *tblCustomerNotes* table, you do not want to allocate an additional column for an occasional note. This would waste storage space. So *tblCustomerNotes* would contain the foreign key CustomerID and a Notes column. CustomerID would serve both as the primary key for the *tblCustomerNotes* table and as a foreign key into the parent *tblCustomer* table. The following notation shows this relationship conveniently:

tblCustomer ^{1}————————>^{1} tblCustomerNotes

Databases often contain tables that have one-to-many relationships with each other. There are several examples in The Coffee Merchant's database. Look again at Figure 3.8. Consider the relationship between the *tblCustomer* table and the *tblInvoice* table. Each customer can have as many unpaid invoices as The Coffee Merchant permits (or none). On the other hand, an invoice row in the *tblInvoice* table can be associated with one and only one customer in the *tblCustomer* table. The relationship between the *tblCustomer* table and the *tblInvoice* table is said to be a one-to-many relationship (in that direction—customer to invoice). Although it is technically correct to talk about "many-to-one" relationships, most database designers indicate the "one" side of the relationship first and use the "one-to-many" phrasing. A one-to-many relationship is shown this way:

$$\text{tblCustomer }{}^1 \text{———————}{>}^M \text{ tblInvoice}$$

Finally, consider the relationship between invoices and the coffee and tea items found on individual invoice lines. Various coffees and teas can appear on the many lines of a single invoice. An invoice might contain a line for 10 pounds of Kona coffee and another line for 5 pounds of Zimbabwe. Similarly, the coffee and tea items in The Coffee Merchant's inventory can appear in several invoices. For example, many different invoices might include Kona coffee. This type of relationship between the Invoice table and Inventory table is called a many-to-many relationship. We depict this type of relationship as follows:

$$\text{tblInvoice }{}^M \text{———————}{>}^M \text{ tblInventory}$$

Many-to-many relationships can be difficult to represent and maintain in a relational database system. Most database designers create a new table to represent the M—M relationship. This table is called a *relationship* table or a *junction* table, and it combines attributes from the tables that participate in the M—M relationship. The relationship table makes the connection between the two tables by converting the M—M relationship into two 1—M relationships. The relationship table in The Coffee Merchant's database is called Invoice Line (*tblInvoiceLine*); it preserves the relationship between invoices (*tblInvoice*) and inventory (*tblInventory*). You can represent this three-table relationship for the M—M relationship as:

$$\text{tblInvoice }{}^1 \text{————}{>}^M \text{ tblInvoiceLine }{}^M{<}\text{————}{}^1 \text{ tblInventory}$$

Thus, it is always possible to break a many-to-many relationship between two tables into two one-to-many relationships by using an intermediate relationship table. The following are some general rules governing relationships among tables.

1. Primary keys must not be null.

2. Create a foreign key from the primary key on the one side of the 1—M relationship.

3. Many-to-many relationships are handled by creating an additional table—the *relationship table*—that consists entirely of the parent tables' primary keys. (The relationship table can contain other columns as well.)

4. Most one-to-one relationships indicate unnecessary tables in the database design. Normally, you should merge the two tables. Exceptions occur when there are just too many columns in one table, or one group of fields is used far more frequently than another group. Then, you can consider separating them into different tables for efficiency's sake.

Fundamental Relational Database Operations

Relational database management systems provide several important and fundamental retrieval operations. Among the most significant are select, project, and join.

SELECT. The select operator chooses a set of rows from a table. Rows are selected based on a set of qualifying factors, often called *selection criteria*. A new, virtual table is created by the select operation. There are several ways to implement a select operation. Some RDBMSs such as Access provide a Query By Example (QBE) graphical interface, in which you can choose example elements to specify selection criteria and check the attributes to be displayed.

Figure 3.19 shows a select operation and the resulting dynaset, another table. The query selects rows from a smaller version of an Employee table. Rows are selected in which the HireDate is after a particular date. Notice that the result returns all columns of the original table satisfying the selection criterion. The result is a table, because queries in relational database systems always deliver answers in table form.

PROJECT. The project operator returns a subset of columns from one or more tables. Columns retrieved are a result of the user indicating them, not as a result of specifying a selection criterion. Figure 3.20 shows an example of a projection of the Name and Gender columns of our example Employee table shown previously in Figure 3.19. Notice that a project operation does not specify which *rows* are retrieved. Projections indicate only which *columns* are retrieved in the result. Of course, you can combine the selection and project operations in one query to produce both a row and column subset of a table.

JOIN. The most important relational database operation is the join operation. It provides the ability to pull together data from associated tables into a single, virtual table. Usually, you join two tables together using a common attribute found in both tables. This is the role of the foreign and primary keys. In the most common form of the join operation, one table's foreign key value is used to locate a matching primary key in another table. Then the selected data from the matching rows in both tables are combined. That is, rows of one table are concatenated

Employee table:

ID	Name	Comm	HireDate	BirthDate	Gender
1301	Stonesifer	5%	07/06/96	03/10/66	F
1364	Pruski	4%	12/01/00	01/26/79	M
1528	Pacioli	6%	08/26/95	05/06/50	M
1695	Nagasaki	4%	01/28/00	04/10/77	M
2240	Stonely	15%	11/05/88	05/03/61	F
2318	Hunter	8%	11/16/93	01/26/54	F
2754	Kahn	5%	05/14/97	05/29/61	M
3370	Kole	9%	02/08/92	03/23/63	M
3432	English	8%	10/01/93	02/14/56	F
3436	Gates	6%	04/11/95	03/09/54	M
3458	Morrison	15%	12/13/89	07/04/56	F
3609	Chang	5%	09/16/97	03/30/77	F
. . .	. . .	. . .	. . .	. . .	. . .
4112	Goldman	11%	12/24/90	03/05/62	M

Result of selection operation: HireDate > 1/1/97

ID	Name	Comm	HireDate	BirthDate	Gender
1364	Pruski	4%	12/01/00	01/26/79	M
1695	Nagasaki	4%	01/28/00	04/10/77	M
2754	Kahn	5%	05/14/97	05/29/61	M
3609	Chang	5%	09/16/97	03/30/77	F

Figure 3.19   Select operation.

with (placed next to) rows of the second table for which the common attribute matches.

For instance, suppose we want to join a slightly altered Employee table with the employee title information found in a table on your Companion CD called *tblEmployeeTitle*. In the Employee table is a number, which stands in place of an actual job title. The number is used so that the title is not misspelled when it is entered over and over in the Employee table. *tblEmployeeTitle* contains the numbers and actual job titles associated with the numbers. Normalization has produced the two tables rather than a single table with repeating job titles, which would violate 3NF rules. The tables are joined on title number columns found in both tables. In the Employee table, this column is called *EmployeeTitleID*, although the Caption property setting for that field has been shortened to *TitleID*. The *EmployeeTitleID* column in *tblEmployeeTitle* is the primary key and contains

Employee table: **Projection:**

ID	Name	Comm	HireDate	BirthDate	Gender	Name	Gender
1301	Stonesifer	5%	07/06/96	03/10/66	F	Stonesifer	F
1364	Pruski	4%	12/01/00	01/26/79	M	Pruski	M
1528	Pacioli	6%	08/26/95	05/06/50	M	Pacioli	M
. . .	. . .	. . .	. . .	. . .	. . .	. . .	. . .
4057	Bateman	9%	02/16/92	05/01/58	M	Bateman	M
4058	Halstead	5%	06/16/96	12/22/73	F	Halstead	F
4082	Flintsteel	11%	03/21/90	08/22/58	F	Flintsteel	F
4112	Goldman	11%	12/24/90	03/05/62	M	Goldman	M

Figure 3.20 Project operation.

a corresponding title field, *Title*. Joining the two tables in TitleID produces the result shown in Figure 3.21. Note that the join column *does not* have to have the same name in both tables. In the illustration, TitleID is a foreign key in the *tblEmployee* table, whereas TitleID is the primary key in the *tblEmployeeTitle* table. Joining is a matter of matching foreign key and primary key values. The join illustration in Figure 3.21 is an example of the most common type of join. It is called an *equijoin*, because rows from the two tables are placed next to each other (concatenated) on matching join column values, and the join column appears only once in the result.

Another join operation type combines rows from two or more tables on the join column, but rows that do not match on the join column are included in the result. This type of join is called an *outer join*. Outer joins are useful for creating reports that show information such as employees who have made no sales or students who have not signed up for a particular class.

There is no theoretical limit to the number of tables that may be joined. For instance, one of the results we can produce with a join operation are invoices. An invoice is created by a query that joins five of The Coffee Merchant's tables whose schemas are shown in Figure 3.9. Tables joined to form an invoice are connected in pairs on common columns, but not all on the same columns. For instance, the *tblCustomer* table can be joined to the *tblInvoice* table via their common column, CustomerID. Continuing, the *tblInvoice* table can be joined to the *tblInvoiceLine* table (individual invoice lines) over the join column InvoiceID, an attribute found in both tables. The Inventory table, *tblInventory*, is joined to *tblInventoryDescription* to link the names of each invoiced item. *tblInventory* is joined to *tblInvoiceLine* on the common column InventoryID. Figure 3.22 illustrates how the join columns of all involved tables are connected to form the single result. All of the joins shown in Figure 3.22 are equijoins.

tblEmployee

ID	Name	TitleID	HireDate	Gender
1301	Stonesifer	2	07/06/96	F
1364	Pruski	1	12/01/00	M
1528	Pacioli	2	08/26/95	M
1695	Nagasaki	1	01/28/00	M
2240	Stonely	3	11/05/88	F
2318	Hunter	2	11/16/93	F
2754	Kahn	2	05/14/97	M
3370	Kole	2	02/08/92	M
3432	English	2	10/01/93	F
3436	Gates	2	04/11/95	M
. . .	. . .	. . .	. . .	. . .
4082	Flintsteel	3	03/21/90	F
4112	Goldman	3	12/24/90	M

tblEmployeeTitle

TitleID	Title
1	Sales Trainee
2	Sales Associate
3	Senior Sales Associate
4	Sales Manager
5	Senior Sales Manager
6	Division Sales Manager
7	Regional Manager
8	Division Manager
9	National Sales Manager

Result of join operation:

ID	Name	TitleID	HireDate	Gender	Title
1301	Stonesifer	2	07/06/96	F	Sales Associate
1364	Pruski	1	12/01/00	M	Sales Trainee
1528	Pacioli	2	08/26/95	M	Sales Associate
1695	Nagasaki	1	01/28/00	M	Sales Trainee
2240	Stonely	3	11/05/886	F	Senior Sales Associate
2318	Hunter	2	11/16/93	F	Sales Associate
2754	Kahn	2	05/14/97	M	Sales Associate
3370	Kole	2	02/08/92	M	Sales Associate
3432	English	2	10/01/93	F	Sales Associate
3436	Gates	2	04/11/95	M	Sales Associate
. . .	. . .	. . .	. . .	. . .	. . .
4082	Flintsteel	3	03/21/90	F	Senior Sales Associate
4112	Goldman	3	12/24/90	M	Senior Sales Associate

Figure 3.21   Join operation.

INTRODUCTION TO DATABASE DESIGN

A well-designed database that accurately models an enterprise's operations is crucial to the success of any database system designed to maintain accounting information. A badly designed database can be worse than using no system at all; information can be misrepresented, difficult to find, or completely lost.

One important aspect of database design is carefully choosing the rows and attributes that you want to include in each table. This activity, often referred to as *modeling*, can be accomplished using any of several methods. We introduce you to two of these methods in this section. The first method draws information from existing business documents. The other method, called entity-relationship (abbreviated E-R) modeling, is described in the context of The Coffee Merchant's invoice system.

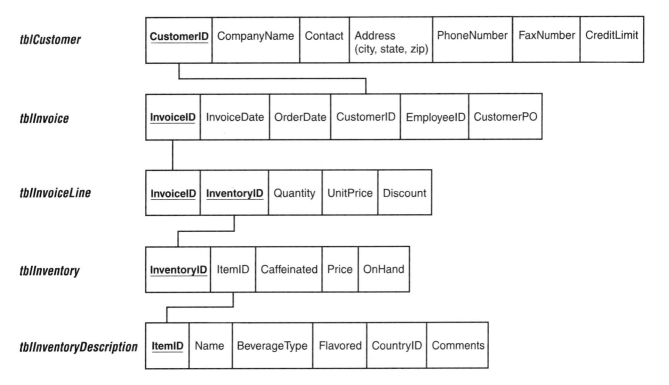

Figure 3.22   Joining tables with primary key/foreign key relationships.

Creating User Views and Tables

One way to approach designing database objects is to use existing documents as a starting point. For instance, we can look at a current customer invoice facsimile used before the database accounting system was implemented. The first step in designing database objects to replace paper forms is to list all the information found on the document and to assign names to the attributes. Next, identify functional dependencies, if any. Then, the entities (tables) can be created by selecting which attributes belong in which tables. Finally, apply normalization rules to the tables to ensure that all tables (entities) conform to third normal form.

The first step is to list potential attributes from an existing document. Attribute names may not be exactly right the first time, but they provide a starting point. Figure 3.23 shows a list of possible attribute names. Other possible attributes have been omitted from the list such as Ship Date, Item Quantity Backordered, and Item Quantity Shipped to keep the example simple yet sufficient to illustrate the modeling process.

The next step is to identify functional dependencies. You can make good guesses as to which attributes determine the value of other attributes. Do not worry about making a mistake. Any errors will be uncovered when you show your design

CustomerContactPerson   ItemExtendedPrice
CustomerName   ItemName
CustomerNumber   ItemNumber
CustomerPhone   ItemPrice
CustomerAddress   ItemQuantity
InvoiceDate   OrderDate
InvoiceNumber   OrderNumber
InvoiceTotalAmount   SalesTax
ItemDescription   ShippingCharges

Figure 3.23   A list of possible attribute names.

to the people that will be using the system. Figure 3.24 shows an example of a dependency list. Dependent attributes are listed below the attributes that determine them.

After making initial assignments of attributes, you might discover that you need to change these assignments. For example, you might determine that the price charged to a customer depends on the CustomerNumber and the ItemNumber. This can happen when particular customers are given price reductions based on volume or other factors. Finally, attributes that are calculated from other database fields

CustomerNumber:
    CustomerName
    CustomerPhone
    CustomerContactPerson
    CustomerAddress

InvoiceNumber:
    InvoiceDate
    CustomerNumber
    OrderDate
    OrderNumber
    ShippingCharges
    InvoiceTotalAmount
    SalesTax

InvoiceNumber, ItemNumber:
    ItemQuantity
    ItemExtendedPrice

ItemNumber:
    ItemDescription
    ItemPrice
    ItemName

Figure 3.24   Tentative dependency list.

should not be stored in the database at all. Examples of such calculated fields in this example would include InvoiceTotalAmount, SalesTax, and ShippingCharges. SalesTax, for instance, depends on additional attributes besides InvoiceNumber. A change in the unit price of an item would not be reflected in SalesTax automatically.

As the last step in this process, you develop a revised list of attributes that conform to third normal form. The attributes upon which each group depends constitute the relation's primary key, and each table's attributes are the primary key and the attributes listed below the primary key. The list of corrected dependencies is left as an exercise for the student (Hint: See Figure 3.9).

Developing Entity-Relationship Models

Another popular modeling technique is called *entity-relationship (E-R) modeling*. Introduced by Peter Chen in 1976, E-R modeling has gained wide acceptance as a graphical approach to database design.

Database designers often use three terms to describe a company's information: entities, relationships, and attributes. *Entities* are objects (people or things) that are important to the company (nouns such as customer, inventory, employee, or vendor) or important activities (nouns such as sale, purchase, or cash disbursement). *Relationships* describe the way in which entities interact or are related to one another. For example, the entity customer is related to the entity sale when the company sells something to a customer. *Attributes* describe the characteristics of entities and relationships.

In the E-R model, diagrams represent entities and relationships. The diagrams contain three symbols: rectangles, diamonds, and lines. Rectangles represent entities and diamonds represent relationships. Lines are the connections between the two. A digit or letter above the line indicates the *degree* of the relationship: one-to-one, one-to-many, or many-to-many. Figure 3.25 shows an example of an E-R diagram for The Coffee Merchant's invoice system.

At first, the E-R model allowed both entities and relationships to have attributes. In an E-R diagram, attributes are often shown as a list near the relationship or entity to which they belong. Another way to show attributes is to have an attribute name attached to a line leading from the entity or relationship to the attribute. Chen later suggested a slight change to the E-R approach. The altered E-R model allowed only entities to have attributes, not relationships.

A problem arises with the refined E-R methodology when a database includes many-to-many relationships. In this case, a new entity—shown with a diamond within a rectangle—is used to redraw two entities as three. The new entity reduces the many-to-many relationship to two relationships: a 1—M degree relationship on one side and an M—1 degree relationship on the other side (see Figure 3.26). 1—M signifies that one record from the table on one side *may* have many related records in the table on the other side of the relationship. For instance, an invoice can have a 1—M relationship to the items on the invoice: one invoice has many possible invoice lines.

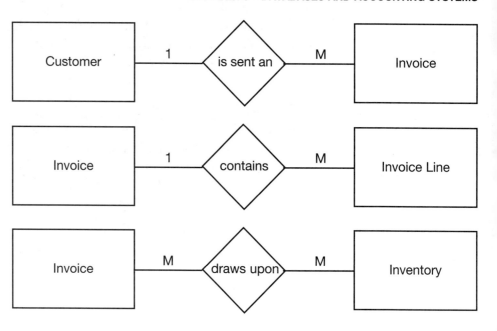

Figure 3.25   Entity-relationship diagram.

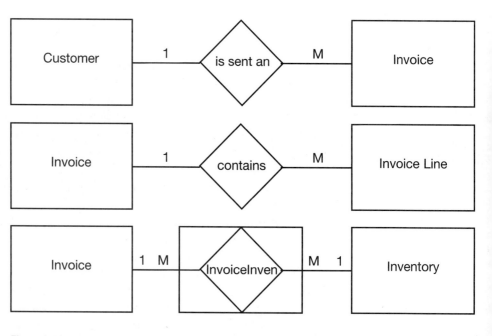

Figure 3.26   Revised entity-relationship diagram.

The newly created entity in the middle is implemented in a database as a *relationship table*, which includes the primary keys of the two joined entities as two elements in its composite primary key. A relationship table is also sometimes called a *junction table* or a *bridge table*.

After the E-R diagrams are complete, they can be combined into a single E-R diagram. This process is called *view integration*. For larger systems the process is started by placing the most often used entity in the center of the diagram. Then, lines connect the related entities as in the original diagrams. From these entities you can identify tables. For each entity, one table is created. Primary keys for each table must be identified next. The relationships between entities, exemplified by lines connecting the entities, are maintained by foreign key/primary key linkages between tables. That is, a line from one entity to another is implemented by a key in one table (a foreign key) that matches one or more primary keys in the other table. In the case of a 1—M relationship, the "one" side of the relationship has a foreign key matching possibly several rows on the "many" side of the relationship.

When a many-to-many relationship exists in the E-R diagram, such as the relationship between *tblInvoice* and *tblInventory*, a relationship table is created. The InvoiceInven table in Figure 3.26 contains the primary key from the *tblInvoice* table and the primary key from the *tblInventory* table. Once the relationship table is created, the three tables have a pair of one-to-many relationships.

A table can also be related to *itself* in a special case in which rows of a table are related to other row(s) in the same table. A typical example is an employee table in which the primary key identifies employees and a Supervisor column contains foreign keys pointing to each employee's supervisor. Supervisors are in the same table because they are themselves employees. A parts inventory is another example. Some parts are made from several other parts, all of which are stored in the same inventory table. When rows of a table are related to rows in the same table, the relationship is called *recursive*.

The last step in view integration is to normalize the individual tables. For best results, all tables should be at least in third normal form.

SUMMARY   In this chapter, you have learned about database accounting systems, business activity classifications, transaction cycles, database management systems, database tables, relationships between tables, and database design. You learned why double-entry bookkeeping was an excellent system for organizing manual data gathering and storage tasks for many years, but you also learned that database accounting systems can now offer significant advantages over computerized double-entry bookkeeping systems. Most firms today have concluded that the advantages of database accounting systems outweigh their disadvantages.

The discussion of business activity classifications showed you how to categorize firms as manufacturing, merchandising, and service businesses. You then learned how these classifications can help you match particular database features to accounting applications. The chapter discussed transaction cycles and the characteristics of database accounting systems for the revenue, purchase, payroll, and production cycles.

This chapter also introduced database management systems and their application to accounting information. Database management systems are the basis of many accounting systems and provide several advantages over nondatabase approaches to managing data. High on the list of advantages are cost savings resulting from the centralization of all data management functions and the enforcement of data integrity and consistency by the database system. Relational database management systems provide the needed capabilities to represent accounting information. Data maintenance in a relational database management system does not require a programmer's help. Usually, people can learn to insert and delete database records, and can learn to query database systems. Valuable accounting information can be retrieved in a variety of formats and aggregation levels; information retrieval is not limited to a standard set of accounting reports.

The chapter also emphasized the importance of representing table objects in normalized form. First, second, and third normal forms have been described. First normal form precludes repeating groups; second normal form requires that all table attributes be dependent on the table's entire primary key, not just part of it. Third normal form includes all the characteristics of first and second normal forms. In addition, tables in third normal form do not contain attributes that depend on other nonkey attributes. Tables in third normal form avoid problems that can impair the integrity of accounting information.

QUESTIONS AND PROBLEMS FOR REVIEW

MULTIPLE-CHOICE QUESTIONS

1. A double-entry bookkeeping system records each transaction
   a. twice.
   b. as an abstraction.
   c. in a relational database.
   d. on the day it occurs.
2. The events-based approach to accounting theory
   a. classifies businesses in terms of their complexity.
   b. requires validity checks on all accounting events that are entered into the database.
   c. supports the use of relational database accounting systems.
   d. supports the use of double-entry bookkeeping systems.

3. Database systems store data only once. This feature
   a. makes *ad hoc* queries possible.
   b. eliminates data inconsistencies.
   c. facilitates cross-functional data analysis.
   d. allows multiple users to have simultaneous data access.

4. One disadvantage of database accounting systems is that they
   a. make data more dependent on applications.
   b. often require duplicate processing.
   c. can be more expensive to install and operate.
   d. fail to adequately control data entry errors.

5. The term *cost of goods manufactured* on a manufacturing firm's income statement is analogous to
   a. cost of goods sold on a merchandising firm's income statement.
   b. revenue on a service firm's income statement.
   c. purchases on a merchandising firm's income statement.
   d. gross profit on a merchandising firm's income statement.

6. A time worked table would normally appear in a
   a. payroll cycle application.
   b. revenue cycle application.
   c. production cycle application.
   d. both a and c.

7. The purchase cycle includes
   a. manufacturers' ordering and receipt of raw materials.
   b. merchandisers' ordering and receipt of goods for resale.
   c. both a and b.
   d. none of the above.

8. A table's primary key field
   a. is always stored in one table column.
   b. is always referenced by a foreign key in another table.
   c. guarantees that each row is unique.
   d. can sometimes be empty or null.

9. When you retrieve related information from two or more tables in a database, what is that operation called?
   a. join
   b. selection
   c. criteria
   d. projection

10. How are many-to-many relationships represented in a relational database system?
    a. by four tables, each having a one-to-one relationship with the other tables
    b. by three tables, one of which is a relationship table containing primary keys from each original table
    c. by combining two tables having the many-to-many relationship into a single table
    d. many-to-many relationships must be eliminated entirely, without creating any other tables

DISCUSSION QUESTIONS

1. Why is double-entry bookkeeping better suited to manual accounting systems than to computerized accounting systems?
2. What prevents accountants from using a database model to automate a double-entry bookkeeping system?
3. In which of the business activity classifications described in this chapter would you include a hospital? Why?
4. Discuss the problems that can arise from storing data in two different places.
5. What is a primary key and why is it so important in a relational database management system?

PROBLEMS

1. Describe the tables that a grocery store would use in its revenue cycle. Be sure to include all necessary relationship tables and foreign keys.
2. Assume you are working for a manufacturing firm that operates 14 factories, each with 16 departments. What tables would you add to those listed in this chapter for the payroll cycle to track employee time worked by factory and department?
3. Redraw Figure 3.5 for a merchandising firm.
4. Discuss the inherent problems of storing an employee's age as one of the attributes of a table. Discuss alternative solutions that would not cause inaccuracies in the database.
5. Suppose you are designing a database that contains information about university classes, students enrolled in classes, and instructors teaching various classes. The Catalog table lists all the courses that the university can offer. The Classes table describes the classes offered during the semester and includes names of students currently enrolled in each class offered. The Students table contains one record for each student enrolled in the university. The Instructor table contains information about instructors including their names, phone numbers, and office telephone numbers. Discuss the relationship between the

Instructor table and the Classes table. Is the relationship 1—1, 1—M, or M—M? Describe the relationship between the Students table and the Classes table. Finally, draw a diagram showing the tables Catalog, Classes, Instructor, and Students and how they might be linked. Use Figure 3.22 as a model of how to represent the tables. Only include the primary and foreign key fields in each table's representation.

4 TABLES AND QUERIES

OBJECTIVES

This chapter extends the knowledge that you gained in Chapters 2 and 3 with detailed information about Microsoft Access. Several hands-on exercises and special Try It exercises reinforce the material in this chapter. You will learn about creating and altering tables and a wide variety of queries. Throughout this chapter, exercises emphasize Microsoft Access techniques critical to building accounting information systems. Like Chapter 2, this chapter is application-oriented and contains very little theory; however, we emphasize *employing* the theory we presented earlier. In this chapter you will learn how to use two important types of Access objects, tables and queries. In particular, you will learn how to:

•Reset the Tables and Queries toolbars to their original configuration.
•Define a table's structure.
•Enter data into a table.
•Alter a table's structure.
•Set a table's field properties.
•Join tables and establish referential integrity checks between them.
•Create queries involving a single table.
•Create queries for tables with a many-to-many relationship.
•Create queries involving multiple tables, derived column values, and expressions.
•Create queries with an outer join relationship to reveal hidden information.
•Create parameter queries.

We continue using The Coffee Merchant's tables as the backdrop application in this chapter. All the tables and queries mentioned in Chapter 3 have been copied to the Ch04 folder on the Companion CD. For all exercises and examples in this chapter, we assume that you have inserted the Companion CD in your CD drive, copied the database *Ch04.mdb* to your hard disk, turned off the database file's read-only attribute, started Microsoft Access, and opened the Ch04 database. If not, then please be sure to do so before doing the exercises in this chapter.

ACCESS OBJECTS

The term *Access objects* refers to several ways you can store and display information in your tables. Like most database systems, Access provides a rich variety of objects for your use. Beginning with the most fundamental, objects include tables, queries, forms, reports, pages, macros, and modules.

Tables

All database information is stored in one or more tables comprised of rows and columns. A row contains all the information about a particular item in the table. Also called a record, a row's columns contain individual values for each attribute that characterizes the row. For instance, The Coffee Merchant's *tblCustomer* table contains a row for each current or potential customer. Columns in the Customer table hold information about ten different attributes of a customer record.

Each column can contain only one data type. Though the exact names of these data types vary from one RDBMS to another, they are all drawn from a small, common set. Data types constrain the type of information that can be entered into a column. Access supports the data types listed in Figure 4.1. Of the listed types, you will probably use the AutoNumber, Currency, Date/Time, Text, and Number data types most frequently.

Queries

A query is a question that you ask about one or more tables in your database. You use queries to locate and display a subset of the rows of a table, combine information from several tables into a single result, or perform calculations on fields. You can also use queries to make massive changes to a table, delete data from a table, or insert rows into a table. These latter queries are known as *action queries*.

Access uses the popular Query By Example (QBE) method in which you select one or more tables to query and then check off the columns you would like to see. By placing values or expressions below particular column names, you can limit the rows that are retrieved. These values or expressions are called selection criteria. By using the appropriate selection criteria, you can, for instance, list all customers who live in the Midwest. Or, you can compute the total value of all outstanding invoices based on an invoice table or tables. Queries are used to reduce the amount of information that is displayed, summarizing it and giving it meaning.

Forms

Forms provide a simpler way of examining data in a table one row at a time. You can look at a great deal of information or only a small amount. Data displayed in a form is exactly the same data found in a table. The only difference is that you

Data Type	Description and Use
Text	Holds characters—anything you can type on the keyboard. Data cannot be used in calculations. Employee names and inventory descriptions are examples. A text field can hold up to 255 characters.
Memo	Lengthy, variable-length text and numbers for comments or explanations. A memo field can contain up to 65,535 characters.
Number	Numeric data that can be used in calculations (unlike identification numbers, which are not used in calculations). Set the FieldSize property to define the specific Number type. Do not use Number type data for calculations involving money; use Currency for these calculations.
Date/Time	Holds date or time information. Several formats are available, or you can establish a custom format.
Currency	Holds monetary data of up to 19 significant digits (15 to the left of the decimal point and 4 to the right). Currency fields are formatted to display a currency symbol and two decimal places. Use currency to avoid rounding errors in financial calculations.
AutoNumber	A unique sequential number that is automatically generated by Access. Numbers no longer needed are retired. The AutoNumber data type is often used for primary keys, because it guarantees unique values.
Yes/No	Yes/No, True/False, or On/Off are all examples of legitimate field values. Choose the Yes/No data type when only two values are possible (gender or invoice paid, for example).
OLE Object	Contains objects from another Windows application such as a picture, graph, or spreadsheet. When you double-click an OLE object, the program that created the object is launched so you can modify or view the OLE object. OLE objects occupy large amounts of space.
Hyperlink	Text or combinations of text and numbers constituting a World Wide Web hyperlink address.
Lookup Wizard	Creates a field that provides the mechanism to automatically look up a value from another table or list of fields by using a combo box or list box control.

Figure 4.1   Access data types.

can format and enhance the data's appearance in a form. Figure 4.2 shows a form displaying data from The Coffee Merchant's Employee table.

A form is especially useful for nonexperts who must enter or change data in a table. Data entry is also much easier when using a well-designed form. Helpful aids, such as drop-down lists or radio buttons, can be embedded in a form.

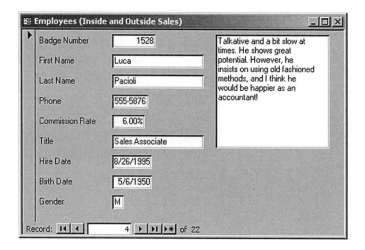

Figure 4.2 Example form.

Drop-down lists, for example, are helpful when you encounter an entry whose possible values are limited but not known to the user. By making a list available, you can choose one of a select set of values by simply clicking your choice. When you move to another row, the changed information is automatically posted to the underlying table.

Form navigation buttons make moving the data around easy. You can move to the first or last row in a table, up or down one row at a time, or to a particular row. You can customize a form so that it precisely matches an existing paper form, making the computerized version less intimidating and more familiar to those who are computer novices. You will learn about forms in Chapter 5.

Reports

While forms provide an excellent way to view and alter data in one or more tables, reports are superb for providing boardroom-quality printed, detailed, and summary information. You can sort, group, and summarize results. Reports can contain subtotals, totals, averages, and counts, all attractively printed. Like other reporting tools, you can include report headers and footers and page headers and footers. You can also create mailing labels using the Access report facility.

Like forms, reports can take advantage of Access' many design tools, including graphic import, lines, boxes, and text, to name a few. Data can be drawn from several tables and combined in one report. Figure 4.3 shows an example of a simple report that can be quickly and easily produced with Access. You will learn about reports in Chapter 5.

Pages

A data access *page* is a special Web page designed to allow you to view and work with data from the Internet or an intranet—data that is stored in a Microsoft Access

Employees Grouped by Title

Title	Name	ID	Hire Date	Birth Date	Gender
Sales Trainee					
	Nagasaki, Ted	2695	1/28/00	4/10/77	M
	Pruski, Kevin	1364	12/1/00	1/26/79	M
Sales Associate					
	Bateman, Giles	4057	2/16/92	5/1/58	M
	Chang, Annie	3609	9/16/97	3/30/77	F
	Ellison, Larry	3700	4/18/94	12/12/54	M
	English, Melinda	3432	10/1/93	2/14/56	F
	Gates, William	3436	4/11/95	3/9/54	M
	Halstead, Whitney	4058	6/16/96	12/22/73	F
	Hunter, Helen	2318	11/16/93	1/26/54	F
	Kahn, Phillipe	2754	5/14/97	5/29/61	M
	Kole, David	3370	2/8/92	3/23/63	M
	Pacioli, Luca	1528	8/26/95	5/6/50	M
	Stonesifer, Patti	1301	7/6/96	3/10/66	F
	Watterson, Barbara	3943	10/10/93	5/1/61	F
Senior Sales Associate					
	Ballmer, Steve	3692	5/16/85	7/13/44	M
	Flintsteel, Hillary	4082	3/21/90	8/22/58	F
	Goldman, Ted	4112	12/24/90	3/5/62	M
	Manispour, Sharad	4029	12/18/90	2/4/69	M
	Minsky, Barbara	4012	10/13/90	4/12/59	F
	Morrison, Alanis	3458	12/13/89	7/4/56	F
	Shoenstein, Brad	3892	9/5/90	3/6/55	M
	Stonely, Sharon	2240	11/5/88	5/3/61	F

Figure 4.3   Example report.

database or a Microsoft SQL Server database. Additionally, the data access page can contain data from other sources such as a Microsoft Excel worksheet.

You will design all your data access pages in Design view; the collection of page designs is found in the Pages collection of the database. When you design a data access page, the page is actually stored as a separate file outside Access, and Access automatically adds a shortcut to the file in the Pages collection of objects in the Database window. Often, data access pages are a convenient way to consolidate and group information that is stored in a database and then publish summaries of the data on the Internet. Data access pages also allow you to view, add, and edit records.

A data access page is connected directly to a database. When users display the data access page in Microsoft Internet Explorer, they are viewing their own copy of a page. Thus, if each user filters, sorts, or changes the way the database is displayed, that affects only their own copy of the data access page. However, any change a user makes to the database—by deleting records, editing fields, or adding data—does affect the database. The changes are available to anyone viewing the database through Access or through data access pages on the Web. A clear advantage of data access pages—a facility not available prior to Access 2000—is that remote users with an Internet connection can view and manipulate an Access database without having Microsoft Access installed, though they must have a Microsoft Office license to do so. Figure 4.4 shows a page generated from Access. It behaves just like an Access form (discussed in Chapter 5).

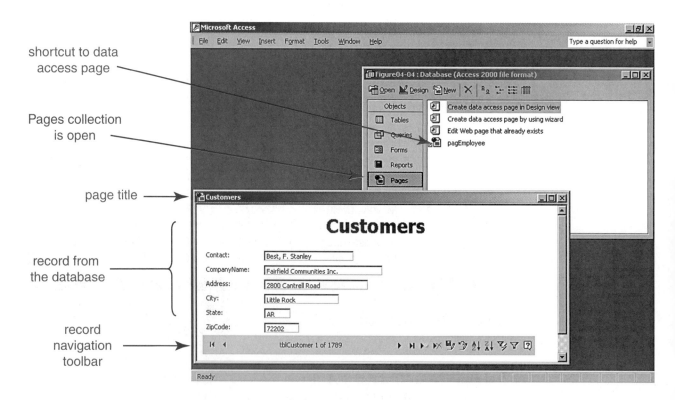

Figure 4.4   Viewing a database record with Internet Explorer.

Macros and Modules

Macros are Visual Basic codes that can be executed at the click of a button or when a form is opened. They define one or more actions that you want Access to perform in response to a particular event. Macros are frequently attached to objects located on a form, but you can write stand-alone code segments that can be invoked by a wide variety of objects in your applications. For example, you can write a small macro to check the value of an entry after the user moves to the next form field. If the field fails a value range test performed by the macro, then the macro can display an error message and move back to the erroneous field.

A *module* is an object containing custom procedures that you code using Visual Basic. Modules provide a finer degree of control and flow that allow you to write a code that recognizes and traps errors—something macros cannot do. Modules are stand-alone, global objects that can be called into action from anywhere within your Access application. Defining modules means the code can be reused by all of your forms, scripts, and other libraries.

Separating Tables from Other Objects

Whether or not you are developing an application for a client server environment, you may find it convenient to separate an application's tables from queries, forms, reports, and other database objects. Doing so allows you to store tables in one database and related, nontable objects in another database. You can then create queries, forms, reports, macros, and modules based on linked tables. A *linked table* is stored in a file outside the open database from which Microsoft Access can access records. You can perform all the normal database operations on linked tables except altering their structure. That is, you can insert, delete, update, and view records in linked tables.

Why would you bother to separate tables—the only database objects storing data—from other database objects? The single most important reason to separate tables from the other application objects is to provide application development independence. As a developer, you can continue to improve and develop the queries, forms, and reports embedded in one of the two application database files. Then, when you replace a client's application with the newest version of the database application you have been independently developing, you simply supplant the database containing the queries, forms, reports, macros, and modules with the new one. The database containing only tables remains unchanged. This way, your client's ever-changing tables are not affected, and the client can continue processing using the database. This method allows you to transparently update software without affecting the firm using your database software. Figure 4.5 shows a graphical representation of table/object separation.

WORKING WITH TABLES

We have described tables in Chapters 2 and 3. In this chapter, you learn how to alter an existing table's structure and how to modify a table whose rows are related to another table. Prohibiting removal of a parent table row until all the rows in

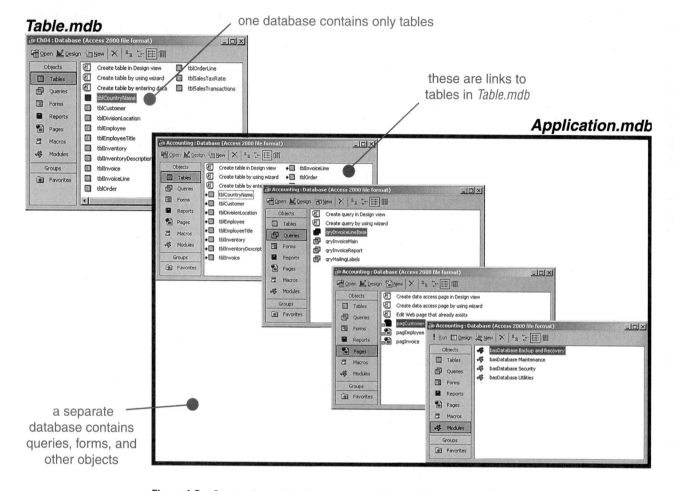

Figure 4.5 Separating tables from other database objects.

another table referring to the parent table are first removed is called *referential integrity*. This is an important feature provided by most relational database management systems. Referential integrity can be enforced, and we will show you how on one of the existing tables for The Coffee Merchant. In this section we show you how to add and delete columns from a table and how to forge a permanent link between related tables. First, let's see how to add and delete table columns.

One of the important tables in the evolving invoice subsystem contains customer names, addresses, and telephone numbers (and other fields) collected from both customers and people who merely expressed an interest in receiving a catalog. Besides periodically sending out promotional material to selected members of the customer "list," customer information appears in the "Ship to," "Sold to," or "Bill to" areas of invoices. The Coffee Merchant sample Customer table is somewhat large (over 1,700 rows), but it is small when compared to the customer database of a company such as Microsoft. The Coffee Merchant Customer table, called *tblCustomer*, is stored in the database called *Ch04.mdb*. The database is found on your Companion CD in the Ch04 folder. We have loaded *tblCustomer* with several rows so you can experience manipulating a nontrivial table. All of the data is real, including company names and addresses. The telephone numbers and contact persons have been randomized sufficiently to protect the privacy of individuals. You will notice that the telephone area codes are correct and correspond to the city in which the business is located.

In the next several sections we want you to create a table from scratch and enter data into it. Rather than have you be mere observers of our data, you will be involved with the entire process, from start to finish, of designing your own table. Doing so prepares you to create quality databases after you finish reading this book and working its exercises. That's why it is instructive for you to build and fill at least one of the tables so that you experience the process. If you have trouble, the Companion CD contains all the tables and other objects for The Coffee Merchant. The next section begins the process by describing how to create a mini-version of the Customer table. The section afterward describes the step-by-step process of filling (called *populating*) your table.

Defining a Table's Structure

From here on in the chapter, you will be doing a lot of work with the Ch04 database. If you have not already done so, copy the database from your Companion CD to the hard drive on your computer. Insert your Companion CD in the drive and copy the file *Ch04.mdb* from the Ch04 folder. Remember to turn off the read-only attribute on the *Ch04.mdb* file after you have copied it to your hard disk. Once the database has been copied to your disk, you can remove the Companion CD and store it for safekeeping. Every change you make to the database will be made to the copy of the database you just created on your hard disk. Of course, you will want to save your database to a floppy disk to preserve the work you have done to that point. (As you know, you cannot write the database file back to the Companion CD.)

Prepare for the first exercise in this chapter using Access by launching Access. Next, select Open from the File menu, and then locate and select in the Open dialog box database *Ch04.mdb*. Follow the steps in the next exercise to create an example Customer table that is a much smaller version of the *tblCustomer* table already stored in the Chapter 4 database.

EXERCISE 4.1: CREATING THE CUSTOMER TABLE STRUCTURE

1. Make sure the Tables collection in the Database window is open, and then click the New button to open the New Table dialog box.

2. Select Design view from the list of choices and click OK to get started. In the upper part of the Table window in Design view are columns in which you can enter a field name, data type, and description for each field. You will do this next.

3. Type **CustomerID** in the first row of the Field Name column in the Table dialog box. Press Tab to move to the Data Type column. Most database experts agree that column names should *not* contain embedded spaces.

   Some database systems disallow spaces, so your table and database cannot be ported to or used by those systems. Always follow the Hungarian notation in which words are given initial capitalization and concatenated to form an object name.

4. Type **N** in the Data Type column (click the list box to see a list of all Access data types). Press Tab to move to the Description field.

5. Type the description **Customer identification number**. (The Description field text appears in the status bar on the left side whenever the cursor is positioned on the corresponding field during data entry. It helps you remember the purpose of the field.)

6. Click the Primary Key button on the toolbar. (The Primary Key toolbar button displays a small key. Move the mouse over it, pause, and the ToolTip "Primary Key" appears confirming you have selected the correct button.) Access places a small key symbol to the left of the field name indicating that CustomerID is the table's primary key.

   If you need to select multiple columns for a composite primary key, simply hold down the Ctrl key and click the row selectors to the left of the fields' names. Then click the Primary Key toolbar button. Press Tab to move to the next row to define the next customer column.

7. Type **CompanyName** in the Field Name column and press Tab. Text is the suggested data type. That is fine. However, the default length, 50, is too large. You will change it in the next step.

8. Double-click the Field Size property in the Field Properties list found in the lower half of the dialog box. (You can press F6 to move to the Field Properties panel and back.) Type **25** in the Field Size cell.

9. Click the Description column in the CompanyName field row and type **Company name**. Press Tab to move to the next row in the Table dialog box.

10. Type **PhoneNumber**, press Tab, select the Text data type, change the default data length (Field Size property, lower panel) to **8**, and type the description **Telephone number**. Press Tab to move to the next row.

11. Type **LastContactDate**, press Tab, type **D** to select the Date/Time data type, and type the description **Date of last contact** in the Description column. Press Tab to move to a new row.

12. Type **CreditLimit** in the Field Name column, press Tab, select the Number data type, and type the description **Credit limit**. Press Tab to move to the next (and last) row.

13. Type **Notes**, press Tab, and type **M** to select the Memo data type. In the Description field type **Miscellaneous notes**

14. To save the newly defined table, click Save in the File menu. The Save As dialog box appears (see Figure 4.6). (Your field names, types, and descriptions should match those shown in Figure 4.6. If not, simply click in the incorrect cell and change it.)

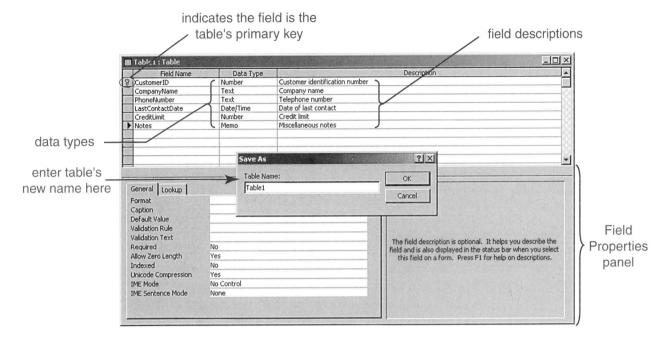

Figure 4.6   Defining a table's structure and saving it.

15. Type **tblMyCustomer** in the Table Name text box and then click OK. Access saves your newly created Customer table, *tblMyCustomer*, in the Ch04 database.
16. Click Close in the File menu to close the table. (Alternatively, you can click the Close button on the table's Title bar to close its Design view.)

Be sure that you save your new table with the name *tblMyCustomer*, not *tblCustomer*. This is a safety feature. This way you still have the original table *tblCustomer*, which is on the Companion CD, for use in the textbook's exercises.

Next, let's enter some data into the table *tblMyCustomer*. This will give you experience entering, altering, and saving data.

Populating a Table

When you *populate* a table, you are simply placing data into a table whose structure already exists. Entering data into a table is straightforward. First, ensure that *Ch04.mdb* is open. Then, locate *tblMyCustomer* in the Tables objects of the Database window. Double-click the *tblMyCustomer* table name to open it in Datasheet view. Maximize the Table window so that you can see the full table.

Next, you will enter the first customer record. Exercise 4.2 uses three different methods to move to the next field: pressing Tab, clicking the next field, and pressing Enter. Select the one that suits you best.

EXERCISE 4.2: ENTERING A RECORD INTO A TABLE

1. In the CustomerID field, type **3101** and press Tab to move to the CompanyName field.
2. Type **Experience Coffee** in the CompanyName field. Move to the PhoneNumber field by clicking the cell just under the PhoneNumber field name.
3. Type **555-1233** in the PhoneNumber field. Press Enter to move to the next column, LastContactDate.
4. Type **5/23/2003** in the LastContactDate field. Press Tab to move to the CreditLimit column.
5. Type **4000** and press Tab to move to the last column, Notes.
6. Type **This is a good customer** in the memo field.

Don't press any keys for a moment. Do you notice the small pencil symbol in the row selector button of the table? This indicates that a record's contents have been changed but not yet posted to the table. You post changes to a table simply by moving to another table record. You will do that in a moment.

If you make a mistake anywhere while entering data, simply use the arrow keys to move left or right in the field, or use the Backspace or Delete keys to delete information. Pressing a key inserts the letter into the field at the insertion point indicated by the cursor. To correct a value in a field to the left of the current field, press Shift+Tab repeatedly until the cursor arrives at the field to be changed. To display the blinking insertion point, simply press F2. Then you can use the arrow keys to move the insertion point within a field. Pressing Tab or Shift+Tab moves to another cell and selects the entire value.

Next, enter the remaining *tblMyCustomer* table data by completing Exercise 4.3. When you move to a new row, the previous row is stored on disk. The last record you enter in a table is saved when you close the table or you close the entire database. Alternatively, you can simply press the up arrow key to move to a previous record to save the latest record.

EXERCISE 4.3: ENTER THE REMAINING *TBLMYCUSTOMER* TABLE DATA

1. With the *tblMyCustomer* table still displayed, click in the CustomerID column of the second table row.
2. Enter the remaining table rows. Figure 4.7 shows all customer table rows. Refer to it as you enter the remaining customer records. You can enter anything you like (or nothing) in the Notes field of each customer record. That's entirely up to you.
3. After you enter the last customer's information, click the Table window Close button to close the table. The last row of the *tblMyCustomer* table will be posted automatically to the database.

CustomerID	CompanyName	PhoneNumber	LastContactDate	CreditLimit
3101	Experience Coffee	555-1233	5/23/03	4000
3122	Gourmet Grinder	555-7826	9/14/02	1000
3245	La Jolla Expresso	555-3919	7/9/03	5500
3658	Starbucks Coffee	555-5561	9/14/02	15000
3702	Kensington Coffee Company	555-6153	12/16/02	1000
3824	Intermezzo Espresso Bar	555-8282	8/5/03	7500
3961	Just Bean Counters	555-9646	3/15/03	2500

Figure 4.7 Contents of the example customer table, *tblMyCustomer*.

Adding a Column to a Table

If you create and use a table and later—perhaps much later—discover you have left out an important column or two, you can add one or more new columns to tables at any time. You can add a column to a table either in Datasheet view or Design view. Adding a column in Design view is the best way, because you can add a column and define all of its characteristics in one window—the Design view window. On the other hand, you can add a column more quickly in Datasheet view.

The Coffee Merchant's Division Location table (*tblDivisionLocation*) contains the city and state in which each of The Coffee Merchant's divisions is located. It is useful to place often-repeated character strings such as cities or organization names in their own table along with a unique identification number. Then, you can refer to the cities with a number in place of the long string in the original table. Among other advantages, this prevents you from misspelling "Cincinnati" or other city names when they occur frequently in a table's columns. This is the purpose of the *tblDivisionLocation* table. A related column, yet to be placed in the *tblEmployee* table, will contain a number that is related to the company division number found in the *tblDivisionLocation* table. Your next job will be to add a new table column to *tblEmployee*—a division number column—which is a foreign key field linked to the primary key of the *tblDivisionLocation* table. A *foreign key* is a column whose values match similar values in another table's primary key column. A foreign key column in one table *always* corresponds to a primary key column in another table. Once the *tblEmployee* and *tblDivisionLocation* tables are linked together through their primary key/foreign key pairs, you will be able to determine the city and state in which each employee and each employee's division are located.

Each employee row should have an entry indicating which division the employee works for. Adding or deleting a column in a table is called *altering* the table's structure. Do not confuse this activity with adding or deleting *data* in a table's columns.

The next exercise shows you how to add a column to a table. In particular, you will add a column called *EmployeeDivisionID* to the *tblEmployee* table. This column is a foreign key to the *tblDivisionLocation* table.

EXERCISE 4.4: ADDING A COLUMN TO THE EMPLOYEE TABLE

1. Click Tables in the Database Objects bar if necessary. Select *tblEmployee*, and click the Design button. Maximize the Table window to display all columns.
2. Select the entire EmployeeTitleID row by clicking its row selector button. Press the Insert key. (Alternatively, you can select Row from the Insert menu.) A new, empty row is added to the table's structure.
3. In the new row, click the Field Name cell, type **EmployeeDivisionID**, and press Tab to move to the Data Type column.
4. Type **N** because the EmployeeDivisionID field will hold a number.
5. Select the Description field and type the description **Identification of the division for which this employee works** to document the field's use.
6. Select the Caption property box in the Field Properties panel and type **Division ID** (with an embedded space). The Caption property text is displayed in place of the column's name in forms, reports, and Datasheet views of tables.
7. Select Save from the File menu. This saves the revised *tblEmployee* table structure.
8. Click the Design view Close button.

   To complete this operation, you need to place data in the newly created EmployeeDivisionID column. This is relatively easy. Make sure you fill in the field for each employee row, because the next exercise will use the EmployeeDivisionID column values to establish a connection to the *tblDivisionLocation* table.

EXERCISE 4.5: PLACE VALUES IN THE EMPLOYEEDIVISIONID COLUMN

1. Open the *tblEmployee* table in Datasheet view and then click any entry in the Phone column.
2. Click Records in the menu bar, point to Sort, and click Sort Ascending to sort the table from low to high on the telephone numbers.
3. Select the topmost Division ID cell corresponding to employee David Kole and type **101** into the cell.
4. Repeat step 3 for the next five employees. The first six employees all work in division 101.
5. Type the value **102** in the next six Division ID cells, indicating that employees Sharad Manispour through Whitney Halstead work in Division 102. (Hint: After entering the value 102 once, use Copy/Paste to rapidly paste the next five entries.)
6. Type **103** for the next six employees' Division ID attributes—employees whose names are Kevin Pruski through Luca Pacioli. (Remember to speed up data entry by pasting—Ctrl+V—copies of the same field into successive rows' cells.)
7. Finally, type **104** for the remaining four employees—Ellison through Flintsteel.

8. Close the table (click the Datasheet view Close button), and click No when you are asked if you want to save changes to the design of the table. (We are not interested in preserving the *view* of the table in sorted order, even though the table is not actually sorted.)

Keep the following distinction in mind. A table's design has to do with its structure—the number of columns and their characteristics, not the columns' contents. You have changed the table's contents just now, and those changes are automatically posted to the table. Remember to save any table structural changes by executing the Save command in the File menu.

Deleting or Renaming a Table Column

It is easy to remove unwanted columns from any table or to give one or more columns a new name. Though you don't need to delete table columns right now, you should learn how to do it. You can delete a column while viewing a table in either Datasheet view or Design view. It is equally easy to delete a column in either view. To delete a table's column in Design view, click Tables in the Database Objects bar, select a table, and open it in Design view. Click the row selector to the left of the column you want to delete and then click the Delete button. Remember to click the Save button (or File, Save) to post the changed table structure to your database. To delete a table column in Datasheet view, right-click the column's field selector, select Delete Column from the pop-up menu, and click Yes when a dialog box asks if you want to permanently delete the column. In Design view, any attribute rows that are below the deleted field are moved up to close the gap. In Datasheet view, any columns to the right of the deleted column move left to close the gap left by the deleted column.

You may decide that a column name no longer makes sense or is otherwise inappropriate. Renaming a column is straightforward. You can change a table column's name either in Datasheet view or Design view. In Datasheet view, simply double-click the column's selector, type a new name, and press Enter. The new name replaces the name originally assigned. Also, the renamed field's Caption property is deleted. (You will learn about field properties later in this chapter.) To rename a table column in Design view, first display the table in Design view. Next, click the Field Name cell that you want to change and type over the old name with its replacement. Finally, click Save in the File menu to store the altered table.

Moving a Table Column

Although the order of columns in a table has no importance whatsoever, you can rearrange table columns so they appear in a different order in Datasheet view. Just like other table structure alteration operations mentioned here, you can rearrange table columns either in Datasheet view or Design view. We think that this is easiest to accomplish in Datasheet view. To move a column or a group of contiguous columns, you begin by selecting the columns. Click the field selector of the column you want to move. To select adjacent columns, click a column field selector and move the mouse to adjacent columns without releasing the mouse. In either case, one or more columns is selected. Click and hold the mouse in the field selector again and drag the column(s) to their new location. Release the mouse button to "drop" the selected columns into their new locations. Click Save in the File menu to save the altered table structure in the database.

Establishing Referential Integrity

Access provides a way to enforce *referential integrity* whereby defined relationships between tables are maintained permanently and automatically. For example, referential integrity rules prevent you from adding a record to a related table if there is no associated record in the primary table. Additionally, the rules prevent you from deleting or changing records in a primary table that would result in orphan records in a related table. Suppose you want to enforce referential integrity between the Invoice table (*tblInvoice*) and the related Invoice Line table (*tblInvoiceLine*). Once you tell Access to enforce referential integrity rules between two tables, you cannot delete an invoice from the parent Invoice table unless there are no related invoice line items in the Invoice Line table. As you work more with Access, you will gain a deeper understanding of how referential integrity works to preserve a kind of "parent/child" relationship between tables falling under the integrity protection rules.

In the next exercise, you will do your work in the *Relationships* window, a window that displays linkages between tables for a given database. You define permanent linkages—primary key to foreign key relationships—to make forming multiple-table queries easier. You can also choose whether or not the Relationships window displays none, some, or all intertable relationships. To illustrate just how this works, you will establish referential integrity between the Employee table (*tblEmployee*) and the Division Location table (*tblDivisionLocation*). This will ensure that a division in the table *tblDivisionLocation* cannot be deleted until all employees (*tblEmployee*) have been reassigned to a new division or first removed completely.

EXERCISE 4.6: ESTABLISHING REFERENTIAL INTEGRITY

1. Close all windows except the Database window.
2. Click Tools on the menu bar and then click Relationships. The Relationships window opens. It may appear empty initially.
3. Click Show Table from the Relationships menu (or click the Show Table button on the toolbar). A Show Table dialog box opens.
4. Click the Tables tab in the Show Table dialog box, if necessary.
5. Double-click the *tblEmployee* table to add it to the Relationships window (see Figure 4.8).

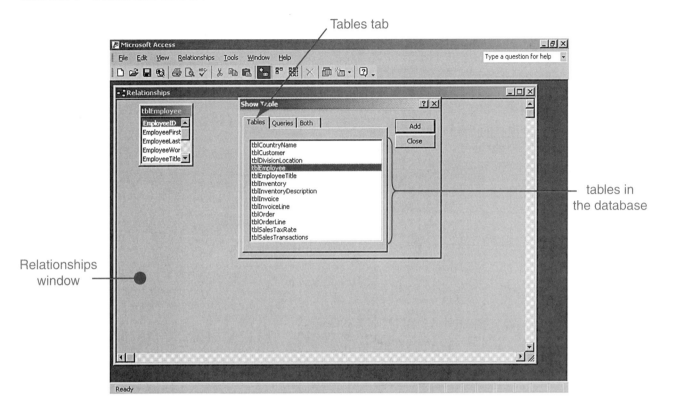

Figure 4.8   Show Table dialog box.

6. Click *tblDivisionLocation*, click the Add button to display that table's field roster in the Relationships window, and then click the Close button in the Show Table dialog box to close it. No more tables are to be added at this time. The two tables and their attribute names are displayed in the Relationships window. (You may want to drag the bottom border of *tblEmployee* to reveal all of its attributes. Drag the right border of *tblEmployee* to reveal the longer field names.)

   Next, let's show the primary key to foreign key connection between the two tables.

7. In the Relationships window, click the DivisionID field in *tblDivisionLocation* and drag and drop the field onto the EmployeeDivisionID field in *tblEmployee* (see Figure 4.9).

8. Click the Enforce Referential Integrity check box to select this option. A check mark is placed in the check box (see Figure 4.10).

9. Click the Create button to establish referential integrity between the two tables.

10. Finally, click the Relationships window Close button and click Yes when you are asked "Do you want to save changes to the layout of 'Relationships'?" This preserves the newly established relationship and the referential integrity constraint. Figure 4.11 shows the line in the Relationships dialog box before

you close it. On one end of the line is the number 1, indicating the primary key side of the relationship. On the other side is the symbol for infinity, which indicates the foreign key side of the relationship. The infinity symbol means that several records can be related to a single record in the "parent" table.

click and drag the DivisionID field
to the foreign key in *tblEmployee*

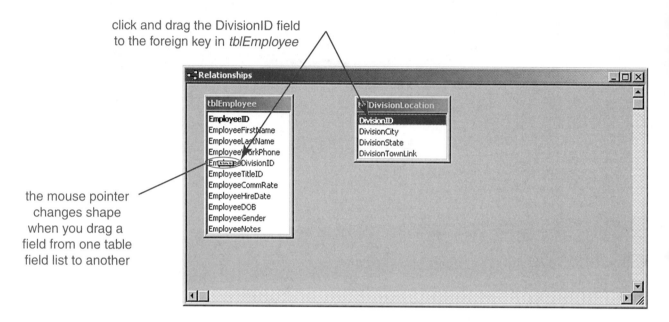

the mouse pointer
changes shape
when you drag a
field from one table
field list to another

Figure 4.9 Establishing a link between related tables.

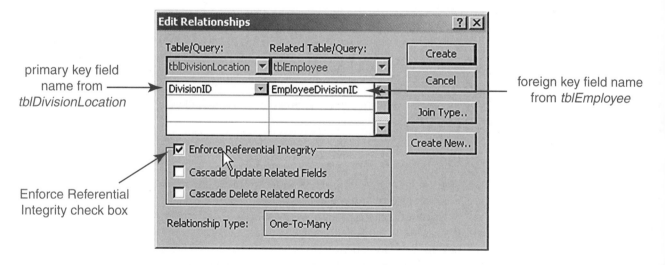

primary key field
name from
tblDivisionLocation

foreign key field name
from *tblEmployee*

Enforce Referential
Integrity check box

Figure 4.10 Enforcing Referential Integrity in the Relationships dialog box.

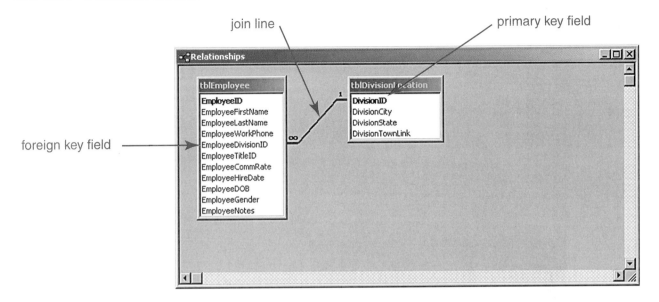

Figure 4.11   A join line connecting two tables.

When you join two tables in the Relationships window as illustrated here, their Datasheet view is slightly different from the way it appears before the tables are joined. A new column called the *expand indicator* appears in the first column of each table that is explicitly linked to another table. The indicator displays either a plus sign (+) or minus sign (–). When viewing a linked table in Datasheet view, you can click the expand indicator attached to any row to view any related records. The next exercise illustrates how to view related records in the *tblEmployee* and *tblDivisionLocation* tables.

EXERCISE 4.7: DISPLAYING RELATED TABLES WITH THE EXPAND INDICATOR

1. Open the *Ch04.mdb* database, if necessary, and close all windows except the Database window.
2. Select Tables from the Database Objects bar and double-click *tblDivisionLocation* to open it. The table opens in Datasheet view (the default view when you double-click a table name).
3. Click the expand indicator of the first *tblDivisionLocation* row, which corresponds to DivisionID 101. A portion of the Employee table opens, revealing which employees work in that division (see Figure 4.12). Notice that the expand indicator, normally a plus sign, changes to a minus sign. The minus sign indicates that the related table rows are open. Of course, if no rows are related to the row whose expand indicator you click, then no related *tblEmployee* rows are displayed.
4. After you examine the results, click the *tblDivisionLocation* expand indicator to close the rows of *tblEmployee*.

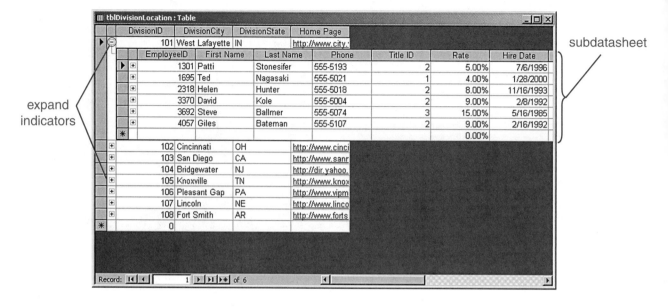

expand
indicators

subdatasheet

	DivisionID	DivisionCity	DivisionState	Home Page					
	101	West Lafayette	IN	http://www.city.'					
		EmployeeID	First Name	Last Name	Phone	Title ID	Rate	Hire Date	
		1301	Patti	Stonesifer	555-5193	2	5.00%	7/6/1996	
		1695	Ted	Nagasaki	555-5021	1	4.00%	1/28/2000	
		2318	Helen	Hunter	555-5018	2	8.00%	11/16/1993	
		3370	David	Kole	555-5004	2	9.00%	2/8/1992	
		3692	Steve	Ballmer	555-5074	3	15.00%	5/16/1985	
		4057	Giles	Bateman	555-5107	2	9.00%	2/16/1992	
							0.00%		
	102	Cincinnati	OH	http://www.cinci					
	103	San Diego	CA	http://www.sanr					
	104	Bridgewater	NJ	http://dir.yahoo.					
	105	Knoxville	TN	http://www.knox					
	106	Pleasant Gap	PA	http://www.vipm					
	107	Lincoln	NE	http://www.linco					
	108	Fort Smith	AR	http://www.forts					
	0								

Record: 1 of 6

Figure 4.12   Clicking the expand indicator reveals related records.

Any table rows revealed after clicking an expand indicator are called a *subdatasheet*. Not all rows in *tblDivisionLocation* have a subdatasheet. For example, no employees are currently working at the Knoxville, Tennessee plant. You can add rows to subdatasheets that are open by simply entering data in the open row at the end of the table—next to the new row indicator. If you add a row to the *tblEmployee* table subdatasheet, Access automatically fills in the foreign key field value for EmployeeDivisionID—the value that corresponds to that group of related rows.

Try It

Click the expand indicator corresponding to Knoxville in *tblDivisionLocation*. An empty row is returned. This indicates that no employee currently is assigned to that location.

Editing and Removing Intertable Relationships

You can remove or edit an existing relationship between pairs of tables by a procedure similar to the preceding one. For example, you can remove referential integrity checks between *tblEmployee* and *tblDivisionLocation* by opening the Relationships window, right-clicking the line connecting the two tables, selecting Edit Relationship, and clearing the Enforce Referential Integrity check box. This edits the relationship between the tables, but does not remove it. Removing a relationship is equally easy. Open the Relationships window (choose Relationships from the Tools menu), click the line that connects the two tables, and then press the Delete key. Similarly, you can right-click the line connecting the tables and select Delete from the pop-up menu that appears. In either case, the connecting line disappears along with the explicit relationship definition. Whenever you change a relationship by editing or removing it, be sure to select Save from the File menu to preserve the relationship changes.

Setting Field Properties

You can customize each field of a table by setting its specific properties. Each field has property settings that affect the way the field looks and behaves. These property settings appear in the Field Properties panel, which is visible when you display a table in Design view (see Figure 4.6). When you set one or more properties for a particular field, Access enforces those properties wherever the field appears—including queries, forms, and reports. The number and type of properties vary slightly depending on the field's data type you select. A field whose data type is numeric, for instance, has a Decimal Places property, whereas a Text field does not. Similarly, a text type field has a Field Size property, but a data type field does not. All together, there are 45 distinct properties available. We will discuss a few of the most important properties here. You can learn about other field properties by pressing F1 to obtain online help.

Next, you will learn about several important properties. We present these in the same order as they appear from top to bottom in the Field Properties panel. After we explain key properties, we present exercises that show you how to set Field Properties values.

FIELD SIZE. The Field Size property allows you to specify the length of text and number fields. Text fields can be from 0 through 255 characters long. The default Field Size for text fields is 50. Number fields have sizes varying from a single-byte integer (Byte), to two integer sizes (Integer or Long Integer), and two floating point number sizes (Single or Double). The size of a text field limits how much information you can enter. Specifying a numeric field size restricts fields to a particular magnitude and to either integer numbers or real numbers (numbers containing decimal places).

FORMAT. You can use the Format property to customize the way numbers, dates, times, and text appear when they are printed or displayed. For example, you can set the EmployeeCommRate (employees' commission rates) Format property to *percent* and the Decimal Places property to *2* so that a value such as 0.057 will be displayed as 5.70% in the tables, queries, forms, or reports—wherever the field is referenced. The Format property uses different settings for different data types. Consult Access help for details about the several format choices.

INPUT MASK. The Input Mask property makes data entry easier and allows you to control the values that users can enter. For example, an Input Mask for a date field can indicate exactly what you expect the user to enter and prevent all keystrokes except digits: __/__/__. It is frequently easier to use the Input Mask Wizard to help you create an Input Mask.

CAPTION. The Caption property provides an alternative field name—an alias—that appears in various views. Field captions specify the heading for the field in a table's Datasheet view or a query's Datasheet view. When a field appears in a report or form, the table's caption appears as the field's label. The Caption property is a string expression that can contain up to 2,048 characters. If you do not specify the Caption property value, then the table's Field Name appears wherever the field is referenced.

DEFAULT VALUE. The Default Value property specifies a value that is automatically entered in a field when you create a new record. For example, if you are entering the names and addresses of members of your Chicago area club or organization, you can set the default value for the City field to Chicago. When anyone adds a new record to the table, "Chicago" automatically appears in the City field. You can either accept this value or enter the name of a different city. Set the Default Value property whenever you can identify a field whose contents are often a particular value.

VALIDATION RULE AND VALIDATION TEXT. The Validation Rule property specifies the requirements for data entered into a record or field. When anyone attempts to enter data that violates the Validation Rule setting, the Validation Text property value contains the message to display. The Validation Rule and Validation Text properties go hand in hand. For example, suppose you want to restrict the values that users can enter in the annual salary field of an employee table. Simply enter into the salary field Validation Rule property the expression *Between 15000 and 87500* to limit the values users can enter into that range. The Validation Text property is a character string that is displayed when a user violates the Validation Rule for a particular field. The text is merely a character string up to 255 characters that indicates the nature of the error. For example, the salary field Validation Text "Valid salaries' values are $15,000 to $87,500" indicates to the user the probable error.

REQUIRED. The Required property specifies whether a value is required in a field. If this value is set to Yes, then whenever you add a new record to a table, you must enter a value in the field. You might want to specify that the LastName field always has a value for each record. When a field's Required property is set to Yes and you are entering a new record, Access will not permit you to go to the next record if any required fields are empty (called *null* by database people).

INDEXED. The Indexed property has the value of Yes or No. When a field's Index property is Yes, Access performs a special operation on that field—called generating an index—to speed up searches on the field. Fields that have an Index property value of No do not have associated indexes. While any nonindexed field can be searched, indexed field searches are much faster. Primary key fields are always indexed. You might want to index a LastName field of a table if you anticipate frequent searches by last name. In a small table, there is no noticeable difference between indexed and nonindexed field searches. In large tables—tables with 50,000 rows for instance—the search times between indexed and nonindexed fields is significant.

To illustrate how to set properties, you will set the field properties of two fields of the *tblEmployee* table. The fields are EmployeeWorkPhone and EmployeeCommRate. The employee phone numbers should be restricted to seven digits (assume the phones are all on a corporate system in which you can call any division without first entering a telephone area code). Furthermore, you want the hyphen between the first three digits and the last four digits inserted automatically. That will save time whenever anyone enters a telephone number and will ensure that the hyphen is placed in the correct position. The caption "Phone" is better than the default column name that is displayed—"EmployeeWorkPhone." So you will set the EmployeeWorkPhone field Caption property to display a more concise field name.

You will make several property changes to the commission rate field, which is called EmployeeCommRate. The commission rate is a small number, so you will indicate that its field size is single to accommodate small numbers with decimal places. Set the format so that the commission rate is displayed in percentage format with two decimal places. For example, the value 0.0895 displays as 8.95% in Datasheet view. You will change the Caption property so that the commission rate column displays the heading "Rate" instead of the default and awkward heading "EmployeeCommRate," the column's field name. New employees and management personnel earn no commission, so you want to set the default value for the commission field to zero percent. Lastly, you will establish a valid range of commission rates so that no one can mistakenly enter an unreasonable commission rate such as 45 percent. A Validation Rule will validate all newly entered commission rates, and an appropriate Validation Text message will display when the commission rate is invalid.

Let's start with an exercise to set three employee phone field properties: Field Size, Input Mask, and Caption. To prepare for this exercise, ensure that *Ch04.mdb* is open and close all windows except the Database window. Then do the following exercise.

EXERCISE 4.8: SETTING FIELD PROPERTIES
FOR THE EMPLOYEEWORKPHONE FIELD

1. Open the table *tblEmployee* in Design view.
2. Click anywhere in the EmployeeWorkPhone row and then press F6 (a shortcut) to move to the Field Size property in the Field Properties panel.
3. Type 7 in the Field Size property.
4. Click in the Input Mask field and type **000\-0000;1;_** (three zeroes, a backslash, a hyphen, four zeroes, a semicolon, the digit 1, another semicolon, and an underline character). We explain these symbols following the exercise.
5. Click in the Caption property and type **Phone**
6. Click Save in the File menu to save your table design changes. A warning dialog box opens and displays the ominous message "Some data may be lost."
7. Click the Yes button in the dialog box. No data will be lost.
8. Close the Design view window.

The Input Mask property symbols require some explanation. The zeroes in the Input Mask mean that a digit is required in the given digit position. A back-slash indicates that the character that follows the backslash, a hyphen in this case, is a literal character and not an operator such as subtraction. The first semicolon ends the first part of the Input Mask. The value 1 between the semicolons indicates that the hyphen in any phone number that a user may enter will not be stored in the field—only the seven digits of the phone number. The second semicolon ends the second part of the Input Mask. Finally, the third part of the Input Mask specifies the character that Access displays for the location where an end user should type a character. In other words, an underline appears in the Phone field wherever no digits appear.

Try It

To see how the Phone field mask operates, open *tblEmployee* in Datasheet view. Then, drag across the digits of the Phone field of any employee and press Delete to erase the current phone number. Notice that the Phone field displays a series of underlines separated by a hyphen. Next, type 5557777 (without entering a hyphen). Notice that the digits 555 are placed before the hyphen and the remaining four digits are placed after the hyphen. Close the Datasheet view window.

EXERCISE 4.9: SETTING FIELD PROPERTIES
FOR THE EMPLOYEE COMMISSION FIELD

1. Open *tblEmployee* in Design view and click in any column of the EmployeeCommRate row.

2. Press F6 to move to the Field Size property in the Field Properties panel.
3. Click the Field Size drop-down list arrow and click *Single*.
4. Click the Format property, click the drop-down list arrow, and click *Percent*.
5. Click the Decimal Places property, drag the mouse to select the current entry, and type **2** to select two decimal places.
6. Click the Caption property and type **Rate**. Observe the comment in the right portion of the Field Properties panel. It has helpful information about the selected property.
7. Click the Default Value property and type **0**
8. Click the Validation Rule property and type **between 0 and 0.15** to indicate the range of valid commission rates. Be sure the second value is 0.15, not 15. A value of 15 means 1500%, which is an unreasonable commission rate! (When you move to another property field, notice that Access changes the expression by capitalizing the words "Between" and "And.")
9. Click the Validation Text property and type **Commission rates range from 0% to 15%**, the message that is displayed when a new, invalid commission rate is entered. Figure 4.13 shows *tblEmployee* in Design view and the new properties you set in this exercise.
10. Click Save in the File menu. A dialog box opens and displays a warning indicating that data integrity rules have changed and that existing data may not be valid. Click No to bypass the validity check for existing data. The warning occurs because you have established criteria for the commission rate field—criteria that were not in place when some records were entered. Access recognizes that existing commission data may fall outside the acceptable range. We know the data is fine.

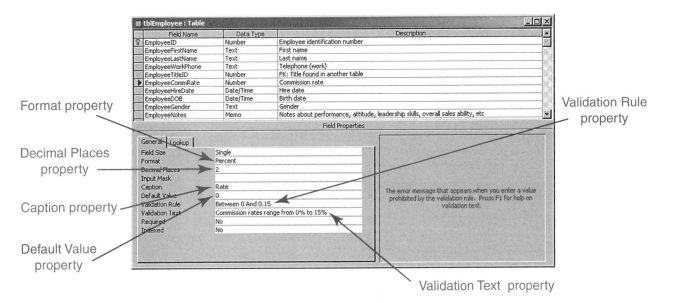

Format property

Decimal Places property

Caption property

Default Value property

Validation Rule property

Validation Text property

Figure 4.13 Setting *tblEmployee* field properties.

11. Click Datasheet view in the View menu. Notice the EmployeeCommRate column has a new caption—Rate. Observe that the commissions are formatted with a percentage sign and two decimal places.
12. Close the Datasheet view window.

Try It

Verify that the new commission rate validation software works as advertised. Go to the bottom of *tblEmployee* in Datasheet view, and enter a new EmployeeID number in the empty row. Continue entering information in the row. When you reach the Rate column, type **0.55** and move to another field. What happens? Type the valid commission rate, **12%**. Move to a new row to post the new employee row to the table. Delete the new employee row you just added: click in any field in the row you just added and press the Delete Record button on the Datasheet view toolbar. Click the Yes button to confirm the record-delete operation.

Be careful whenever you set both a field's Default and Validation Rule properties. They can come into conflict with each other if you aren't careful. For instance, suppose you set the default value of a field to 2 and subsequently type the Validation Rule *Between 3 And 25*. Clearly, the default value is not in the range of allowed values set forth by the Validation Rule property. That conflict can occur inadvertently when you skip the field and Access attempts to insert the default value, 2, into the field—violating the Validation Rule.

CREATING AND USING QUERIES

A database's ability to retrieve selected rows and columns from tables lies at the heart of its information retrieval ability. Managers seeking information about employees can retrieve rows and columns from an employee table, but information gathering would be limited if retrieval was restricted to a single table. Without the ability to select which rows are retrieved and without the ability to select information from multiple, related tables, a database's retrieval capabilities would be no better than those of a flat file system. Further, suppose someone wants to display an entire customer table in an attempt to locate all customers from Idaho, or inventory items supplied by manufacturers from California or Oregon. Manually scanning a list for candidate table rows satisfying those criteria would be time-consuming, frustrating, and error-prone.

There are two general classes of queries you can use: action queries and selection queries. *Action queries* are queries that allow you to change, insert, create, or delete sets of data in your database. *Selection queries* are queries that allow you to retrieve and display data from one or more tables or queries. Chapter 2 introduced you briefly to both of these query types. In this section, we will focus on selection queries.

Selection queries pose questions to the database. Unlike tables, which hold information, queries actively search specified tables and return answers to your questions. For instance, you can use a query to return a list of all employees in the San Diego branch office in order by department and last name within department. A query can be used to list all invoices that are over 30 days past due. Although you can do a lot of work with datasheets—including sorting, updating, filtering, and printing—you will quickly find that manually manipulating a table's Datasheet view is restrictive. Queries provide you with a convenient way to filter, sort, and manipulate data. Furthermore, you can store the query so that you can repeat the operations on one or more tables. For instance, you can create a query to scan an airline reservation system's database and display the names of passengers on TWA Flight 711 from Memphis to Los Angeles. By creating a query to perform the actions of searching the flight data, extracting passengers' names for a particular flight, and sorting them in name order, you automate the multistep information retrieval process. When you run the stored query next week, the same query (a stored definition) returns a completely new result. The result is called a *dynaset*, which is a temporary table. Called a *closed set*, relational database queries examine, on input, tables and then produce, as output, a table-structured result.

Relational database systems differ in how they deliver a query facility to users. Some systems use a widely accepted RDBMS interface language called Structured Query Language (SQL). Other systems use an interface called Query By Example (QBE). Microsoft Access provides both, but most people use QBE because it is both easier to learn and straightforward to use.

Perhaps the most important feature of queries is their ability to join tables together. Related tables can be linked in a query. Then, you can apply selection criteria to eliminate unwanted data and sort it on any number of fields. For example, suppose you wanted to query The Coffee Merchant tables. You might write a query to list the names and addresses of all customers whose invoices are more than 30 days past due. Two tables, *tblCustomer* and *tblInvoice*, are joined on their linking fields—their CustomerID column. The query's selection criteria limit retrieved rows to those whose InvoiceDate value is more than 30 days ago.

Building queries is not difficult. Here is an overview of the steps. This chapter provides you with a lot of practice using these steps to build actual queries to retrieve information. The steps to creating and saving a database query are:

• Select Queries in the Objects bar of the Database window and click New.

• Select Design view from the list and click OK.

• Add the table(s) to be included in the query.

• Drag the fields you want returned in the dynaset to the QBE grid.

• Enter selection criteria so that Access returns only rows that match the criteria.

• Open the query in Datasheet view to see the query's results.

- Select Design view, if necessary, to revise the query to achieve the results you want.

- Save the query if you want to rerun it later.

When you build queries involving more than one table, you follow the same basic steps outlined above except that you select additional tables for the query design. Tables cannot be arbitrarily selected to form a query. They must be related to one another. You can either indicate the relation of one table to another as you design the query, or you can establish a more permanent relationship between tables in the Relationships window. Before continuing, take a moment to look at all the intertable relationships already established for your Ch04 database. Figure 4.14 shows nearly all the tables in your database and the relationship between each pair. Take a moment to study the figure.

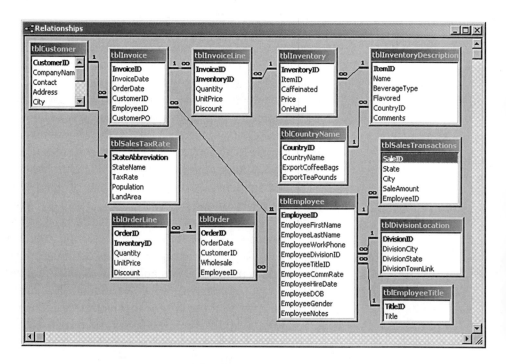

Figure 4.14   Relationships among tables.

Tables related to one another contain a line that connects the primary key of one table to a foreign key of the related table. For all tables in *Ch04.mdb*, the relationships are one-to-many (1—M). For example, *tblCustomer* (upper left corner of Figure 4.14) is on the "one side" of a one-to-many relationship with *tblInvoice*. That means that for each customer record in the Customer table, there may be zero, one, or several related customer invoice records. The line connecting the tables indicates the "one" side of the relationship with the digit 1 above the line next to the primary key. Similarly, Access displays the symbol for infinity to indicate the "many" side of the relationship next to the table's foreign key. Of course, any given table may be related to several other tables in the database. For example, *tblEmployee* has established relationships with four other tables, including *tblDivisionLocation* and *tblEmployeeTitle*. You must explicitly establish any relationships between tables yourself. You must either create a relationship in the Relationships window where relationships persist when you create new queries, or you must create the relationship each time you create a query. Unless the *name* of a primary key in one table is spelled the same as the foreign key of another, Access will not automatically forge a relationship between table pairs.

We introduce queries by starting with a single-table query—a query whose data is retrieved from one table. Then, you will build more complex queries involving some rows and some columns of a single table. Finally, you will build queries that draw data from many related tables.

Retrieving Selected Rows from a Table

A query is the best way to examine a large table and select a group of records from it. A one-table query is easy to construct, and it reduces the list you look at to a manageable size. We will illustrate a one-table query with the *tblInventoryDescription* table. It contains several important product descriptors including the beverage type (the allowed values are only *c* or *t*, which stand for coffee and tea) and whether or not the coffee or tea is flavored (yes/no). Other descriptors include the country of origin (an identification number pointing to the *tblCountryName* table) and lively comments about the particular coffee bean or tea leaf. Figure 4.15 shows some of the rows of the Inventory Description table.

Inventories without quantity or back-order values for each inventory item are not very helpful. A related table, *tblInventory*, holds additional inventory information such as unit price and quantity in stock. (See Figure 4.14.) Together, the *tblInventory* and *tblInventoryDescription* tables supply all the inventory information for our small example. The two tables have a one-to-many relationship because each coffee listed in the *tblInventoryDescription* (for example, Jamaican Blue Mountain) can have both decaffeinated and caffeinated choices. In reality, the "many" side of the relationship, *tblInventory*, has at most two entries for every named coffee or tea. When necessary, we join the two tables on their common fields—both named ItemID in this case.

Let's create a simple query to locate and display all unflavored coffees whose beans are described as "hard bean" in the inventory. (Hard bean coffees are grown at higher altitudes than others and generally yield a better coffee.) Do the following exercise.

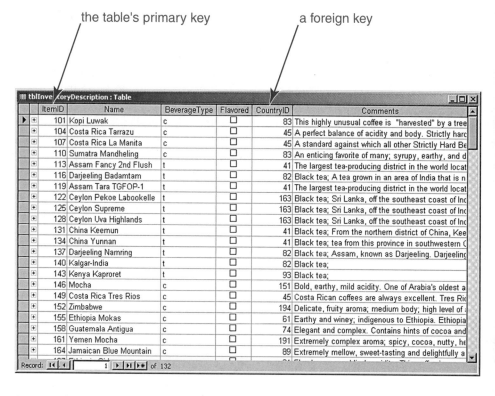

the table's primary key   a foreign key

Figure 4.15   Some rows of the *tblInventoryDescription* table.

EXERCISE 4.10: CREATING A ONE-TABLE QUERY

1. In the Database window, click Queries in the Objects bar, and then click the New button on the Database window
2. Select Design view from the list, and then click OK. (When creating queries, it is often easier to *not* use the Query Wizards.)
3. Select the *tblInventoryDescription* table from the list presented in the Show Table dialog box, click the Add button to add it to the query, and click the Close button.
4. Drag the fields ItemID, Name, Comments, BeverageType, and Flavored from the *tblInventoryDescription* field roster to the first through fifth cells in the Field row of the QBE grid.
5. Clear the Show check boxes under BeverageType and Flavored in the QBE grid, because you do not want to display these fields in the result—they are in the query so we can use them to specify criteria.
6. Enter three selection criteria in the Criteria row:
   • under the Comments column type **Like "*hard bean*"** (including the quotation marks and asterisks at both ends of the string),
   • under the BeverageType column type **"c"** (with the quotation marks),

- and under the Flavored column type **no** (letter case does not matter, but *do not* place quotation marks around this criterion or any other Yes/No criterion).
7. If you omit quotation marks when entering character string data, Microsoft Access automatically surrounds the data with quotation marks. Because the two selection criteria are in the same Criteria row of the QBE grid, both criteria must be true for a row to be returned. This is a classic AND criteria.
8. Select Datasheet view from the View menu to see the query results (dynaset).

Your dynaset should look like the one shown in Figure 4.16. We have saved this query as *qryHardBeanCoffee* on your Companion CD, so you need not save yours. Simply close the query without saving it.

What if you wanted to see all inventory items that were either not flavored *or* are coffees? We would place one criterion on one Criteria row and the other criterion on the "or" row below the previous criteria. (This type of query is a classic OR question.) Figure 4.17 shows the OR query and part of the result. As indicated in the status line, the query returned many rows—all unflavored beverages (tea or coffee) and all coffees (flavored or not).

query definition

dynaset

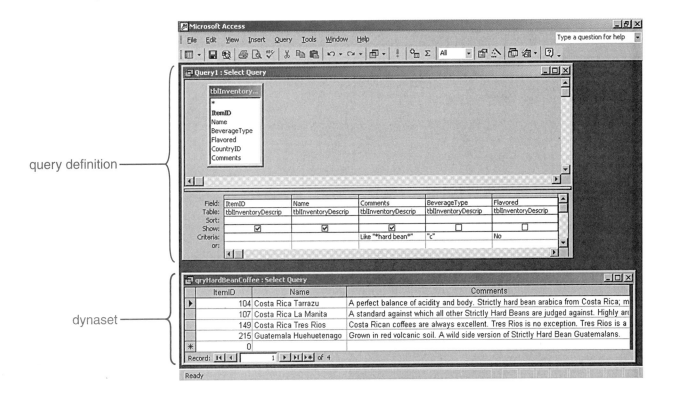

Figure 4.16   One-table query definition and dynaset.

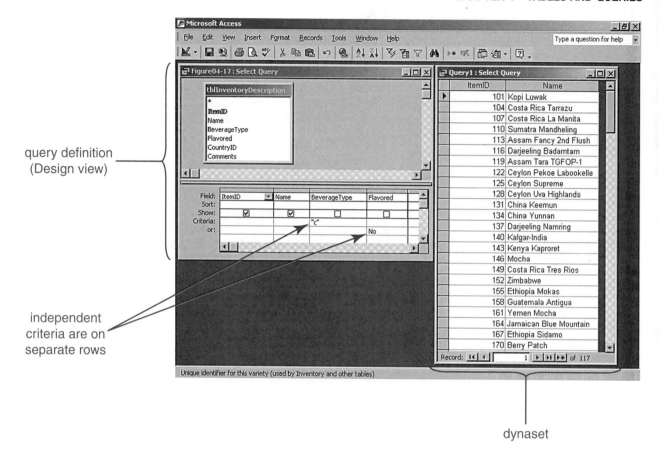

query definition
(Design view)

independent
criteria are on
separate rows

dynaset

Figure 4.17   Query with multiple, independent criteria.

Working with a Dynaset

Access returns query results in a dynaset. Similar to a table in behavior and structure, a dynaset is only temporary. It is replaced every time you rerun the query. For most queries, you can alter information displayed by the dynaset while in Datasheet view simply by typing in new information. The new information replaces the appropriate row and column of the underlying table. Thus, most dynasets present live, updateable views of underlying table data. Some dynasets are not updateable, and Access will warn you when you attempt to update data through one of the non-updateable dynasets. Most of the dynasets presented in this textbook are updateable.

You can alter the appearance of the dynaset so that the rows are arranged differently, the columns are displayed in a different order, or the columns are formatted in a special way. The next section illustrates how easy it is to make changes to the dynaset.

PRODUCING SORTED QUERY RESULTS. Suppose you want to rearrange dynaset rows so they are displayed in a more useful form. For instance, the list of coffees and teas shown in Figure 4.15 would be easier to use if it appeared in name order. Sorting dynasets is easy. By default, Access displays dynaset records in ascending order on the table's primary key, if it has one, whether or not the primary key is displayed in the dynaset. Creating a query to sort data in other ways is particularly useful. For example, a list of employees in order by their last and first names is particularly handy when you want to look up someone on a printed list. We'll show you how to sort the dynaset next.

Suppose you want to list all flavored teas in stock in order by their names. First, you would construct a one-table query based on the *tblInventoryDescription* table. In the QBE Field row you might include the fields ItemID, Name, Flavored, and BeverageType. Only ItemID and Name would have their Show check boxes marked. Flavored and BeverageType would contain the criteria values *Yes* and *t*, respectively, to retrieve only flavored teas (both criteria must be met). How about the sorting part of it? Simple! Follow along in the next paragraph and try it.

Try It

Open in Design view the query *qryFlavoredTea*, which selects flavored teas and displays them in a dynaset. To sort the dynaset results by Name, click the Sort row under the Name column—the attribute by which you want the rows sorted—and select Ascending from the drop-down list (or type a). Select Datasheet view from the View menu to see the dynaset. Notice that the rows are in Name order beginning with *Apricot* and ending with *Vanilla with Vanilla Bean*.

You can specify a sort order for more than one column. Access sorts by the leftmost field first followed by the next sort field to the right, and so on. Therefore, you should arrange the columns you want to sort, relative to each other, from left to right in the QBE grid. Note that the sort columns do not have to be the first group of columns in the QBE grid. You can sort by fields whose Show check box is cleared and thus does not display, though the reasons may seem obscure at this point. We will explain later why this may be necessary.

ALTERING THE ORDER AND SIZE OF COLUMNS. You can alter the order of the dynaset table columns. The dynaset columns' order is established by the query. For instance, the first field whose Show box is checked in the QBE grid is the first column in the dynaset, but you can alter the dynaset's column order either by altering the query's design or by altering the dynaset's column ordering after Access displays the dynaset. The former method is the best way.

To rearrange query columns, display the query in Design view and move the mouse pointer to the column selector of the field to be moved. (The column selector is the area just above the field name.) When the mouse pointer is on the column selector, it turns to a down-pointing arrow. Click the column. The entire column is darkened, indicating you have selected it. (Be careful not to move the mouse.) Release the mouse but keep it poised over the column selector. Next, click and drag the column to its new location. A rectangle appears below the pointer, indicating you are about to move the column. Finally, release the mouse when the column is in its new location. A vertical bar appears as you drag the column, which indicates where the column would reside if you were to release the mouse. When you release the mouse, columns to the right of the vertical bar move to the right, making room for the new column to be dropped in place.

If desired, you can enlarge individual columns by moving to the column selector area of a column so that the mouse is over the right line of the column selector. When the mouse changes from a down-pointing arrow to a double-headed arrow, drag the right edge to the right to enlarge the column, or drag it to the left to shrink the column.

You can change both column order and column size in the dynaset—after Access executes a query. When the query results appear, you can move columns or change their size following the procedures outlined in the preceding paragraphs. You can move the cursor to a dynaset column and then select Column Width from the Format menu. The Column Width dialog box is displayed (see Figure 4.18). Click the Best Fit button to size the column so it is just wide enough for the widest entry. (The shortcut for Best Fit is to move the cursor to the right edge of the column selector and then double-click the pointer after it changes to a double-headed arrow.) You can also size multiple columns at once. Drag the mouse across all the column selectors to select multiple contiguous columns. Move the mouse to the right column line of any one of the selected columns. When it changes to a double-headed arrow, double-click the pointer to optimize the column width.

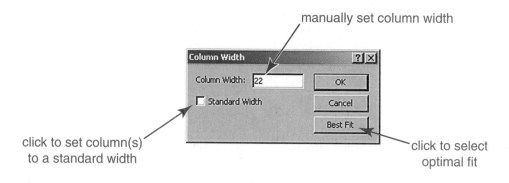

Figure 4.18   Column Width dialog box.

ALTERING COLUMN DISPLAY PROPERTIES. Like other dynaset characteristics, column display formats can also be changed. First, display the query in Design view. Then, move the mouse to the Field row in the QBE grid of the column whose format you want to change. When you right-click a column, a pop-up menu displays several choices. Click the Properties selection. A Field Properties dialog box opens. You can experiment with changing characteristics such as format yourself. For instance, try changing the format of the ItemID dynaset column so that the data is displayed in Currency format. After you are done experimenting, there is no need to save the altered query.

Saving a Query and Printing Dynasets

SAVING A QUERY. You should save queries that you anticipate using more than once. Save a query by selecting Save from the File menu with the query displayed in either Design or Datasheet view. Access saves the query design in the database on your disk under the name you type in the Query Name text box. If the query has been saved before, it is simply saved under the original name, replacing the older copy.

PRINTING DYNASETS. Printing query results simply means that you print the dynaset displayed in the Datasheet view. You can select the stored query name and print it, or you can open the query and view it. In either case, you select Print from the File menu (or click the toolbar Print button) to print the dynaset. When the Print dialog box displays, make any necessary adjustments to the page range to print (or print all pages) and click OK to give final authority to print the table. Note that you do not have any control over the page headers or footers. Table and dynaset outputs are somewhat "raw" and undisciplined, especially when you compare them to Access reports.

Dealing with Many-to-Many Relationships

The relationship between *tblInvoice* and *tblInventory* is many-to-many. Any particular invoice can contain several items drawn from inventory. From another perspective, any particular inventory item (for example, Kona coffee) may be found in several invoices. Recall that whenever an M—M relationship exists between two tables, you must create a *relationship* table. Minimally, the relationship table contains primary keys from both the *tblInvoice* and *tblInventory* tables for every item on a particular invoice and all invoices.

There are as many rows in the relationship table as there are invoice line items for all invoices. We have removed invoice lines from the *tblInvoice* table and placed them in the *tblInvoiceLine* table (see Figure 4.14). Matching the invoice number with the InvoiceID attribute of *tblInvoiceLine* can retrieve all the items of a particular invoice. InvoiceID is the primary key of the *tblInvoice* table, whereas the attribute InventoryID in *tblInvoiceLine* is the primary key in *tblInventory*. Thus, InventoryID in *tblInvoiceLine* is a *foreign key*. The other attributes in the relationship table are Quantity, UnitPrice, and Discount. Quantity is the amount invoiced for a particular item (coffee or tea) for a given invoice line. UnitPrice is the price charged for this item. It can be different from the Price column stored in the *tblInventory* table. The Discount field holds the percentage discount for a line item on a particular invoice. Discounts vary from customer to customer and from one time of the year to another. The two *tblInvoiceLine* table attributes, InvoiceID and InventoryID, form a *composite primary key*, because they are both required to form a primary key for the relationship table called *tblInvoiceLine*.

If you encounter other tables having a many-to-many relationship, which cannot be handled easily by a RDBMS, the remedy is simple. Create a relationship table containing a composite primary key that is formed from the primary keys of the two tables having the M—M relationship—just as we have done with the *tblInvoiceLine* table. Once a relationship table is in place, then both of the original tables have a 1—M relationship with the relationship table. In other words, the relationship table provides the "glue" connecting two tables in a one-to-many relationship.

Producing Queries Involving Multiple Tables

We created the various tables for The Coffee Merchant to normalize them in order to avoid problems such as data redundancy and data inconsistency, and to reduce data entry errors. Data is found in several related tables, and we need a way to connect the tables to retrieve information not found in a single table. When you connect tables together, you are *joining* them. Related tables are joined by indicating which columns are common to the tables to be joined. For instance, you could join the *tblCustomer* and *tblInvoice* tables on the common column CustomerID found in each table. Although these columns have the same name, it is not necessary. It is often simpler to remember the join columns by naming them identically.

JOINING RELATED TABLES. Linking two or more tables is not difficult. You connect a table's primary key to another's foreign key to explicitly indicate how tables are linked. In many cases, Access can automatically determine how tables are linked when tables to be linked (*joined* is the preferred term) have identically named fields or they have been joined permanently via the Relationships window. If Microsoft Access does not create join lines for you automatically, you can join tables manually.

You join tables manually by creating a query and adding all the related tables to the query in the Show Table dialog box. Then you can create a join line between each table pair by selecting the primary key field in one table and dragging it to the equivalent foreign key field in the other table. Of course, you can join tables by performing the preceding actions in the Relationships window. Once you join tables in the Relationships window, you never need to do so inside individual queries. Access remembers table-to-table relationships that you create in the Relationships window until you explicitly delete them.

CREATING CONDITIONAL QUERIES. Queries containing conditions are very useful. A *condition* provides a way for you to specify a range of values, or minimum and maximum values, for a field. For example, suppose you would like to locate all inventory items that are back-ordered. The coffee buyer is preparing to order more coffee and tea from the ranches around the world. One of the important questions that the buyer must answer is which products are back-ordered. In The Coffee Merchant system of tables, a product is back-ordered when the OnHand field in *tblInventory* is *negative*. In order to make intelligent product buying decisions, the buyer needs to know the product identification number, product name, and back-order volume column values. From that listing, he or she can order the correct quantity and types of products from the various suppliers.

To answer the buyer's question, we must construct a query involving two tables that are to be joined. The tables are *tblInventory*—the Inventory master table—and *tblInventoryDescription*. We will use a special operator called a comparison operator to create the selection criterion in a new query. A *comparison operator* is a special symbol that compares one value to another. The comparison operators are shown in Figure 4.19. In particular, we will use the less than (<) comparison operator in the selection criterion of the exercise that follows. We begin presenting you with more condensed exercise steps by combining several separate steps into one numbered step.

Operator	Meaning
<	Less than
<=	Less than or equal to
>	Greater than
>=	Greater than or equal to
=	Equal to
<>	Not equal to
Between	Test for a range of values where two extreme values are separated by the And operator
In	Test for "equal to" any member in a list
Like	Test a text or memo field to match a pattern string

Figure 4.19 Comparison operators.

EXERCISE 4.11: CREATING A TWO-TABLE QUERY   🐟
THAT USES A COMPARISON OPERATOR

1. Create a new query joining the tables *tblInventory* and *tblInventoryDescription*: click Queries on the Database window Objects bar, click New, select Design view, click OK, double-click *tblInventory* and *tblInventoryDescription* to add the two tables, and close the Show Table dialog box. Access automatically links the tables on their common field, ItemID, because we previously defined the relationship between them in the Relationships window.

2. Drag the columns ItemID (from *tblInventory*), Name, BeverageType, and OnHand to the Field row of the QBE grid. (You can double-click field names in the field roster to automatically place them in the next available column of the Field row.)

3. Click in the Criteria row of the OnHand column and type <0 (the less than symbol followed by zero).

4. Select Datasheet view from the View menu to display the dynaset. Figure 4.20 shows both the query design and the resulting dynaset. Your screen may be arranged differently, but the dynaset should show the same rows as the figure. (This query is named *qryStockOut* on your Companion CD.)

5. After observing the result, click the Datasheet view Close button and click No when you are asked if you want to save changes to the query.

USING WILDCARDS IN CRITERIA. A *wildcard* character allows you to find information when you are unsure of the complete spelling of an alphanumeric field. Used with the *Like* operator (see Figure 4.19), the wildcard characters define positions that can contain any single character, a single number, or zero or more characters in a text string match pattern. There are three *Like* wildcard characters available in Access. They are shown in Figure 4.21. Here's an example of how you can use them. Suppose you want to check The Coffee Merchant's stock for any beverages whose name contains the word *chocolate* (for example, Dutch Chocolate). You are interested in how much is available, if any. You can use the * (asterisk) wildcard character and the partial word *choc* to return any beverages whose Name field contains *choc* anywhere within it.

The preceding query involves two tables, *tblInventory* and *tblInventory-Description*. The key search criterion is the wildcard expression **choc**. This criterion is placed in the Criteria row just below the Name column in the QBE grid. (After you type the preceding expression, Access automatically surrounds it with double quotation marks and precedes the entire phrase with *Like*.) The asterisk preceding *choc* indicates that any word, phrase, or character string can appear before the word—or none at all. Similarly, the asterisk following *choc* indicates that any characters may follow the word—or none at all. That is, the search criterion requests any rows in which the partial word *choc* is found anywhere within the name. Figure 4.22 shows a query and the resulting dynaset.

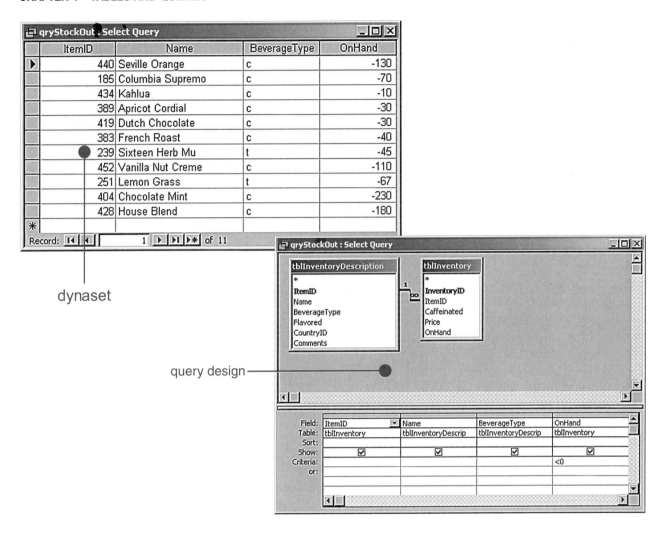

Figure 4.20 Two-table query using a comparison operator.

Wildcard Character	Meaning	Example Pattern Matches
?	Any single character	*b?lk* matches balk or bulk
*	Zero or more characters	**or* matches door, floor, and matador *or** matches ordinary, order, and organize **or** matches bored, category, and fluoride
#	Any single digit	*6#4* matches 604, 644, and 664

Figure 4.21 LIKE wildcard characters.

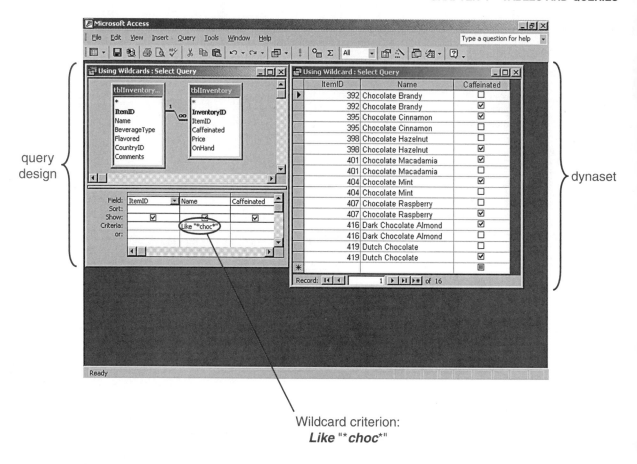

Figure 4.22   Query using a wildcard in its criteria.

USING LOGICAL OPERATORS IN QUERY CRITERIA. Some other useful operators helpful in forming selection criteria are called logical operators. *Logical operators* provide a way of bonding two comparison or wildcard criteria. There are several logical operators, but the ones used most often are AND, OR, and NOT. Using the AND operator, you can specify a condition in which two criteria must be true simultaneously. For example, suppose you want to examine the invoices issued during the first week in November 2003. A temporary employee was used to process the invoices that week, and you heard that some invoices were handled incorrectly. You can use the AND operator to bound the range of invoice dates you want to inspect. Specifically, you write the criterion expression **=#11/2/03# And <=#11/8/03#** in the Criteria row below InvoiceDate in the QBE grid. This selection criterion states a range of acceptable invoice dates. The range encompasses dates that are greater than or equal to November 2, 2003 *AND* (simultaneously) less than or equal to November 8, 2003. (The # characters always surround dates so that Access doesn't confuse dates with arithmetic expressions. Do not mistake this use of the pound sign with the wildcard character used to match a single digit.) Thus, the criterion limits rows from the Invoice table to invoices issued during the first week. An equivalent and simpler way of writing the preceding criterion using the Between comparison operator is **Between #11/2/03# And #11/8/03#**. Any dates between or matching the two dates satisfy the criteria.

Performing Calculations with Queries

Recall that in Chapter 3 we emphasized the importance of omitting from a table any information that can be calculated or derived from other columns in the table. For instance, good database design and normalization rules preclude the inclusion of a column of extended prices in any of The Coffee Merchant's invoice tables. This is because the extended price is calculated from the fields Quantity, UnitPrice, and Discount stored in *tblInvoiceLine*. Because the extended price can be calculated, it should not be stored in the table. Why? Suppose the extended price is stored in *tblInvoiceLine* along with Quantity, UnitPrice, and Discount. What if someone discovers a mistake in the Quantity or UnitPrice values in one or more invoices? Changing either renders the extended price value inaccurate. Database experts say that the database is *inconsistent*.

That leads us to this question: How do you produce the extended price and other useful calculated results? One answer is that you include any calculations in a query. Access allows you to write expressions that sum, average, and count values as well as write expressions that involve the arithmetic operators, fields, summary operators (we will discuss these in the next section), numeric constants, and comparison operators. The arithmetic operators are the familiar ones: +, -, *, and /, and you have been introduced to comparison operators. You reference other query or table fields by enclosing their names in brackets. To compute a result and display it in a query, you simply write an expression in its own Field row cell.

Let's write an expression to see exactly how to calculate results and display them in a dynaset. In the next exercise, we will join the *tblInvoiceLine*, *tblInventory*, and *tblInventoryDescription* tables and display invoice line items for invoices in the database. The query you will construct displays the extended price, among other columns, using the following formula:

[Quantity]*[UnitPrice]*(1-[Discount])

(Surround field names with brackets when you include them in expressions.) For example, if someone ordered 20 pounds of a particular coffee priced at $10.00 per pound and received a discount of 5 percent, then the extended price would be:

20*10*(1-0.05)

(Though the Inventory table, *tblInventory*, contains a price field, Price, for each item carried, customers may or may not be charged that *suggested* price. The actual price charged is stored in UnitPrice, an invoice line field [*tblInvoiceLine*], and may vary from one customer to the next.) The extended price that is calculated by the preceding expression is $190.

EXERCISE 4.12: WRITING EXPRESSIONS IN QUERIES

1. Close all windows except the Database window.
2. Create a new query, adding the tables *tblInvoiceLine*, *tblInventory*, and *tblInventoryDescription* to it. Access will draw join lines connecting the three tables on their respective primary and foreign keys. Close the Show Table dialog box.
3. Drag the fields InvoiceID, ItemID, Name, UnitPrice, Quantity, and Discount to the first six Field row cells in the QBE grid (in the order listed).
4. Click in the Sort row beneath the InvoiceID column in the QBE grid, click the drop-down list box arrow, and select Ascending from the drop-down list box. This will list the invoices in ascending order by invoice number.
5. Click in the seventh cell in the Field row, the first empty cell in the Field row of the QBE grid, and press Shift+F2 to open a Zoom dialog box. A Zoom dialog box opens a larger area in which you can see the entire expression as you type it.
6. Type the following expression. When you are done, click OK to close the Zoom dialog box and then press Enter.

   Extended Price: [Quantity]*[UnitPrice]*(1-[Discount])

7. Right-click the cell containing the preceding expression and select Properties from the pop-up menu that appears.
8. Click Format and then Click Currency from the drop-down list (see Figure 4.23). Doing this will format the calculated expression to display the result rounded to two decimal places and will include a currency symbol and commas (if necessary). Click the Format dialog box Close button to close the dialog box.

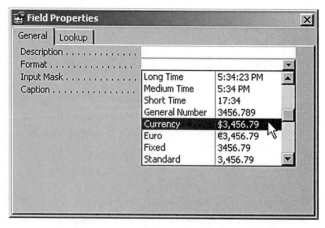

Figure 4.23 Formatting a query's calculated column.

9. Select Datasheet view from the View menu to see the dynaset (see Figure 4.24). We have saved the query as *qryExtendedPrice* on the Companion CD.
10. Close the query without saving it once you are finished examining the results.

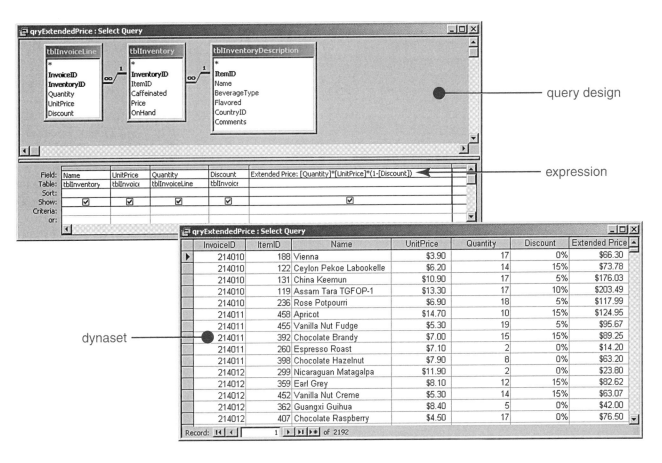

Figure 4.24 Query design and dynaset with calculated column.

Step 6 of Exercise 4.12 illustrates how you write an expression—the product of three fields: Quantity, UnitPrice, and Discount—in Access. Whenever you refer to Access table field names, always enclose them in brackets. Otherwise, Access becomes confused. *Extended Price* is an alias for the field. It precedes the expression. To rename a column (an expression in this case), simply begin with the new name (it can be several words) followed by a colon and a space. Then write the expression. If you omit an alias in an expression, Access assigns a unique, default field name such as *Expr1* or *Expr12*. Access-assigned field names are neither particularly attractive nor informative.

Grouping and Summarizing Data

Summary information can reveal situations that are not obvious from examining detailed data. Access provides several functions that produce aggregate information for data groups or an entire table. Figure 4.25 lists seven of the most popular aggregate functions along with a brief description of what each function does. Of the listed functions, the most useful to those of us in the accounting profession are Avg, Count, Max, Min, and Sum.

Sometimes you will want statistics for all rows of a table or joined set of tables. At other times, however, you will need summary statistics on smaller groups of records. For instance, it may be revealing to know the total number of pounds of each type of coffee and tea ordered each month. This would disclose the more popular choices. Or, the accounts receivable department might be interested in a statistic such as the average elapsed days, by customer, between the time invoices are sent and their corresponding payments are received. When Access summarizes information for several sets of rows, that calculation involves *grouping*. Grouping information simply means forming groups of rows that share some common characteristic such as having identical values for a client name, customer identification number, invoice number, or other attribute.

Frequently, the summary functions are used in queries (but they can also be used in forms and reports). To compute an average of a numeric field in a query, simply click the Totals toolbar button. Access adds a new row to the QBE grid, called the *Total* row. When the row appears, type *Avg* in the Total row beneath the field whose values you want to average. Then, run the query. You can compute multiple summary statistics on a particular field as long as you include multiple copies of the field name in the QBE grid Field row.

Function	Meaning
Avg	Computes a field's average value (ignores null fields)
Count	Counts the number of non-null (empty) items in a field
Max	Computes largest value in a field
Min	Computes smallest non-null value in a field
Sum	Computes the total of all items in a field
StDev	Computes the standard deviation of non-null values in a field
Var	Determines the variance of non-null values in a field

Figure 4.25   Access aggregate functions.

In the next exercise, you will try out a summary function and learn how to meld two character fields into one field by *concatenating* them. Let's try some of the summary functions. You will join together three tables so that you can compute and display the total sales grouped by salespersons' names. In other words, you want to know how much each salesperson sold. The three tables involved in the query are *tblEmployee*, *tblInvoice*, and *tblInvoiceLine*. The fields required to form the query summarizing sales are all found in just two tables—*tblEmployee* and *tblInvoiceLine*. However, the relationship between *tblEmployee* and *tblInvoiceLine* is many-to-many. Because Access cannot link many-to-many tables together directly, the *tblInvoice* table serves as a "bridge" table that restructures the M—M relationship into two 1—M relationships.

Whenever you want to combine text fields from a table into a single field, you simply write an expression containing the two fields separated by the symbol for ampersand, &. Suppose you want to produce a listing of employees for a telephone book listing their last name, a comma, a blank, and their first name. Combine text fields in a single cell of the Field row in a query to get the desired result. For instance, the following expression provides the required single text field:

Name: [LastName] & ", " & [FirstName]

The ampersand adds one string onto another. In this case, the previous expression is "adding" three text strings together, back to back. This is a handy tool to keep in mind whenever you need to combine disparate fields from a table into a single field in a query, report, form, or Web page.

Prepare for this exercise by closing all windows except the *Ch04.mdb* Database window. Click Queries on the Database window Objects bar.

EXERCISE 4.13: USING SUMMARY FUNCTIONS IN A QUERY

1. Create a new query (select Design view from the New Query dialog box), add the three tables *tblEmployee*, *tblInvoice*, and *tblInvoiceLine* to the query, and close the Show Table dialog box.
2. Select Totals from the View menu to insert in the QBE grid a new row called Total. (You can also click the Totals button on the Design view toolbar.)
3. In the first cell in the Field row enter the following expression, which combines the two name fields together, separated by a blank. Be sure to place a space between the two quotation marks.

   Name: [EmployeeFirstName] & " " & [EmployeeLastName]

   (You can place a blank on either side of the two ampersand symbols, but you don't have to. Access will do that for you automatically after you move to another cell in the QBE grid.)
4. Click the Show box in the first column so that a checkmark appears in it. This causes the employee name you created with the preceding expression to display when you run the query.

5. In the second cell in the Field row enter the following expression to compute and display sales totals, including any discount applied for each customer.

   Sales: [Quantity]*[UnitPrice]*(1-[Discount])

   You may want to press Shift+F2 to produce a larger view of the cell in the Zoom dialog box. The larger display makes it easier to see the whole expression. When you are finished writing the expression in the Zoom dialog box, click OK to close the Zoom dialog box.
6. Click in the QBE grid Total row beneath the second cell—the expression you just typed—and select the Sum function from the drop-down list (click the list box to display the list of summary functions).
7. Click in the QBE grid Sort row beneath the second cell and select Descending from the drop-down list. You want to see the sales summary sorted from highest sales total to lowest.
8. Set the format of the second cell to Currency by right-clicking the Field row cell containing the expression, clicking Properties, and then clicking Currency from the drop-down list in the Format box of the Field Properties dialog box.
9. Close the Field Properties dialog box.
10. Select Datasheet view from the View menu to see the results. Figure 4.26 shows both the query design and its dynaset.
11. Select File, Save, and then type **qryTotalSales** to name and save the new query.

The dynaset calculates total sales for 19 salespersons. Switch back to the query Design view in preparation for a little experiment. (*Do not* close this query yet.) Can Microsoft Access compute the grand total of all invoices that are in the database? In other words, is it possible to sum all the sales amounts for all the invoices by using a query? The answer is yes. As a matter of fact, you can make a simple change to the query you created in the preceding exercise to yield the grand total.

Try It

Display the previous query in Design view. Move the mouse pointer just above the Field row of the Name field (an expression) in the QBE grid. When the pointer changes to a solid, dark, down-pointing arrow, click it to select the entire Name column. Press the Delete key to delete that column. Select Datasheet view from the View menu to see the grand total of all invoices in the database. Your altered query should display a single row with the value of $176,729.37—the current total of all invoices stored in the system. Close the Datasheet view window. Click No when the dialog box displays a message asking if you want to save the query's design, because you want to preserve the original query you created in Exercise 4.13.

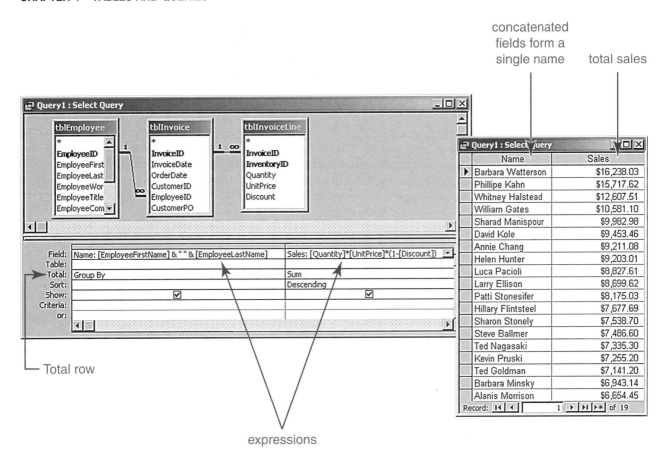

Figure 4.26   Sorted sales totals for each employee created with the Sum aggregate function.

Remember the following when using summary functions. Place the summary function in the field for which the computation is to be performed (beneath an expression in our previous example). Rename a summary column when desired by typing the new name, a colon, a space, and then the field name. (This technique works equally well to create aliases for fields, too.)

Using an Outer Join in a Query

When you join two tables, you may find that one or more rows in one table do not have matching rows in the other table. Knowing this may be important for someone. For example, a sales manager would want to know if there are any salespersons who have sold nothing during a particular period. There are examples of hidden information in your databases, too. In your *Ch04.mdb* database, for example, it is not apparent which cities have no employees simply by performing a standard join of the *tblEmployee* and *tblDivisionLocation* tables on matching primary and foreign keys. Instead, you produce this kind of information by using an *outer join*, which lists *all* rows from one table and only matching rows from another table.

The next exercise shows you how to create an outer join. The exercise uses as its starting point the query you created in Exercise 4.13 called *qryTotalSales*. You will modify the join properties for both of the existing joins to form an outer join. (The query's two joins are called *inner joins*.) The new query, when completed, will reveal the names of people who sold nothing in addition to those that did. Prepare for the exercise by copying *qryTotalSales* in the Queries collection of the Database window. (Simply click *qryTotalSales* and press Ctrl+C and Ctrl+V to cut and paste the query. Then type **qryOuterJoin** to name the new query.) Follow the steps in the following exercise.

EXERCISE 4.14: CREATING AN OUTER JOIN QUERY

1. Open *qryOuterJoin* in Design view.
2. Double-click the join line between the field lists of *tblEmployee* and *tblInvoice* in the upper part of the Query window. The Join Properties dialog box opens. If you double-click on the gray area and not on the join line, the Query Properties dialog box opens. If that is the case, close the Query Properties dialog box and place the tip of the mouse arrow directly on the join line and try again.
3. Select the second option in the dialog box (see Figure 4.27) and click OK. You should now see an arrow on the join line pointing from the *tblEmployee* field list to the *tblInvoice* field list, indicating you have asked for an outer join with all records from *tblEmployee* regardless of whether or not corresponding records are found in *tblInvoice*.
4. Repeat steps 2 and 3 for the join line between the field lists of *tblInvoice* and *tblInvoiceLine*.
5. Display the query in Datasheet view. Notice that the Sales column is empty for Melinda English, Giles Bateman, and Brad Shoenstein. That means that they have no records in the *tblInvoiceLine* table, which means they have no sales for the period.
6. Display the query in Design view, move to the criteria row beneath the Sales column, and type **Is Null** into the Criteria cell. That reduces the Datasheet view to those employees who did not report sales for the period. Figure 4.28 shows both the query design and the dynaset.
7. Save and close the query.

Designing and Using a Parameter Query

So far you have seen and created queries containing selection criteria directly in the design grid of the Query window. However, you can create a special type of query that allows you to specify selection criteria when you *run* the query. Known

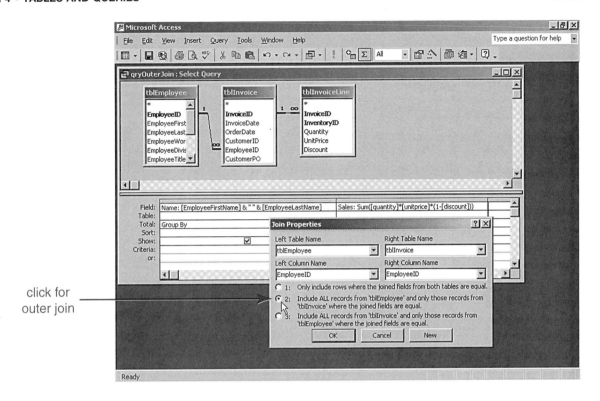

click for
outer join

Figure 4.27 Creating an outer join.

as a *parameter query*, it prompts you to enter the selection criteria just before running the query. The advantage of a parameter query over conventional queries is versatility. For example, you could create and run a query that lists all customers that live in Minnesota. Using the query to pass information to a report (Chapter 5), Access could create a form letter that you mail to all Minnesota residents. When the northwest sales region decides to run a similar promotion, it can revise the Minnesota query, substituting "Oregon" for "Minnesota" in the criteria row to extract those residents. Imagine creating 50 such queries simply to generate a listing for each of the U.S. states. Creating those queries would be time-consuming, and your database would be filled with 50 copies of a query whose basic forms are identical except for the criteria each contains.

A single parameter query can be used in place of the 50 individual queries. The only action required by a user running the query is to type the state name or abbreviation when prompted by Access. One query does the work of many. You can extend the use of parameter queries to an unlimited number of other accounting applications. A parameter query provides a perfect way to extract a group of invoices for varying time periods. Simply create a parameter query with two parameters—the beginning and ending dates for the billing period—

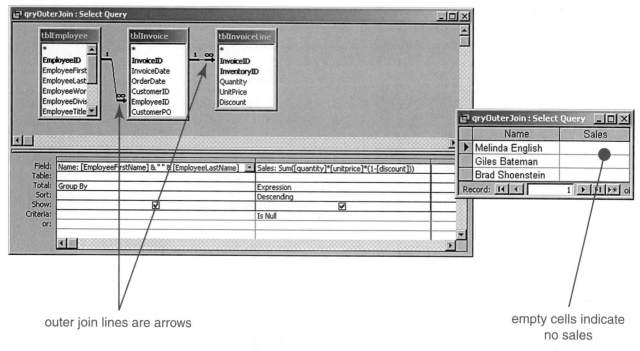

outer join lines are arrows

empty cells indicate
no sales

Figure 4.28 Using "Is Null" to display rows with empty fields.

and anyone can retrieve invoices from the date ranges a user enters when the query begins execution. Further, you can imagine a simple search engine query that retrieves a sales tax rate from a table when a user types the state name or state abbreviation. Simply enter the state name and the query returns the sales tax rate for that state.

The best way to understand parameter queries is to build one. Let's create a parameter query that displays a list of customers, retrieved from the table *tblCustomer*, for any state that the user wishes. When you run the query, you are prompted to enter a two-character state abbreviation. The query then retrieves addresses for customers in that state. In preparation for the next exercise, open *Ch04.mdb* and close all windows except the Database window. Follow the exercise steps to create and save a parameter query.

EXERCISE 4.15: CREATING A PARAMETER QUERY

1. Click Queries in the Objects bar, click New, select Design view from the list in the New Query dialog box, select and then add the table *tblCustomer*, and close the Show Table dialog box.

2. Double-click the following fields found in the field roster in this order: Company-Name, Address, City, State, and ZipCode. Access places each field in the Fields row of the QBE grid.
3. Type **[Enter a two-character state abbreviation:]** into the Criteria row in the State column. This sequence of characters, enclosed in beginning and ending brackets, defines a parameter.
4. Select Datasheet view from the View menu to test your new parameter query before you save it. An Enter Parameter Value dialog box appears.
5. Type **ne** in the Enter Parameter Value text box. This indicates you want to display addresses for Nebraska customers (see Figure 4.29). Recall that the capitalization of search strings doesn't matter. Lowercase "ne" will match table entries such as "Ne" or "nE."

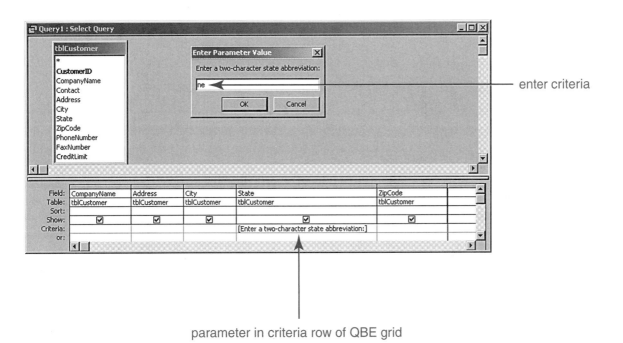

Figure 4.29   A parameter query design and run-time prompt.

6. Click OK in the *Enter Parameter Value* dialog box to test the query. If you constructed the query correctly, Access will display a list of 11 companies—all from Nebraska, of course (see Figure 4.30).
7. Select Save from the File menu and type **qryParameter**; then, click OK to save the query under the name you entered.
8. Close the Datasheet view window.

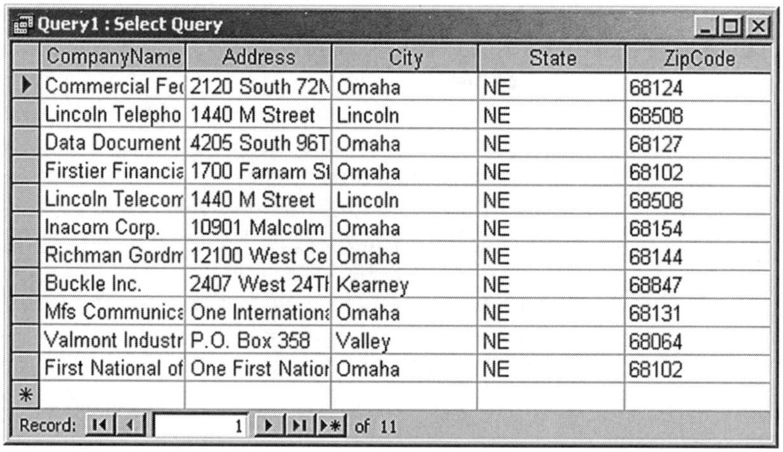

Query1 : Select Query				
CompanyName	Address	City	State	ZipCode
Commercial Fed	2120 South 72N	Omaha	NE	68124
Lincoln Telepho	1440 M Street	Lincoln	NE	68508
Data Document	4205 South 96T	Omaha	NE	68127
Firstier Financia	1700 Farnam St	Omaha	NE	68102
Lincoln Telecom	1440 M Street	Lincoln	NE	68508
Inacom Corp.	10901 Malcolm	Omaha	NE	68154
Richman Gordm	12100 West Ce	Omaha	NE	68144
Buckle Inc.	2407 West 24TI	Kearney	NE	68847
Mfs Communica	One Internationa	Omaha	NE	68131
Valmont Industr	P.O. Box 358	Valley	NE	68064
First National of	One First Natior	Omaha	NE	68102
*				

Record: 1 of 11

Figure 4.30 A parameter query dynaset.

SUMMARY

This chapter has emphasized using Access to create tables and queries. You have learned how to create table structures, enter data into tables, and set limits on the type and size of information that one can enter into a table. In addition, you learned how to establish referential integrity between tables. We have stressed the importance of specifying primary keys when constructing tables. Tables, you learned, hold all of the data in a database system. Queries, on the other hand, access one or more tables to produce combined results that display related data fields from several tables. You know how to write and save queries that involve both single and multiple tables. Queries can contain expressions comprised of comparison operators, arithmetic operators, example elements, and wildcard characters. Using queries, you can focus on the data elements important to you. Finally, you learned that parameter queries are quite versatile and can provide varied results depending on what criteria you enter when you run queries.

QUESTIONS AND PROBLEMS FOR REVIEW

MULTIPLE-CHOICE QUESTIONS

1. If you want to list all male employees in the Accounts Receivable department, which object would you use to reduce the possible results to just the requested persons?
   a. table
   b. form
   c. query
   d. report

2. If you wish to add a column to an existing table, you must
   a. first enter Edit mode.
   b. display a table in Design view.
   c. change the table's Datasheet view properties.
   d. disable referential integrity checks.

3. A query involving more than one table must indicate how the tables are related to each other by
   a. minimizing them.
   b. displaying their property sheets.
   c. linking them.
   d. drawing link diagrams.

4. You can design a table's salary field to automatically restrict legitimate values by entering an expression in the field property called
   a. Field Size.
   b. Default Value.
   c. Validation Text.
   d. Validation Rule.

5. In which window can you link two tables permanently so that any new queries involving these tables automatically link them?
   a. Query design
   b. Relationships
   c. Datasheet
   d. Table design

6. The comparison operator meaning "is not equal to" is which of the following symbols?
   a. <=
   b. < >
   c. <=>
   d. \ =

7. The QBE grid contains a(n) _____ row.
   a. Field
   b. Table
   c. Sort
   d. all of the above
8. Access supports two classes of queries. They are called
   a. Action and Field.
   b. Selection and Referential.
   c. Selection and Action.
   d. Active and Passive.
9. You can add special functions that allow you to group and summarize numeric data. An example is the Sum function. Collectively, these functions are known as _____ functions.
   a. summary
   b. table
   c. aggregate
   d. equijoin
10. What is the general name for a query that prompts you for criteria values to filter dynaset rows when you run the query?
   a. filter query
   b. criterion query
   c. update query
   d. parameter query

DISCUSSION QUESTIONS

1. Discuss the advantage(s) of providing a data validity check in the Validation Rule field property. What might happen if you omitted validation rules from text fields, and how could that affect the integrity of your database tables?
2. Explain why referential integrity is so important when dealing with a database, such as The Coffee Merchant's, involving several related tables. Give a scenario in which the lack of referential integrity could cause problems. Be specific.
3. Discuss the problem with storing an extended price (an invoice item quantity multiplied by an item's wholesale or retail price) in the *tblInvoiceLine* table. Why could you not simply add a column called ExtendedPrice to the Invoice Line table?
4. Discuss the advantages of an outer join query. Give an example, different from the one used in the textbook, of using an outer join to display information from two tables related in a query with an outer join. What role does the expression "Is Null" play in outer join queries?
5. Suppose the table *tblStudents* contains the first and last names of students and that *tblClassRosters* contains the list of students enrolled in each class in the

university. Discuss the relationship between *tblStudents* and *tblClassRosters*. Is it 1—1, 1—M (or vice versa), or M—M? Are there any problems representing the relationship of these two tables to one another?

PROBLEMS

1. List the first name, last name, commission rate, and gender of all male employees from the Employee table (*tblEmployee*) whose commission rate is at least 7 percent. Sort the rows in ascending order by last name. Print the dynaset. Be sure to write your name on the output before you turn it in.

2. Create a query to list the ItemID, OnHand, and Name values for all inventory items whose on-hand amount is between 1 and 139 pounds, inclusive. Sort the result in descending order by the OnHand value. Print the dynaset. (You should have fewer than a dozen rows in the dynaset.)

3. Create and run a query that retrieves all teas whose inventory price is at least $16.00. List only Name, BeverageType, and Price in the dynaset. Sort the list into ascending order by Name. Print the dynaset and write your name and course section number on your paper.

4. Write and execute a query based on the *tblInventoryDescription* and *tblCountryName* tables that lists all products that originate from either Ethiopia or Kenya. List the name of the coffee or tea (Name from *tblInventoryDescription*) and the country name (in that order). Give the CountryName column an alias of *Country*. Sort the dynaset rows by the Country column in ascending order. Print the dynaset and write your name on it.

5. Create and run a query that displays all employees from the Employee table (*tblEmployee*) who have the title *Senior Sales Associate* (*tblEmployeeTitle*). In the dynaset only display each qualifying employee's last name and gender (in that order). Sort the dynaset by gender and then by last name within gender groups. (The sort will group females and then males and then sort them by last names within the group.) Print the resulting dynaset. Remember to write your name on the output.

6. You want to examine the invoices issued in November 2002 in order by date. You are interested only in general information. To answer this question, form a query that joins The Coffee Merchant tables *tblInvoice* and *tblCustomer*. Display the company names, invoice dates, and invoice numbers (InvoiceID) for invoices issued only during the period 11/1/02 through and including 11/30/02. Sort the dynaset in ascending order by invoice date and then by company name among the same invoice dates. Print all pages. Save the query. (Figure 4.14 contains the schemas of all tables for The Coffee Merchant.)

7. Create a query joining tables *tblInventoryDescription* and *tblCountryName*. Display with the query the columns (in this order from left to right) Name, BeverageType, CountryName, and Comments. Include only the countries of

Kenya and Costa Rica in your results. Sort the rows by country name. Print the resulting dynaset. Reviewing the output, which of the two countries displayed produces more coffee varieties?

8. Write a query that displays the five most densely populated states in the United States. Use criteria to eliminate the District of Columbia. Include in the dynaset the long state name, the short state name, and the calculated field, density. Assign the column alias *Density* to the population density column. Format the Density column so that it displays two decimal places. Sort the dynaset in descending order by Density. (Hints: *tblSalesTaxRate* contains state names, populations, and area—in square miles—of each state. Density is, of course, the measure of the number of people per square mile. Right-click the blank area above the QBE grid to locate and set the Top Values property of the Query Properties so that only the top five results are displayed.)

9. Create a query that produces invoice information from The Coffee Merchant's tables: *tblInvoice*, *tblInvoiceLine*, *tblEmployee*, *tblCustomer*, *tblInventory*, and *tblInventoryDescription*. Display the following columns: InvoiceID, ItemID, Quantity, UnitPrice, Discount, InvoiceDate, OrderDate, CustomerID, EmployeeLastName, CompanyName, and PhoneNumber. Write the expression for extended price, Quantity*Price*(1-Discount), and rename the resulting column Extended Price. Format the Extended Price column to display a dollar sign and two decimal places—the Currency format. After you have completed the query's design, run it. Use Page Setup to print in landscape instead of the default, portrait. The output is very long, so print only the first three pages. Write your name on the first page of the output.

10. The boss has decided to split the table *tblInventoryDescription* into teas and coffees, dropping the "beverage" field in the process. Write two make-table queries to split the table, making a coffee-only table called *tblCoffee* and a tea-only table called *tblTea*. Run the make-table queries, and then print the two tables.

5 ACCESS FORMS AND REPORTS

OBJECTIVES

This chapter extends the knowledge you gained by providing detailed information about Microsoft Access forms and reports. You will learn about the advantages of using forms and reports, and about defining and using accounting forms and reports. Throughout this chapter, exercises emphasize Microsoft Access techniques critical to building accounting information systems. Like the chapters before it, this chapter is application-oriented and contains very little theory. Exercises actively engage you in using the theory you learned earlier to create typical accounting forms and reports. In particular, you will learn how to:

• Put forms to work in a variety of accounting applications.
• Create a form replete with formatted fields and aesthetic enhancements.
• Add a label, text box, and list controls to a form.
• Build forms and associated subforms from queries and tables.
• Examine the details of a report's structure.
• Produce a grouped data report.
• Design and print reports ranging from one-table reports to more complex multiple-table reports employing summary information.

We continue using The Coffee Merchant's database system as the backdrop application in this chapter. All the tables, but no queries, that you used in Chapter 4 have been carried over to the *Ch05.mdb* database found in the Ch05 folder on your Companion CD. For all exercises and examples in this chapter, we assume that you have inserted the Companion CD in the CD-ROM drive, copied the database *Ch05.mdb* to your hard disk, removed the database's read-only protection, started Microsoft Access, and opened the Ch05 database. If not, then please be sure to do so before doing the exercises in this chapter.

CREATING AND USING FORMS

A form displays information from one or more tables in an easily understood, attractive format on a computer screen. Unlike a Table window, a Form window can show one row of a table at a time. One advantage of a form over a Datasheet view of a table is that a form can resemble any of a company's paper forms. When database forms match paper forms, the computer forms are almost always intuitive and familiar to those using them. And because the computer forms look familiar, they are not intimidating to new computer users. Forms are the primary interface between users and database applications. As far as your users know, forms *are* the application—not the tables and other objects that are behind the scenes. Forms can be used to store information and pass it from one form to another or from one phase of your application to the next.

Forms can have a plain but functional design, or they can be elaborate, with drop-down lists, built-in help, attractive field designs, graphics, and buttons that activate predefined activities when users click them. Forms, like queries, do not store any information. They simply display information retrieved from one or more tables. Data exhibited in a form can be retrieved from a single table or from multiple tables joined on a common key field. Forms can also display data directly from a query of arbitrary complexity. Any of the queries we created in the previous chapter could be the basis of a form.

Putting Forms to Work

Forms provide a convenient way to control application flow and organize your database application. Using command buttons on a form, you can create macros or code (VBA) that automates all major database procedures. When a user clicks one of the buttons, it activates a procedure such as producing a report or displaying invoices. Forms can contain a special code that runs when a specific event occurs. For example, you can easily create a code, stored with one of your forms, that performs a specific action when someone clicks a button, opens a form, or moves to a particular text box on a form.

Forms are a particularly attractive and effective way to control the data users enter into a database. For example, you could create a special form for entering new information into an invoice table. The new form contains control information that prevents a user from entering an already-assigned invoice ID number or entering an unreasonable value for a unit cost field. You can provide these types of data consistency checks as part of the logic of a form that are far more versatile and robust than the elementary table property checks. Figure 5.1 shows an example of an inventory input form.

Forms are by far the most widely used interface for entering, editing, and checking database information. You can use forms to add, change, or delete information from one or several tables at once. Forms allow you to lock selected table

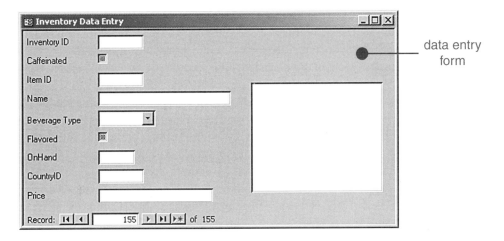

data entry
form

warning
dialog box
form

Figure 5.1   Example of two ways to use forms.

fields to prevent their alteration. Other options allow forms to fill in values with default and calculated values based on other entries the user makes.

Creating forms that display the progress of a database application is an effective way to communicate with the user. During a particularly lengthy database update process, for example, you can display a form that contains a progress chart indicating how far along the update operation is. Forms are the favored way to display informative messages such as warnings or error conditions in various parts of the database. For example, a form can simply display the message "Ordered item, ID number 123445, is now out of stock." when you ship the last of an inventory item. Figure 5.1 shows a sample warning dialog box—a form. Notice the warning dialog box has no close button and no control menu.

Although forms are designed primarily for viewing on a screen, you can print them. An invoice form can serve the dual role of input and output. Data entry personnel can use a form to enter invoice information, and accounts receivable personnel can use the same form to generate individual invoices to mail to customers. The differences between the input form and the printed form may be slight. An input form may have different headers and footers—one for the customers and one for the company's data entry personnel.

Viewing Form Types

You can create several different types of forms either manually or by using the Form Wizard. Normally, the Form Wizard is your best choice for creating most forms—at least until you become comfortable with creating forms.

A form can contain several sections, or subdivisions. These include the Page Header and Page Footer sections, Form Header and Form Footer sections, the Detail section, and any number of Group Header and Group Footer sections. Headers or footers for each section can appear independently of each other. That is, a Page Header may appear in a form without its corresponding Page Footer. Similarly, a form may contain a Group Header listing the department to which a list of employees belongs but no Group Footer. As you have probably guessed, Page Headers and Footers occur at the beginning and ending of each page, respectively. Likewise, a Form Header appears at the top of each form, and a Form Footer appears at the bottom of each form—regardless of whether a form is displayed or printed. The Detail section contains information from the database and labels to identify individual items. Typically, information in the Detail section is variable, because the information there is obtained from queries and tables in the database. Figure 5.2 shows an example of a form containing Header, Detail, and Footer sections. Unless you see a multipage printout of forms, it is difficult to distinguish a form's Page Header from a Form Header.

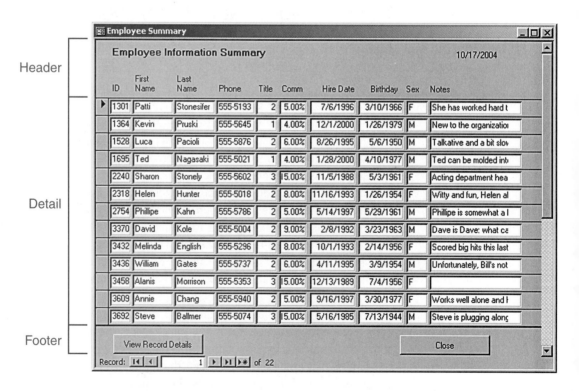

Figure 5.2   Example form with Page Header, Detail, and Page Footer sections.

A form type that is particularly useful for browsing through several records at once is a continuous form. A *continuous form* displays several records simultaneously on one form. The form resembles a spreadsheet, because labels appear at the top of each field and row selectors appear on the left side of each record. Figure 5.2 is an example of a continuous form showing all of the fields of several employee records. To view the remaining records, you click the scroll bar on the right side of the form or you can click the record number box and navigation buttons in the lower left portion of the form.

Forms designed to display a lot of information are usually designed as *multiple-page forms*. Multiple-page forms contain too much information to be displayed on a single screen. Thus, they group information into page-sized pieces. A user simply scrolls down the form to view its other parts. There are many examples of multiple-page forms in use. An employee form might contain many text boxes with name, address, date of birth, and similar information in the first screen-sized form piece. Lower in the form could be a large text box containing the employee's resume, a salary history, and other longer text passages.

Periodically in a database application it is helpful to have a window that remains the topmost window on the Windows desktop. Known as a *pop-up form*, the form might display an opening statement the first time you open a database file, or the pop-up form might provide users with information about the person who developed the database application. Unlike most windows, a pop-up window remains the topmost window, regardless of which other windows you activate on your desktop. This is especially useful to ensure that the database user reads the important information found in the pop-up form. Pop-up forms always contain a button—usually labeled OK—that closes the window. A special version of a pop-up form is called a modal form. A *modal form* is one that requires a response before the user can continue working on any other part of the application. A modal form might provide a stern warning about some action that is about to occur, or it may simply list critical information. In either case, a modal window will not let you click and activate any other window in the database application. Modal windows really get your full attention, and you should use them sparingly. Figure 5.3 shows an example of a pop-up form. (Of course, it would be impossible for you to determine if a form is modal simply by examining a textbook figure.)

A *subform* is especially useful when you want to display information on the "many" side of a one-to-many relationship. For example, a subform is a perfect way to display invoice lines that make up a larger form that is the entire invoice. An invoice's main form displays customer information while a subform displays details about the line items. You will see several examples of this form/subform relationship in this chapter—particularly when you create invoice forms by following this chapter's exercises. Figure 5.3 shows a form and subform example.

We begin our exploration of forms and their utility by creating a rather simple form from a single table. Then we will create a form whose data is derived from multiple related tables. The last form will be created from a query.

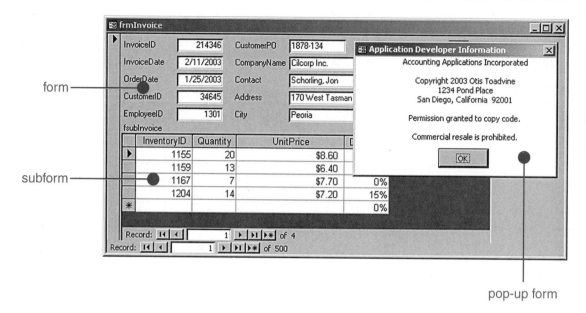

Figure 5.3 A pop-up form displays information about an application's developer.

Building a Simple Form

It is much easier to enter data and alter data in the Customer table using a form. The next exercise shows you how to create an *AutoForm* from the Table window. Subsequent exercises will enhance the form's appearance. First, start with a clean slate. Launch Access if necessary and open your copy of *Ch05.mdb*. Close any open windows except the Database window. Then create a form by doing the steps in the following exercise.

EXERCISE 5.1: CREATING A FORM FROM A TABLE

1. Click Tables in the Objects bar of the Database window and select the table *tblCustomer*. You do not need to open it to perform the remaining steps in this exercise, but you can if you wish.
2. Click AutoForm in the Insert menu. Access quickly builds a form and a related subform (see Figure 5.4).
3. Save the newly created form by clicking Save from the File menu and then typing **frmMyCustomer** in the Form Name text box of the Save As dialog box. Click OK to store the form in the database. (The string *frm* is the customary form name prefix—one of the database world's rules that is equivalent to accounting's "GAAP.")

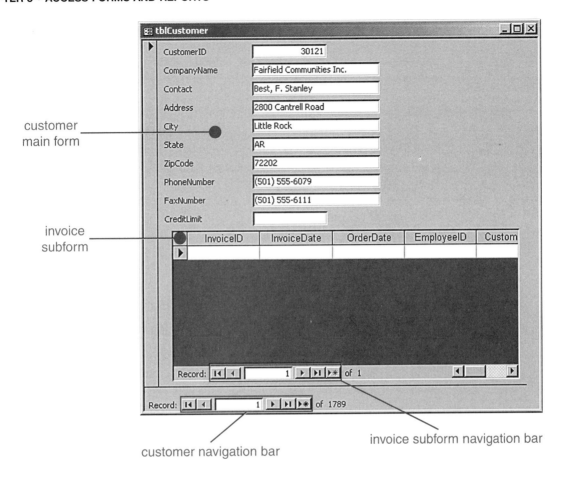

Figure 5.4 AutoForm generated for the table *tblCustomer*.

Try It

Notice that the first row of *tblCustomer* is displayed along with an empty row in the subform beneath the main customer record. Two rows of navigation buttons appear. The top row of navigation buttons moves the record pointer through invoices that are stored in *tblInvoice* and are related to the *tblCustomer* table. The lower row of navigation buttons moves from one customer record to another. Whenever you move to a new customer, the associated invoice rows change to those of the new customer. Click the Next Record navigation button for the customer—the lower set of navigation buttons—and view different customers' information and invoice records. Click the Last Record navigation button to view the last customer's information. Click the toolbar View button and select Design View to examine the form's *design*. Close the form. Click Forms on the Objects bar to see the new form's name, *frmMyCustomer*.

Whenever you want to create a form to enter or examine data in a table, the easiest way is to first create an AutoForm-style form for a table. Subsequently, you can customize the default form to suit your needs, making it more attractive and functional. One of the fundamental operations you will use in the Form Design window is moving and sizing fields and other form objects. To move an object, you first select it and then drag it to its new location. When you select an object, small square handles appear around it. Passing the pointer over any of the object's handles causes the pointer to change shape. By dragging a handle, you can enlarge or shrink the object by dragging the handle away from or towards the object, respectively.

You can move several objects at once by selecting them and dragging the entire group. As with other Windows programs, you select multiple objects by holding down the Shift key while clicking each object in turn. Alternatively, you can simply drag the mouse so that the dashed line touches or surrounds all objects you wish to select. When you release the mouse, handles appear around all the objects that you selected.

Let's rework the default form you created previously—first by changing the title.

EXERCISE 5.2: ALTERING A FORM'S TITLE

1. Display *frmMyCustomer* in Design view and then click the Maximize button on the Form window to make the window larger.
2. Select Form Header/Footer from the View menu. Form Header and Form Footer sections are added to your form.
3. Select Toolbox from the View menu to display the toolbox on the work surface (see Figure 5.5). You can also display the toolbox by clicking the Toolbox button found on the Design View toolbar—it has a hammer and wrench on it. You can move the toolbox anywhere on the screen by dragging its Title bar, or you can drag it to the top, left, right, or bottom of the screen to dock it there.
4. Click the Label button to add a title to the form; move the mouse to the upper left corner of the form header, and drag it down and to the right until the outline is approximately 0.25" by 2.0". Release the mouse. An empty label appears in the Form Header section of the form.
5. Type the label **Coffee Merchant Customers** in the label box. Click outside the label box to see the text.
6. Remove the toolbox from the screen by clicking its Close button.
7. Right-click the label box in the Form Header and select Properties from the shortcut menu. (Alternatively, you can click the Properties button on the Design View toolbar.)
8. Click the Format tab.
9. Scroll to the Text Align property, near the end of the list of properties, and type **Center** (or select it from the drop-down list) in the Text Align box.

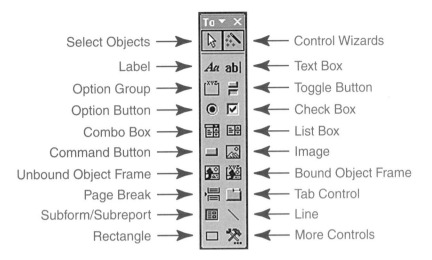

Select Objects ——➤ | | ◄—— Control Wizards
Label ——➤ *Aa* abl ◄—— Text Box
Option Group ——➤ | | ◄—— Toggle Button
Option Button ——➤ ⦿ ☑ ◄—— Check Box
Combo Box ——➤ | | ◄—— List Box
Command Button ——➤ | | ◄—— Image
Unbound Object Frame ——➤ | | ◄—— Bound Object Frame
Page Break ——➤ | | ◄—— Tab Control
Subform/Subreport ——➤ | \ ◄—— Line
Rectangle ——➤ ☐ | ◄—— More Controls

Figure 5.5   Access Toolbox.

10. Type **14** in the Font Size property to indicate you want a point size of 14. Close the property sheet by clicking its Close button.
11. If the title is not entirely visible in its text box, move the mouse to the right-edge sizing handle. When the pointer turns to a double-headed arrow pointing left and right, drag the sizing handle until the entire title is visible.
12. Select Form View from the View menu to see the altered form.
13. Close and save your form.

Your revised form, called *frmMyCustomer*, should resemble the one shown in Figure 5.6. We have saved it as *frmCustomer* on your Companion CD.

Using a Form

By using a form-based interface to a database and its tables, you will realize that data entry with a form is more intuitive and easier than entering data directly into a table. In your database is a simple form called *frmOrder* (remember to use the prefix *frm* for all your form names) that will introduce you to the look and feel of a typical form. The form *frmOrder* found on the Companion CD provides a convenient work surface to enter new orders into the tables comprising the order database. The form provides all the requisite mechanisms to automatically place order information into two tables called *tblOrder* and *tblOrderLine*. Furthermore, the form supplies a helpful table lookup feature in two key locations: the Customer No. (customer identification number) field and the Sales Rep. (sales representative) field.

A table lookup field is helpful to anyone entering information with which he or she is not familiar. For instance, if you do not know a customer's number—

form header ———

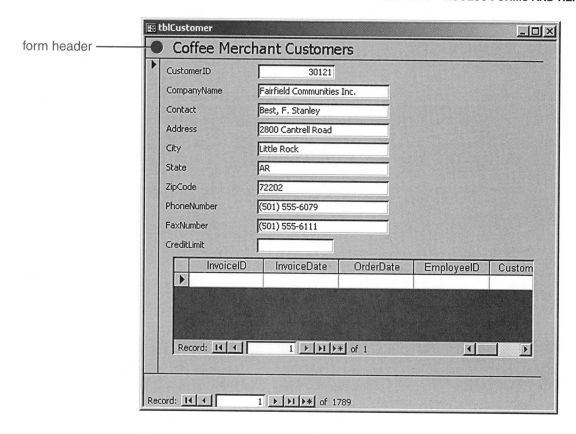

Figure 5.6   Customer form with a form header.

a normal situation—you can click the *combo* box (a combination of a text box and a list box) to display customer names. When the cursor is on the customer number entry, you can click the down-pointing arrow to peruse the list of existing customer numbers and names. Similarly, you can look up a sales representative's name by clicking the *list* box arrows associated with the field. Let's enter one order into the system using the order form.

Prepare for the next exercise by launching Access, if necessary, and by closing all windows except the Database window. Follow the steps in the next exercise to enter and save information in an existing order entry table.

EXERCISE 5.3: USING THE ORDER ENTRY FORM

1. Click Forms on the Objects bar and double-click *frmOrder* found in the list of forms. The Order Entry form opens.
2. Type **5678** into the Order Number field. Press Tab to move to the next field.

3. Enter a date in the form *mmddyy* (for example, type **071803**) into the Order Date field. (Access will automatically supply the / separator between the month and day and between the day and year.) Press Tab to move to the next field.
4. With the cursor in the Customer field, click the combo box arrow on the right side of the field to display a list of customer numbers and names (see Figure 5.7).

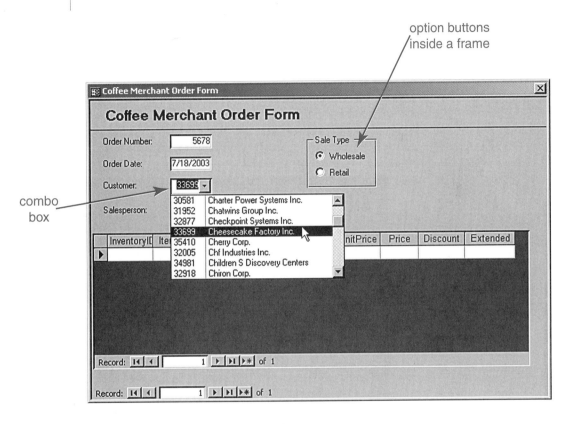

Figure 5.7 Using a combo box to select a customer.

5. Scroll through the list of customers until the company name *Cheesecake Factory Inc.* appears. Click that name. After you select the name, its corresponding customer number is inserted into the field and thus the underlying table.
6. Click the down arrow on the Salesperson combo box and select (click) the name *English, Melinda*.
7. Press Tab to move to the Sale Type option group. Click the Retail option button. Option buttons within a group are mutually exclusive due to their behavior: clicking one button deselects any other previously selected option button in the group.
8. Click the Inventory column in the first row of the subform. This is another way to move the focus in a form. (The *focus* is the active field on a form into which you can type or press the spacebar.)

9. Type **1128**, press Tab, and type **20** in the Quantity column. Press Tab to move to UnitPrice.

10. Type **8.5** and press Tab twice. The cursor moves to the next row in the sub-form. Notice that the ItemID, Name, and Price are automatically inserted into the form; the extended price is calculated and inserted also. Discount takes on its default value, 0.00, if you do not enter a value.

11. Continue entering values into the subform, using Figure 5.8 as a guide. In addition to entering Inventory, Quantity, and UnitPrice values for each row, remember to type **5%** and **15%** (type the percent sign) in the Discount column for the last two entries, respectively. (What happens if you type 15 in the Discount column—without typing a trailing percent sign—and then press Enter? Try it. It won't hurt anything.)

12. Click the Form view Close button to cease entering values or continue on with the Try It examples.

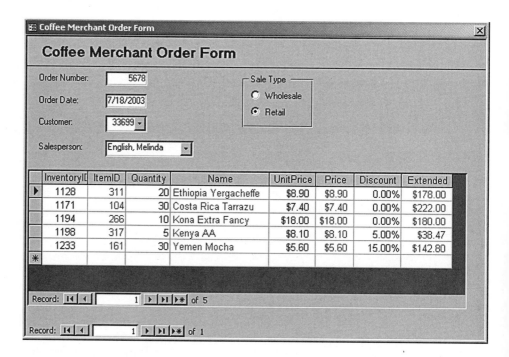

Figure 5.8   Completed order entry form.

Try It

You may not have noticed that there are helpful hints available called *ControlTips* that display when you hover the cursor over a field in the form. *Hovering the cursor* simply means that you move the mouse pointer over a control and pause (but do not click the mouse). After a brief pause, a tip displayed in a yellow box appears. Hover over the Order Number, Order Date, and Customer fields and observe their ControlTips.

If you want to try the form again, first clear it by clicking the Next Record navigation button located at the bottom of the form. Whenever you move to another record, Access automatically posts the current data to various tables. Then Access clears the form to make way for new data. When you are done entering information, click the form's Close button. Don't be concerned that you might lose data. Microsoft Access automatically posts any newly entered data to the database when you move off the current record or close the form.

You have used a Table window's navigation buttons to view the data in a table. Similarly, you can examine all the data in the Order form—from multiple tables—through a form. Assuming you have entered additional orders, you can click the First Record button to go to the first order you entered, or click the Last Record button to go to the last order entered in the system. Other navigation buttons work in a familiar way.

Editing data couldn't be simpler. In a Form view window, click on any field you would like to change and type the change. For form fields using lookup tables (fields having list boxes or combo boxes), click the arrow near the field to display the list of values; then enter a new value or select one of the displayed entries. It is best to use a lookup table when available, especially for noncontiguous values such as sales representative identification numbers. As budding form designers, you should incorporate lookup tables for fields whose values are limited to a specific and small list of acceptable values. This saves much frustration and confusion on the part of form users.

With forms, you can view particular records or groups of records using either the Filter By Form or Filter By Selection techniques. When you filter objects, you are restricting what is displayed to some subset of the total objects available. Filtering records being viewed through a form is no different. You simply specify the criteria—similar to query criteria—that are used to restrict your view of the records and then select Apply Filter/Sort from the Filter menu. Records are displayed in the usual way in the form, but you will notice that only a select group of records is available. The total number of records in the filtered set is indicated to the right of the navigation buttons at the bottom of the form. Try it yourself.

Try It

Display, in Form view, the form *frmCustomer* found on your Companion CD. Notice that there are 1,789 customer records. All are available for viewing. Next, click the

Records menu, point to Filter, and click Filter By Form. Let's see how many customers from California there are in the database—and who they are. Click the Clear Grid button on the Filter/Sort toolbar. Click the State form field and type CA in either uppercase or lowercase letters. Click Filter in the menu bar and then click Apply Filter/Sort. (Be careful not to click Advanced Filter/Sort. That will have a different consequence.) Access reveals that there are 196 customers in California (see Figure 5.9). Use the navigation buttons to go to the next record and the last record. Select Remove Filter/Sort from the Records menu. The form indicates all records in the table are available again. Close the form, *frmCustomer*. If a Save dialog box appears, click the No to All button.

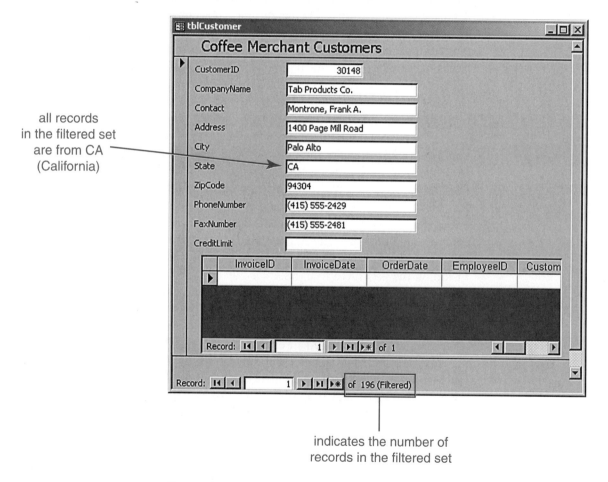

all records in the filtered set are from CA (California)

indicates the number of records in the filtered set

Figure 5.9   Filter By Form example.

Filter By Selection works in almost the same way as Filter By Form. You select a field, such as City, which has an entry by which you would like to filter and then choose Filter By Selection from the Records menu. Access displays only records whose fields match that of the selected field.

Display in Form view the form *frmCustomer*. Move to the first customer in the Customer table, Fairfield Communities Inc. Click the City form field and drag the cursor across the entire city name to select it. Let's see how many other customers we have in the selected city of Little Rock. Click the Records menu, point to Filter, and click Filter By Selection. Access indicates that currently there are six customers in Little Rock. Click Records in the menu bar and then click Remove Filter/Sort. The form indicates all (1,789) records in the table are available again. Close the *frmCustomer* form.

You can do more with Filter By Form and Filter By Selection. However, you will have to discover those details on your own. We have a lot more to cover on other topics, so we'll move on.

Creating a Multitable Form and Subform

Many forms display data from more than one table. The Coffee Merchant's Order form is an example of a multitable form, because data such as the order number, order date, and sales representative number are stored in a table called *tblOrder*. Details about the items ordered (item ID and quantity ordered) are stored in another table called *tblOrderLine*. The Inventory table, *tblInventory*, is also referenced by The Coffee Merchant's Order form, although no new inventory items can be entered via the form. Finally, the *tblCustomer* table is consulted to locate and display customer numbers in the Customer field. Four tables are joined and referenced by The Coffee Merchant's Order form.

Although using The Coffee Merchant's Order form is an informative exercise, you will benefit much more from *building* a form from scratch. Once you create a form, it is only a short time until you will be designing elaborate forms for your own applications. Figure 5.10 shows you an example of a multitable invoice review and data entry form that displays data from several of The Coffee Merchant's tables. That form has the look of the finished form we are striving for in this section. When finished, your form should start to resemble the one in Figure 5.10.

The invoice form that you will build in this section is actually two forms: a main form and a subform. The main form displays one record from the *tblInvoice* table. Simultaneously, the subform displays several related records that are line items in the invoice. Information on the subform includes item number, item name, quantity ordered, unit price, discount, and extended price. Subform information is synthesized by a query supplied on your CD-ROM called *qryInvoiceLineItem*.

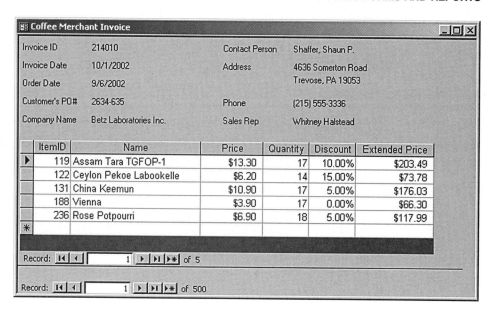

Figure 5.10   Example invoice review and data entry form.

Creating a Form Containing a Subform

Access allows you to create forms and reports that use data found in more than one table or query. The best way to create a main form and its subform is to use a Form Wizard. The following exercise outlines how to create an invoice form. Prepare for the next exercise by closing all open windows except the Database.

EXERCISE 5.4: CREATING AN INVOICE FORM AND SUBFORM

1. Click Forms in the Objects bar, and then click the New button on the Forms collection of the Database window. Access displays the New Form dialog box.
2. Select Form Wizard from the list of form choices, click the list box arrow in the lower portion of the window, and select **qryInvoiceMain** from the list. (When creating forms with subforms, it is usually best to use the Form Wizard.) You base the top half of the form on the table or query that contains the data to appear on the main form (the data on the "one" side of the one-to-many relationship). In this case the main form will contain customer invoice information. The subform will contain invoice detail lines with products, quantities, prices, etc.
3. Click the OK button to begin the form-building process. The first of several Form Wizard dialog boxes appears.
4. Click the >> button to move all fields on the Available Fields list entries onto the Selected Fields list. The latter list contains the fields that Access will display on the completed form.

5. Click the drop-down list arrow beneath the Tables/Queries list box to display the queries and tables in the database, allowing you to add subform fields to the form.

6. Locate *qryInvoiceLineItem* in the list and click it. The query-supplied fields appear in the Available Fields list (see Figure 5.11).

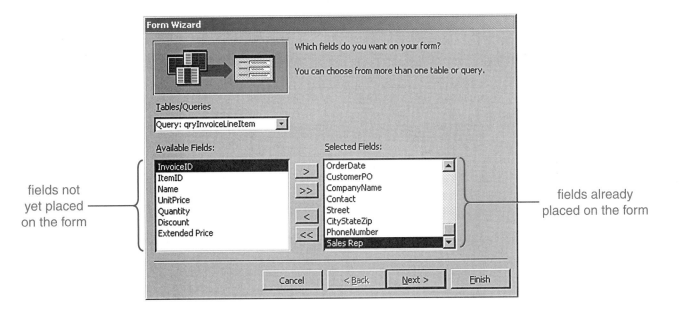

fields not yet placed on the form

fields already placed on the form

Figure 5.11   Selecting main form and subform fields.

7. Click the >> button to move all the subform fields onto the Selected Fields list.

8. In the Selected Fields list, locate and select the field called *qryInvoiceLineItem.InvoiceID*.

9. Click the "<" button to remove the extra InvoiceID field, moving it from the Selected Fields list back onto the Available Fields list. (Alternatively, you could select each field in turn, clicking the ">" button to place each onto the Selected Fields list. The way that we suggest here is faster.)

10. Click the Next button to proceed to the next step.

11. When the dialog box appears asking you how you want to view your data, click the Next button to accept the suggested default.

12. Select the suggested Datasheet layout for your subform by clicking the Datasheet option button. Click Next to go to the next step.

13. Select the suggested "Standard" style (near the bottom of the list) and click the Next button. Be careful on the last Form Wizard dialog box: change the form and subform names by altering them in the text boxes. If you do not do it here, it is more difficult to do later.

14. In the Form text box type **frmInvoice2** and in the Subform text box type **fsubInvoice2**. (Be sure to enter the prefix *fsub* for the subform. This prefix indicates a form is a subform and is the accepted standard for naming subforms.)

15. Click the "Open the form to view or enter information" option button, if it is not already selected.
16. Click the Finish button to conclude the form-building process.

Access takes a few moments to build both the form and subform and then opens it for your use (see Figure 5.12). Scroll through the records to experience how the form works. Occasionally, you may want to scroll through the subform to display all the invoice items for a particular invoice. Keep in mind that the outermost set of navigation buttons pages through whole invoices, while the inner set skips from line to line on invoice details in the subform.

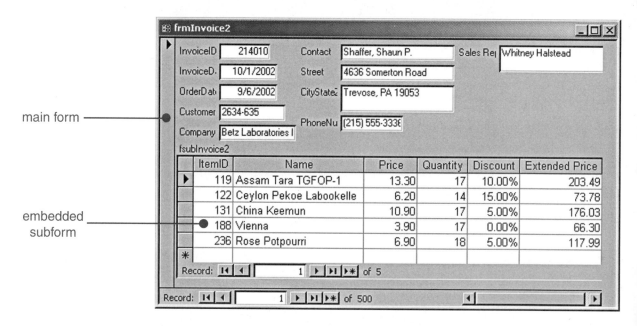

Figure 5.12   Main form and embedded subform created by the Form Wizard.

Modifying a Subform's Column Widths and Labels

Some of the subform's fields are not sufficiently wide. Consequently, some fields are completely visible while others are not. For example, notice in Figure 5.12 that the Extended Price column, which is the rightmost field of the subform, is not visible. Similarly, the UnitPrice column seems far too wide. Let's modify the widths of some subform columns so that they are just large enough to display their information but not too large. Then, we will change the subform column label from *UnitPrice* to *Price*. The next exercise shows you how to accomplish these tasks.

Prepare for this exercise by closing all windows except the Database window. Notice *frmInvoice2* and *fsubInvoice2* are among the list of forms.

EXERCISE 5.5: MODIFYING A SUBFORM'S COLUMN WIDTHS AND LABELS

1. Click Forms on the Database window Objects bar to display the list of forms in your database.
2. Double-click the subform *fsubInvoice2* to open it. If necessary, select Datasheet View from the View menu so the information is displayed as a datasheet, not a form.
3. Alter all the columns to an optimal width: move the mouse to the leftmost column label, ItemID. When the mouse turns to a down-pointing arrow, drag it to the right until all columns are selected. (Selected columns are displayed in black.) Release the mouse button.
4. Move the mouse to any border between two columns in the label area or move it to the rightmost border of the rightmost label. When the mouse pointer changes to a double-headed arrow with a vertical line dissecting it, double-click the mouse. All columns change size, adjusting to the smallest width that is wide enough to display the largest values or column labels.
5. Click any datasheet cell to deselect the columns. Now the columns display the widest values in the column without truncating them. If you wish to further customize individual column widths, you can do so by dragging the line to the right of a column's label when the mouse pointer is a double-headed arrow. Dragging the right column line to the right widens the column; dragging to the left narrows the column.
6. Click Design View from the View menu to display the form in Design view.
7. Double-click the UnitPrice label (not the UnitPrice text box) field in the Detail section of the form to display its property sheet. The UnitPrice label is located to the left of the UnitPrice text box on the form. (If you find this difficult— double-click timing is everything—then right-click the field and select Properties from the pop-up list.)
8. Click the property sheet tab labeled *Format*, double-click the value displayed in the Caption property, and type **Price** to replace the UnitPrice Caption.
9. Click the property sheet Close button.
10. Close the *fsubInvoice2* subform (click the form's Close button) and click Yes when asked if you want to save the changed design.

What you have learned here is that to resize subform fields displayed as a datasheet, simply resize the table fields. This automatically causes the fields to be displayed in their new widths in any subforms constructed from the changed tables.

You will do additional work on this form, but it is always a good idea to preserve the partially complete work. This way, you don't risk losing a large amount of work if something should happen to the power to your computer.

There are several controls on the forms with which you are working. *Controls* are all the objects that appear on forms or reports. For example, the label *InvoiceID* is a control as is the field displaying the value 214010 in the InvoiceID field. There are three general types of controls in Access: bound controls, unbound controls, and calculated controls. A *bound control* has as its data source a field in a table. The invoice date field in Figure 5.12 is a bound control. An *unbound control* has no data source and is used to display a title or label on forms and reports. It does not change from one record to the next. The invoice date label (*InvoiceDate*) in Figure 5.12 is an example of an unbound label. A *calculated control* has as its data source an expression rather than a table field. The Extended Price field is an example of a calculated control. Access database users and developers use the term *control* frequently when referring to objects on forms or reports.

Altering a Subform's Column Widths

When you want to alter an item's property such as its display format, you open the item's property sheet and make the necessary changes. You use the property sheet to set, view, or change the properties of a table, query, form, report, or controls on forms and reports. Available in the Design view of a Table, Query, Form, or Report window, the property sheet is displayed whenever you click the Properties button on the toolbar. It remains on the work surface, even when you select other controls or objects, until you close it. You can also display the property sheet for a selected object by right-clicking the mouse and then choosing Properties from the pop-up menu.

The next exercise illustrates how to change the display properties of two numeric values found in *fsubInvoice2*. Currently, the Price and Extended Price columns display their values in currency format. This may not be desirable in some situations. Let's change the display format for the columns to eliminate the currency symbols.

EXERCISE 5.6: CHANGING A COLUMN'S DISPLAY CHARACTERISTICS

1. Open the subform, *fsubInvoice2*, in Design view. Then, select both the UnitPrice and Extended Price controls (*not* their labels) in the Detail section by holding down the Shift key and then clicking each one. (Be careful not to *move* the controls as you click them. If you accidentally do move them, then simply click Undo in the Edit menu.)
2. Click the Properties button on the toolbar. The property sheet appears with the Title bar displaying *Multiple selection*, which indicates more than one object will be affected.
3. Click the Format tab. The group of properties associated with the way data appears when displayed are called Format properties.
4. Click the Format property text box, click its list box arrow, and locate and then click Standard (see Figure 5.13). (You will have to scroll down the Format list to locate Standard.)
5. Close the property sheet.
6. Close and save the subform (click the subform's Close button and click the Yes button to save the changed subform).

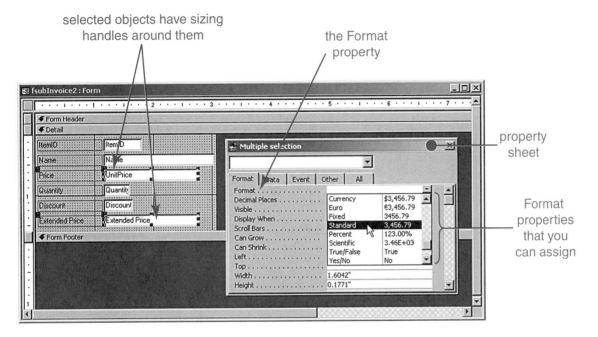

Figure 5.13 Changing objects' properties.

If you want to verify the property changes you have just made, then simply open the form in Form view. Observe that currency symbols no longer appear in either the Price or the Extended Price fields. Figure 5.14 shows the altered invoice form and subform.

Rearranging Form Fields

You can easily rearrange controls on a form by selecting them and then dragging them to a new location. For example, you can move the CompanyName control closer to the customer's address controls on the right side of the form. You move controls by displaying the form or subform in Design view. Then, after you click the bound control, you can move the mouse over the selected control. When the mouse pointer changes to a small hand, click and drag the bound control and its attached unbound control (its label) to a new location. If you want to move a group of controls, simply Shift-click each of them and then move them as a group. To deselect controls, simply click outside the selected control or group of controls.

If a subform's data is not fully visible because the form is not wide enough (a likely case), click the View button and select Design View, click the subform frame to select it, and drag the right border handle to the right to widen the entire frame. (You may have to switch back and forth between Design view and Form view until you have adjusted the subform frame to your satisfaction.) Though your

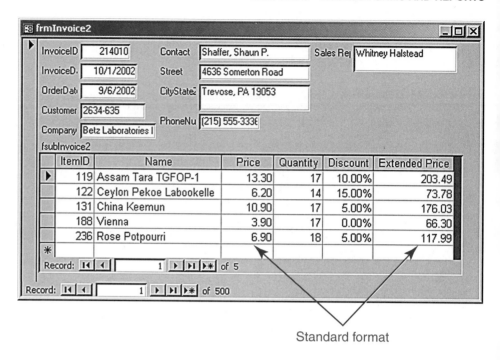

Figure 5.14   Altered invoice subform and form.

form does not exactly match our Invoice form, it is very close. Only a few embellishments remain to make them identical. You can do that on your own, if you want to practice the techniques.

Printing a Form

Usually, you do not print forms to produce printed output. However, printing one page of a form is a good way to keep track of all the forms you have developed for any accounting system. Printing a form is probably the easiest task of all. First, select and open in Form view the form you want to print from the list on the Forms sheet of the Database window. Optionally, you can use the form navigation buttons to display a particular record, or you can simply print the first record displayed. In either case, select Print from the File menu. When the Print dialog box opens, click the "Selected Record(s)" option button so that Access prints only one form (see Figure 5.15). Click OK to start the print process. If your form is wider than can be accommodated by the current print setup, you will receive a warning similar to the one shown in Figure 5.16. In that case, click the Cancel button to close the warning dialog box and click Page Setup in the File menu. Next, click the Page tab and click the Landscape option button. That should fix the print problem.

You can print properties, permissions, and design information for database objects, including your forms' designs. Printing the design characteristics of your database objects helps you document your database's design and the accounting

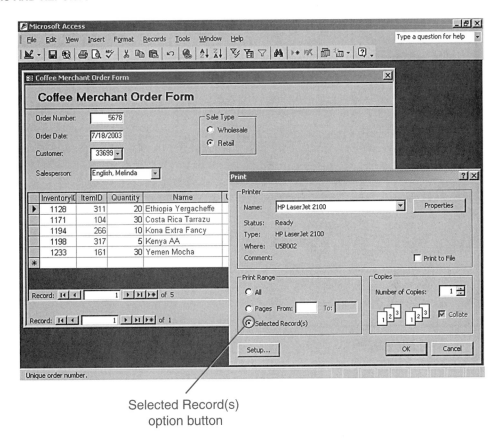

Figure 5.15   Printing a single form.

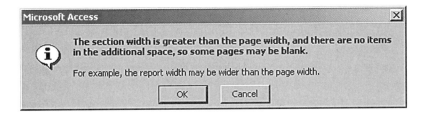

Figure 5.16   Print width warning dialog box.

application you develop. Click Tools on the menu bar, point to Analyze, and then click Documentor. Then, check the objects for which you want printed definition information. Click OK and Access will create the report and display it in the Object Definition window. If you decide to print the report, simply click the Print button on the toolbar. If not, click the Close button on the toolbar to discard the report and return to the Database window.

Try It

Close all windows except the Database window. Click Tools, point to Analyze, and then click Documentor. Click the Forms tab of the Documentor dialog box, and click the check box to the left of the form *frmInvoice2*. Click OK. Access takes a second or two to construct a report and display it in the Object Definition window. Examine the report. Click the Zoom button on the toolbar and click inside the Object Definition window to alternately zoom in and then zoom out. Close the Object Definition window after you are done and close the *Ch05.mdb* database. Take a break if you wish.

When you want to see a comprehensive list of information from one or more tables, then printing forms is not adequate. Instead, you need a report. Reports and how to produce them are described next.

BUILDING AND PRINTING REPORTS

Reports provide the mechanism to produce high-quality printed database information. While you can use a form for viewing or altering information in the database, you cannot enter or alter information in a report. Reports are strictly for output. Like forms, reports are based on information found in tables or supplied by queries. Unlike forms, reports allow you to group information from one table. With forms, you must join two or more tables to group information by using a form/subform combination.

Using Reports

Reports are used in accounting database applications to provide hard copy output that compares, summarizes, and subtotals data found in customer and billing data. An Access report can produce printed shipping labels, purchase orders, bill of materials lists, or invoices that mimic paper-only forms used by businesses. Producing mailing labels from database customer records using Access reports can save money for larger mailings because Access can presort the information into zip code order prior to producing a report. When you group mail by zip code, the U.S. Postal Service provides lower postage rates.

Using Report Wizards

Microsoft Access provides two ways to create reports. You can create a report from scratch, starting with a blank form, or you can use a Report Wizard. You will probably prefer using Report Wizards because the process is easier and faster than creating reports from scratch.

Report Wizards offer several styles of reports, including Columnar AutoReport, Tabular AutoReport, Chart Wizard, and Labels Wizard. The

AutoReport Wizards create preformatted, single-column (Columnar) or multi-column (Tabular) reports with very little involvement from you.

You invoke a Report Wizard from the Database window after clicking Reports on the Objects bar and then clicking the New button on the Reports page. Of course, reports get their data from tables or queries. So, you must designate the table or query that produces the data that is placed in the report. Next, you select one of the report types, such as Report Wizard, from the list displayed in the New Report dialog box. Once you click OK, an Access Wizard guides you through the process of creating a report—step by step. Simply follow the Report Wizard's dialog boxes and respond to its questions. When you click the Finish button in the last step of the Wizard-guided report creation process, Access quickly builds an attractive report that it displays in the Print Preview window.

Examining a Report's Structure

The Report window has three views: Design, Print Preview, and Layout Preview. You change the layout and design of a report in Design view. You use Print Preview to check all the data and its appearance in the report. You review the general layout and appearance of a report in Layout Preview. Design view is where you will spend most of your time, because you create and modify report layouts in that view.

An Access report is divided into *sections*, which appear at prescribed locations on the report. There are seven different types of sections, but a report does not have to include all seven sections. Each section appears once in Design view. When you print a report, some sections are repeated as needed. Figure 5.17 shows an example of a report's design with several of the seven sections.

The Detail section is required in each report. However, all the other sections are optional; thus, you can omit them. Beginning at the very top of the report is the Report Header section. It is printed once at the beginning of the report. The Page Header's contents are printed at the top of every page. The Group Header's contents are printed every time the grouping field value changes. Contents of the Detail section are printed for each record selected from the underlying table(s) or queries. The Group Footer prints at the end of each group. The Page Footer prints at the bottom of each page. The Report Footer prints on a page at the end of the report.

Creating a Tabular-Style Report with a Report Wizard

In many ways, creating a report resembles creating a form. You design a report, including its field layouts, headings, and other details, in the report Design view window. When you want to see the report replete with data, you click the Print Preview button on the toolbar. We introduce report creation by showing you how to build and print a tabular-style, one-table report.

Let's experiment with the Employee table. It is a good one to start with. Suppose you want a printed list of employee names and other information sorted by the employees' last names. All the requisite information is found in one table,

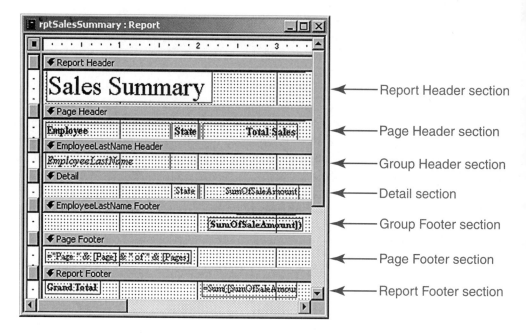

Report Header section

Page Header section

Group Header section

Detail section

Group Footer section

Page Footer section

Report Footer section

Figure 5.17   Report sections.

tblEmployee. Follow the steps in the next exercise to create a report with the help of the Access Report Wizard. As usual, prepare by clearing the work surface: open *Ch05.mdb*, and close all Access windows except the Database window.

EXERCISE 5.7: CREATING A REPORT

1. Click Reports in the Database window Objects bar and then click the New button.
2. Click Report Wizard, which is found in the upper panel of the New Report dialog box.
3. Click the list box arrow to display all the database's tables and queries, click *tblEmployee* in the list of tables and queries, and click OK to start the Report Wizard. A new dialog box is displayed in which you choose which fields will appear on the report.
4. From the Available Fields list, double-click the following fields, one at a time, to move them onto the Selected Fields list: EmployeeID, EmployeeLastName, EmployeeHireDate, EmployeeDOB, and EmployeeGender (see Figure 5.18). Click the Next button when you have entered all the preceding fields. (You can also select a field and press the ">" button to move a field onto the Selected Fields list, but it is faster to double-click field names.)
5. The Report Wizard displays several more dialog boxes. The next one asks if you want to create a grouping level. Because you do not want to for this report, click Next without making any changes.

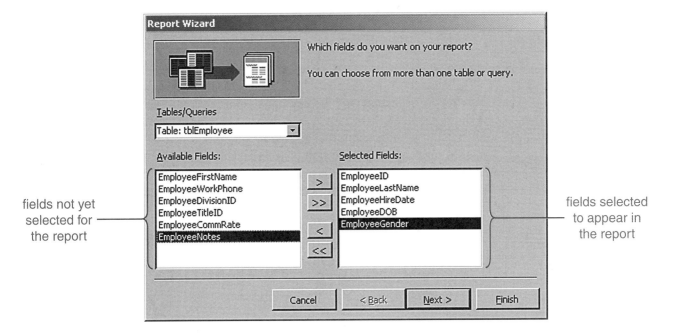

Figure 5.18 Selecting fields for a report.

6. The next dialog box asks if you want to sort the report records. Because we want the report to display the employee information in name order, click the list box arrow next to the first sort box and select *EmployeeLastName* from the list of report fields. Click the Next button to proceed.

   Note: If you discover you have made a mistake on an earlier Report Wizard dialog box, you can simply click the Back button repeatedly until you reach the dialog box containing the mistake. Make any changes and then click the Next button to return to where you left off.

7. Ensure that the Tabular option (in the Layout option group) and the Portrait option (in the Orientation option group) are selected. Also ensure that the "Adjust the field width so all fields fit on a page" check box is checked. Click the Next button.

8. Select the Formal report style and press the Next button.

9. Type **Coffee Merchant Employees** in the text box. Click the Finish button to finalize your choices and generate your report.

10. After reviewing the report preview, click the Design View button on the toolbar to view the report's design. Finally, click the Design View Close button to close and save the report.

    Note: The report title that you entered in step 9 is also used to name the report. That is not a good feature of Access reports. You should rename the report *rptMyEmployee* immediately after you save it. To rename a report, select the report from the list of reports, press F2, type **rptMyEmployee**, and press

Enter. You can rename any object that way. We have saved this report as *rptEmployee* on your Companion CD.

Access creates the report and displays it in Print Preview (see Figure 5.19). The report lists employee records in name order. Did you notice that some report column labels such as *Last Name*, *Hire Date*, and *Birth Date* are different from their table column names? The reason for this is that we included less cryptic names for them in the Caption property of the table design when we created the *tblEmployee table*. (To verify this, examine the Employee table in Design view and pay particular attention to the Caption property as you select field names in the upper portion of the Design view.) Print the report, if you wish, by selecting Print from the File menu.

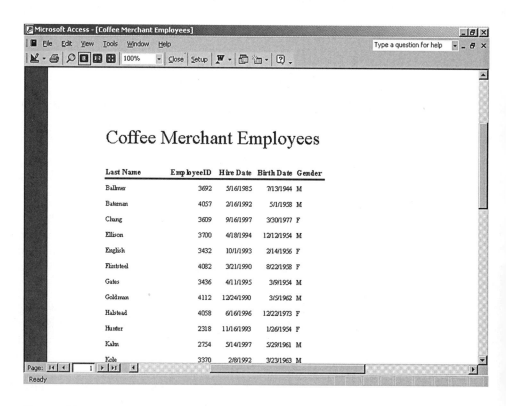

Figure 5.19   Print Preview window showing a tabular-style report.

Modifying a Report Field's Data Alignment

You can enhance the appearance of a control's data or label by adjusting its alignment (its Text Align property). Some of the data columns in the Employee report do not line up well with their column labels. For example, the column label

EmployeeID is far to the left of the actual identification number column values. Similarly, the Gender data values appear misaligned when compared to their column label. You can alter the *alignment* of labels (unbound controls) or data (bound controls) to achieve the effect you want. Briefly, we will illustrate how to alter the data alignment in the next exercise. Follow the steps in the next exercise to alter the data alignment of several report column data controls.

EXERCISE 5.8: ALTERING REPORT CONTROLS' DATA ALIGNMENT

1. Display your newly minted Employee report, *rptMyEmployee*, in Design view.
2. Move the cursor to the Detail section and select the EmployeeID and EmployeeGender bound controls: hold down the Shift key and click each one in turn. Be careful not to *move* the controls when you select them. (It is very easy to do that.)
3. Select Properties from the View menu (or click the Properties button found on the toolbar) to display the property sheet.
4. Click the Format tab to reveal that collection of format-related properties.
5. Scroll the property list until near its bottom, click the Text Align property text box, and click the Text Align list box arrow to reveal the alignment choices.
6. Select Center from the five alignment choices (see Figure 5.20).
7. Close the property sheet, click File in the menu bar, and click Save to save your design changes.
8. Click the Design window Close button.

Deleting Controls and Report Sections

Because the *rptMyEmployee* report is short, there is no need for a Page Footer section. Currently, the Page Footer section contains a single control that displays the current page number, which is unnecessary in a one-page report. Deleting a report section—the Page Footer section in this case—is straightforward, so we will skip a formal exercise and simply describe the steps in the following Try It paragraph. Before eliminating the Page Footer section, you must first remove all its controls. There are three controls in the Page Footer section: two calculated controls and an unbound control.

Try It

Display *rptMyEmployee* in Design view. Using the horizontal scroll bar, move to the left edge of the report and locate the control in the Page Footer section containing the Access function =Now( ). Click it (handles appear around it when it is selected) and press the Delete key to remove it. In a similar way, remove the second control that resides in the Page Footer. Move to the right edge of the report

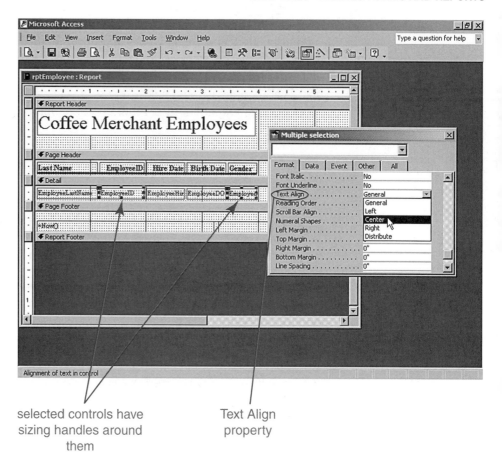

selected controls have
sizing handles around
them

Text Align
property

Figure 5.20 Altering the alignment property of multiple controls.

and locate the Page Footer control containing the expression =*"Page " & [Page] & " of " & [Pages]*. Select the control—a rather long expression—and press Delete to remove it. Finally, select the thin line (the unbound control) that appears near the top of the Page Footer section. Press Delete to remove it. Once all controls in a section are gone, you remove the section by dragging up the bar below the section. That is, you move the mouse to the *bottom* of the Page Footer section until it turns into a double-headed arrow pointing up and down, dissected by a small horizontal line. Then drag the arrow up until the Page Footer section is eliminated. Release the mouse button. Click Save in the File menu to save the altered report. Close the Design view window after you save the report.

In the step you executed above prior to saving the report, you reduced the height of the Page Footer section to zero. That removes it. Removing *both* the

Page Header section and the Page Footer section is even simpler. Simply click Page Header/Footer in the View menu to remove the checkmark to its left. The two sections are removed simultaneously, and any controls in both are removed automatically.

Saving and Printing a Report

You should save any reports that you anticipate running periodically. On the other hand, you need not save any reports that are used only once. You can save a report in Design view or Print Preview: select Save from the File menu. For new reports, you must supply a name before Access will save the report definition in the database.

Reports exist to be printed, so let's print this report. You can print a report from either the Design view window or the Print Preview window. Before actually printing a report, you may want to check and alter some global report settings such as margin settings, page orientation (portrait or landscape), or paper size. You alter any of those settings by clicking the Setup button in the Print dialog box or by clicking Page Setup in the File menu. You should print the report *rptMyEmployee* so you have a copy of its final form. We will not be using this report further, so you can either save it or delete it from the database.

Is it possible to produce a report similar to *rptEmployee* or *rptMyEmployee* but sort the rows into order by division location and by employee names within each division? The answer is yes—by using the Report Wizard to form report groups. You learn how to do this next.

Producing a Grouped Data Report

You learned that either tables or queries can be the basis of any forms you create. The same is true for reports. When you base a report on a query, you can alter the query's selection criteria, save the query, run another report, and produce different report results. For example, we could create a query that selects invoices that are 30 days past due, base a report on that query, and then run and print the report. Printing a list of invoices that are 31 to 60 days past due would then be easy. Simply modify the existing query to select rows whose invoice date is 31 to 60 days ago, save the modified query, and rerun the report. Alternatively, you could create a parameter query that prompts you for the value of "days past due" and run the report after the query processes your input.

Building a report that lists employees and their division locations involves information from at least two tables: *tblEmployee* and *tblDivisionLocation*. There are two general approaches to producing the report. One way is to first create a query that joins the two tables and then create a report based on the query. The other way is to create a report, with the help of a Report Wizard, by including all the tables involved and let the Report Wizard join the tables. The latter approach produces a report through the use of a "behind the report" query. A *behind the report* query is one that is stored inside the report's definition and is not available for general use in the Queries collection. When you create a specialized report whose query will not have widespread use, the latter report method is preferable. That's what we will illustrate here. In preparation for the next exercise, close all windows in *Ch05.mdb* except the Database window.

EXERCISE 5.9: CREATING A GROUPED DATA REPORT WITH A REPORT WIZARD

1. Click Reports on the Database window Objects bar, click the New button on the Database window toolbar, and click Report Wizard in the upper panel of the New Report dialog box.
2. Click the list box arrow to display all the database's tables and queries, click *tblEmployee* in the list of tables and queries, and click OK to start the Report Wizard. A new dialog box is displayed in which you choose which fields will appear on the report.
3. From the Available Fields list, double-click the following fields, one at a time, to move them onto the Selected Fields list: EmployeeLastName, EmployeeID, EmployeeHireDate, EmployeeDOB, and EmployeeGender.
4. Click the Tables/Queries list box arrow to display the database's tables and queries once again, and then click the entry Table: *tblDivisionLocation*. You may have to use the scroll bar to locate the table, which is just above the entry *tblEmployee* in the drop-down list.
5. From the Available Fields list, double-click DivisionCity and then click the Next button to move to the next step in the report-building process.
6. The Report Wizard asks how you want to view your data. Click the choice *by tblDivisionLocation* listed in the left panel. That causes Access to group the report's rows by city (see Figure 5.21). Click the Next button to move to the next step.
7. The dialog box requests whether or not you want additional grouping levels. Because you do not, click the Next button to move to the next step.
8. The next dialog box asks if you want to sort the detail records. Click the list box arrow next to the first sort box and select EmployeeLastName from the list of report fields. Click the Next button to proceed.
9. Ensure that the Stepped option (in the Layout option group) and the Portrait option (in the Orientation option group) are selected. Also ensure that the "Adjust the field width so all fields fit on a page" check box is checked. Click the Next button.
10. Select the Formal report style and press the Next button.
11. Type **Employees by Location** in the text box. Click the Finish button to finalize your choices and generate a preview of your report.
12. After reviewing the report preview, click the Design View button on the toolbar (*not* the Close window button) to view the report's design. Finally, click the Design View Close button to close and save the report.

Remember that the report is saved under the name you typed for the report title—a nonconforming database object name. Be sure to rename the report

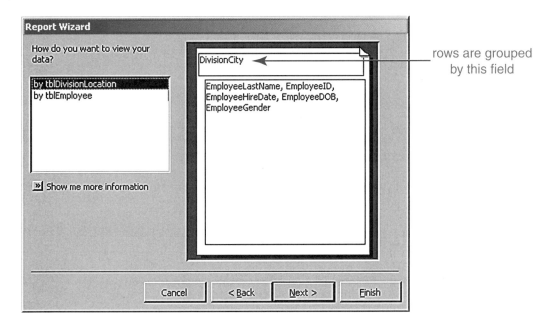

Figure 5.21   Selecting a grouping field.

rptEmpLoc. For your convenience, we have placed the report on your Companion CD. It is called *rptEmployeesByLocation.* Examine that report, or print it if you wish.

A *Group Footer* is displayed just after the grouping element, the employee's city in our example, changes. Currently, our report does not have a Group Footer because the report contains no numeric fields whose sums or averages need to be displayed after a complete group is printed. Let's add a Group Footer to see how it's done.

Try It

Open the *rptEmployeesByLocation* report in Design view (drag the window's borders to widen and lengthen the report if necessary), and then select Sorting and Grouping from the View menu. When the Sorting and Grouping dialog box appears, click under the heading Field/Expression in the DivisionID row, and then click the list box arrow to the right of the DivisionID row. Click DivisionCity from the drop-down list. (This will group and sort entries by city name rather than city identification number.) Click the row selector to the left of the entry DivisionCity to select it. Then, double-click the Group Footer list box located below in the Group Properties panel. This will change the value from "No" to "Yes," which means that a Group Footer will appear in the report (see Figure 5.22). Close the Sorting and Grouping dialog box. Notice the new Group Footer section in the report.

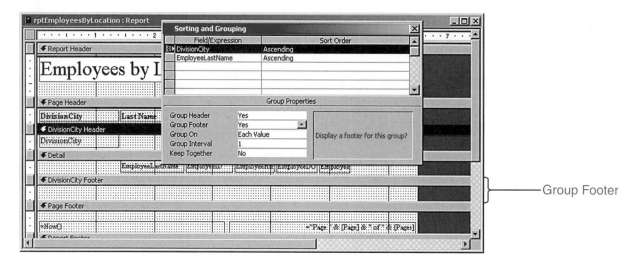

Figure 5.22   Inserting a Group Footer into a report.

When you place a *page break* in a report, it causes the printer to skip to the top of a new page. You can place a page break in any section of a report. For instance, you can place a page break in the Group Footer section. That way, Access prints each city and the employees located in it on a separate page.

Try It

Place a page break in the *rptEmployeesByLocation* report so that each group prints on a new page. First, display *rptEmployeesByLocation* in Design view. To insert a page break, display the toolbox (click the Toolbox toolbar button if needed), click the Page Break button, and move the mouse to the left side of the report within the Group Footer section. Click the mouse to drop the page break into the report's Page Footer section (see Figure 5.23). Close the toolbox. Save the report again and print the first two pages to examine the changes you made to the report. Close the report but leave the Database window open. We are done changing the design of the *rptEmployeesByLocation* report.

Building Reports with Queries and Expressions

Next, we will design a report that produces invoices. You will participate in building the invoice report, and we will help. We merely outline some of the easier procedures, however. You are familiar with all of the steps needed to build the Invoice report except for a few. We will explain these carefully in individual exercise steps. We begin with the query—one that you have not seen before—that joins six tables to assemble all the fields we need for an industrial strength invoice.

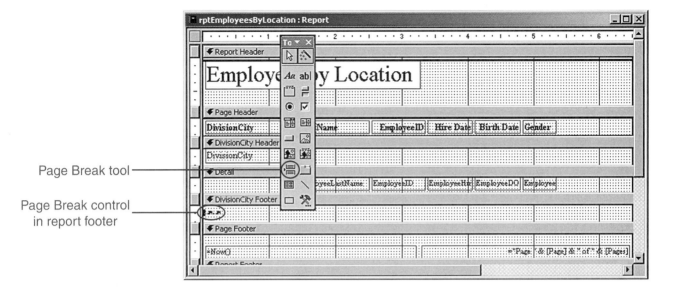

Page Break tool

Page Break control
in report footer

Figure 5.23   Report design containing a Page Break control.

Figure 5.24 shows the query that will produce the fields needed for each invoice. The QBE grid columns are narrow so that you can see several of the Field row entries, though most fields are out of view. Before continuing, please open the query, which is the foundation of our Invoice report, and study it briefly. The query is saved on your Companion CD as *qryInvoiceReport*. Observe how the tables are joined.

The *tblCustomer* and *tblInvoice* tables are joined on the column CustomerID. The table *tblInvoice* is joined to the table *tblInvoiceLine* on the column InvoiceID found in both tables. Other joined tables are *tblInvoice* to *tblEmployee* on the column EmployeeID, *tblInvoiceLine* to *tblInventory* on the column InventoryID, and *tblInventory* to *tblInventoryDescription* on the key column ItemID. Thus, the six tables are joined by five sets of primary key to foreign key pairs. Figure 5.25 shows a typical invoice that we would like to produce with Microsoft Access. The report produces one customer invoice per page and is ready to be mailed to customers.

Begin by generating the initial report using the Access Report Wizard. However, before you proceed, examine this brief list of the steps needed to create the Invoice report from the *qryInvoiceReport* query:

- Use the Report Wizard, which will automatically group data on the InvoiceID value, to produce the initial report with data supplied solely from the query *qryInvoiceReport*.

- Move selected report fields from the Page Header into the InvoiceID Group Header.

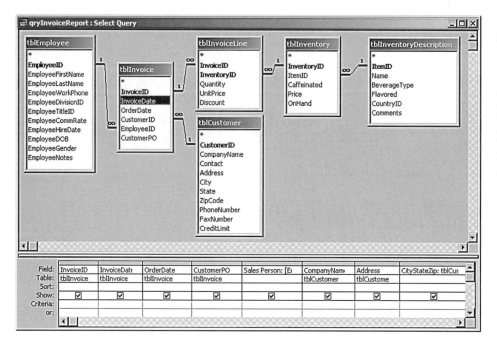

Figure 5.24 Query to select fields for an invoice report.

- Move selected report fields from the Report Header into the Page Header.

- Delete the Report Header, Report Footer, and Page Footer sections.

- Create expressions in the InvoiceID Footer that calculate the invoice subtotal, sales tax (if any), shipping, and invoice total amounts for each invoice.

- Add miscellaneous graphics and other labels as needed to embellish the invoice.

Creating the Report's First Draft

It is almost always best to create the first draft of a report with the Report Wizard. Creating a report with no help is difficult work, and the Report Wizard is sophisticated and resourceful. The Wizard determines that we need a report with groups because the data is produced from a query whose tables are joined in a chain of several one-to-many relationships. That's just what we want. In particular, we want all the invoice detail lines—the item name, quantity, price, discount, and total price—in any given invoice grouped by invoice number.

Let's begin building the first version of the Invoice report. Ensure that the database *Ch05.mdb* is open. Then follow the steps in the following exercise to create the initial draft of the Invoice report.

Invoice

Invoice Number: 214010
Invoice Date: 10/1/2002
Order Date: 9/6/2002
Customer PO #: 2634-635
Sales Person: Whitney Halstead

The Coffee Merchant
5998 Alcala Park
San Diego, CA 92110

Sold to:

Betz Laboratories Inc.
4636 Somerton Road
Trevose, PA 19053

Item #	Qty	Description	Price	Discount	Extended
119	17	Assam Tara TGFOP-1	$13.30	10%	203.49
122	14	Ceylon Pekoe Labookelle	$6.20	15%	73.78
131	17	China Keemun	$10.90	5%	176.03
188	17	Vienna	$3.90	0%	66.30
236	18	Rose Potpourri	$6.90	5%	117.99

Subtotal:	$637.59
Sales Tax:	0.00
Shipping:	20.75
Invoice Total:	$658.34

Figure 5.25   First page of the invoice report.

EXERCISE 5.10: USING THE REPORT WIZARD

1. Click Reports in the Database window Objects bar, click the New button on the Database window, select Report Wizard, and click the drop-down arrow on the list box to display the names of tables and queries in your database. Click *qryInvoiceReport*, and then click OK.

2. Make these choices (and click the Next button as needed) as you go through the remaining Report Wizard steps:
   • Select all available fields from the query to appear on the report.
   • Choose to view data with the "by tblInvoice" group.
   • Select no other grouping levels.
   • Sort your records in ascending order by the ItemID field. On the sort field step, click the Summary Options button and check the box under the Sum column of the Extended row to sum that field for both detailed and summary fields (see Figure 5.26). Click OK to confirm your choices.
   • Accept the Stepped report layout in Portrait orientation.
   • Select the Formal report style.
   • Type the report title **Invoice** in the text box on the last dialog box.

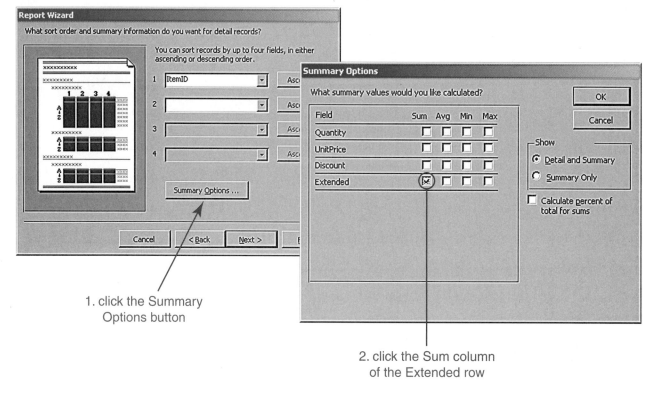

1. click the Summary
Options button

2. click the Sum column
of the Extended row

Figure 5.26   Report Wizard Summary Options choices.

3. After reviewing the draft report, close it and its Design window.
4. Rename the report by selecting Invoice from the list of reports, pressing F2, and typing **rptInvoiceCut1**. This name allows you to keep each successive, improved version so you can compare and contrast them.
5. Reopen the **rptInvoiceCut1** report in Design view.

Figure 5.27 shows the initial report in Design view. Notice that we have removed the rulers and grid lines. While viewing a report in Design view, you can remove the rulers or the grid lines by clicking Ruler or Grid in the View menu. The check mark beside the Ruler choice or the Grid choice is removed, indicating they won't display. These items are toggle commands: select either one again to reestablish them.

Rearranging and Deleting Report Fields

The next step is to move selected text fields from the Page Header section to the InvoiceID Header section. Follow the discussion as we outline how to rearrange fields. All the fields in the Page Header will be either moved or eliminated. First,

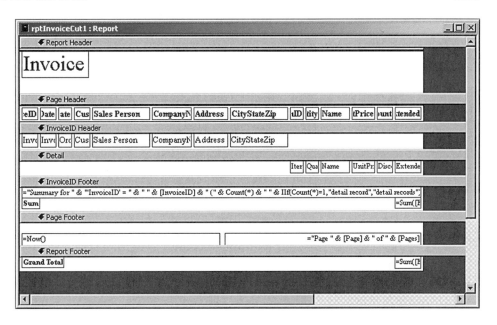

Figure 5.27   Initial Invoice report layout.

we must make room in the InvoiceID Header section. Drag the bottom of the InvoiceID Header section—just above the Detail bar—down until the InvoiceID Header section is about two inches tall. Then, select all fields in the Page Header section (they are all labels). Remember that you first press and hold the Shift key and then click each field in turn to select all of them. (Be careful not to accidentally move them as you click.) Drag the selected fields down into the InvoiceID Header area and release the mouse. Click anywhere to deselect the items. In the Page Header, delete the two horizontal lines (select each and press Delete). Move the large label *Invoice* and its attendant horizontal line from the Report Header section to the Page Header section.

Move the ItemID, Quantity, Name, UnitPrice, Discount, and Extended text labels down so that they are just above the bar labeled Detail and about one inch in from the left edge of the report border. With those six controls still selected, move the pointer to the right side of any one object and double-click its side handle to enlarge all labels so that their full names are visible. (Label controls are bold, whereas you notice that bound controls displaying field values are not bold.) In a similar way, select the Detail section bound controls and spread them out from one another a bit. With all Detail section controls selected, drag any one of the bound controls' right selection handles to enlarge all selected controls. Delete the labels *CompanyName*, *Address*, and *CityStateZip*. Be careful to not delete the bound controls of the same name! They contain the actual customer information.

Continue to rearrange bound and unbound controls. Do not worry when the labels and associated bound controls do not line up horizontally or vertically. You can fix that later. For now, simply rearrange objects so that their approximate location matches Figure 5.25. Eliminate the very long character string in the InvoiceID Footer and the label *Sum*, leaving in place only the expression *=Sum([Extended])*. (The expression sums the extended prices from each invoice line's extended price, yielding the subtotal.) Using Figure 5.25 as a guideline, rearrange each of the Group Header labels and bound controls so they resemble the layout shown. Switch to Print Preview periodically to see how the data and labels line up and to ensure bound controls are wide enough to display the data.

The Coffee Merchant's name and address shown in Figure 5.25 are bold, 12 point, Times New Roman typeface. Create them by opening the toolbox and dragging three labels to the Group Header section; change the Format properties of all three using the property sheet; and type the name and address information you see. Below The Coffee Merchant's address is the customer's address. It consists of four bound controls referring to the fields *CompanyName*, *Address*, and *CityStateZip*, which are all supplied by the query. The latter is a concatenation of the three *tblCustomer* fields City, State, and ZipCode. The expression found in the query that "glues" these three fields together is:

[City] & ", " & [State] & " " & [ZipCode]

The ampersands are character string operators that "add" one group of characters to the end of another. Once your design is fairly close to Figure 5.25, select Save As from the File menu, type **rptInvoiceCut2**, and click OK to save your new report design.

Next, you can simplify the report by eliminating the Report Header, Report Footer, and Page Footer. These contain unneeded lines and summary information—information that is unsuitable for our Invoice report. It is simple to eliminate entire report sections, and you don't need to remove any fields from the sections beforehand. Remove the Report Header and Footer first by clicking the Report Header/Footer selection in the View menu. Click Yes when the warning dialog box appears. Because you want to retain the Page Header, you cannot use the same technique to eliminate the Page Footer. Instead, simply delete all controls in the Page Footer. This removes the Page Footer itself because nothing prints there or below that band.

Modifying Existing Labels

Notice in Figure 5.25 that the label to the left of the invoice number is *Invoice Number:* (with a colon), not the original label taken from the field name, *InvoiceID*. It is easy to alter labels. Click the label you wish to change once and the entire label is selected. Click a second time (do not double-click the label), and an insertion point style cursor is placed in the string so you can add and delete characters. If you find the activity of clicking twice slowly a bit difficult to master, you can use an alternate technique. Double-click the label to bring up its property sheet. Then click the property sheet's Format tab and type in the Caption property text box the corrected label. You can close the property sheet or leave it open. Leaving it open makes it simpler to change other labels' Caption properties. Change all labels in the InvoiceID header to match Figure 5.25. Now is a good time to save your design. A lot of work has gone into the invoice since you last saved it. Select Save As from the File menu and type **rptInvoiceCut3**, which indicates that this is version three of the report design.

Creating Calculated Fields

Writing an expression involving arithmetic operators, numeric or character constants, table field names, and report objects creates a *calculated control*, the third major type of control. For example, the query *qryInvoiceLineItem*, which supplies information to a form, contains an expression that forms the product of the Quantity, UnitPrice, and Discount fields. You can create calculated controls, or expressions, in forms and reports also. For example, Subtotal, Sales Tax, Shipping, and Invoice Total in Figure 5.25 are calculated fields. They are not values stored in tables, because that would violate normalization rules and quickly lead to inconsistent data.

Because the Subtotal, Sales Tax, Shipping, and Invoice Total fields are calculated, their values change with each invoice printed or displayed on the console. The Report Wizard automatically created the Subtotal report field in the InvoiceID Footer when you selected Summary Options and checked Sum for the Extended field. The calculated control computes the sum of the Extended Price fields for every invoice. Let's rename the Subtotal calculated control so we can refer to it by an appropriate name in subsequent calculated controls, such as the Invoice Total control's expression. Other fields such as Sales Tax and Invoice Total will reference the field holding the summation of Extended Price. Here is how you rename an existing control—assigning it a new internal name that other controls can reference.

Try It

With *rptInvoiceCut3* open in Design view, click the field in the InvoiceID Footer that sums the Extended Price field. Display its property sheet (select Properties from the View menu). Select the tab labeled *Other*. Type ctlSubtotal in the Name property text box, replacing the current entry. Close the property sheet. That assigns the control a new and meaningful name.

Prefixes such as *ctl* identify the source of the value—a report control, not a table field. Assigning objects names such as *ctlSubtotal* or *ctlSalesTax* accomplishes two important things. First, the names document the meaning of the fields you create on a design document (report or form). Second, names are mnemonic and easy to remember when you construct other calculated expressions.

Creating a new field that contains an expression is straightforward. The next two exercises explain how to create the *ctlSalesTax* and *ctlShipping* calculated controls that are placed just below the Subtotal field in the InvoiceID Footer. First, create more room in the InvoiceID Footer so that it can accommodate the additional fields. Move the mouse to the bottom edge of the footer. When the pointer changes to a double-headed arrow, drag the bottom edge of the InvoiceID Footer down so that it is approximately two inches high.

EXERCISE 5.11: CREATING A SIMPLE SALES TAX CALCULATED CONTROL

1. Display the latest version of the invoice report (*rptInvoiceCut3*, for example) in Design view, display the toolbox, and click the toolbox Text Box tool. (Hover the mouse pointer over a tool for a second or two and a ToolTip displaying the tool's name will appear.)
2. Move the mouse to a position just below the subtotal control in the InvoiceID Footer and drag the mouse to create a control that is the same size as the *ctlSubtotal* control. When you release the mouse, an unbound text box control appears on the form.
3. Display the new control's property sheet and change the control's name: type **ctlSalesTax** in the Name property. (Remember, click the Other tab to locate the Name property.)
4. Click the property sheet Format tab, select the Format property, and type **Standard** (or select it from the drop-down list).
5. Click the Data tab in the property sheet.
6. Click anywhere inside the Control Source text box and then click the Build button that appears at the right side of the Control Source property. (The Build button has three dots, called an ellipsis, on it.) The Expression Builder dialog box opens.
7. Because our customers are wholesale customers, we will not charge sales tax (a simplifying assumption). In the Expression Builder box, type **=0** and then click OK to close the dialog box. (Notice that Access expressions resemble Excel spreadsheet expressions. They begin with an equal sign and are followed by an arbitrarily complex expression, though just a constant in our example here.)
8. Edit the label control to the left of the sales tax control: click it twice and type **Sales Tax:**
9. Click outside the sales tax label and then click the label to reselect it.
10. Click the Format tab and change the label's Text Align property to Right. (The Text Align property is far down in the list of Format properties. Use the scroll bar to locate it.) Click outside the label to deselect it.

Leave the property sheet and toolbox open for the expression you will build in the next exercise. Next, let's construct the expression to calculate the shipping cost. To keep things relatively uncomplicated, assume that it costs $0.25 per pound to ship everything, regardless of the size of an order. The number of pounds is determined by summing the Quantity bound control (Quantity is recorded in pounds). The next exercise builds the shipping cost control expression.

EXERCISE 5.12: CREATING A SHIPPING CALCULATED CONTROL

1. Display the Invoice report in Design view and click the Text Box tool in the toolbox. (Hover the mouse pointer over the toolbox's objects so ToolTips reveal which tool is the Text Box button.)
2. Move the mouse to a position just below the sales tax control, *ctlSalesTax*, in the InvoiceID Footer, and drag and release the mouse to create a control that is approximately the same size as the *ctlSubtotal* control.
3. Click the property sheet's Other tab and type **ctlShipping** in the Name property to change the control's name.
4. Click the property sheet Format tab, select the Format property, and select Standard.
5. Click the property sheet Data tab, click inside the Control Source property text box, and click the Build button (labeled with the ellipsis).
6. Type the expression **=0.25*Sum([Quantity])** to calculate shipping costs (see Figure 5.28).
7. Click OK to close the dialog box.
8. Type the text **Shipping:** into the label control and right-align it. Place the label control to the left of the calculated control, *ctlShipping*.

Click the Print Preview button to verify that the subtotal, sales tax, and shipping values are correct. Click any of the navigation buttons to verify that other invoices display correct values for the three controls you have created so far. Switch back to Design view to complete the remaining work on your report. If you haven't already, create a label to the left of the subtotal calculated control and type the text **Subtotal:** in the label.

Following the two previous exercise examples, create the Invoice Total calculated control. Name it **ctlInvoiceTotal**, type the expression

=[ctlSubtotal]+[ctlSalesTax]+[ctlShipping]

for the Control Source, and choose the Currency format. Edit and right-align the label to the left of the Invoice Total control, typing **Invoice Total:** for its Caption property. Though labels attached to text boxes are bold by default, you can put in bold other controls' contents by selecting the control(s) (shift-click if more than one) and then changing the Font Weight property (found on the Format sheet) to Bold. Save the report once again to preserve your work.

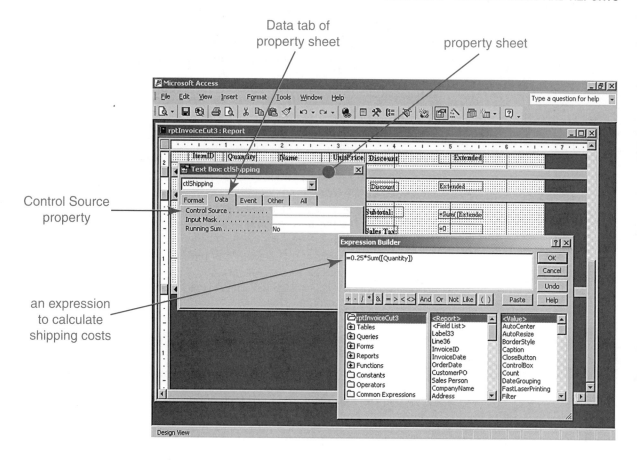

Figure 5.28   Writing an expression for a calculated control.

Aligning and Sizing Fields

It is important to know how to align report controls (fields) and size them so that your report looks professional. Up to this point you have not been concerned with how labels and data are aligned. For instance, we have ignored the fact that the Extended label in the InvoiceID Header appears far to the left of the actual prices in the detail lines below it. A simple exercise will illustrate how to align one column of values. Once you have aligned and sized one column, you can repeat the same steps for other labels and values. In preparation for the next exercise, ensure that the report *rptInvoiceCutx*, where *x* is the number corresponding to your latest version of the report, is displayed in Design view.

EXERCISE 5.13: ALIGNING AND SIZING MULTIPLE FIELDS

1. Select the following six objects: the label control Extended in the InvoiceID Header, the bound control Extended in the Detail section, and the four calculated

controls *ctlSubtotal*, *ctlSalesTax*, *ctlShipping*, and *ctlInvoiceTotal*. Release the mouse when all six objects are selected. Quick tip: Select all the objects by clicking above the topmost label and then drag down and through the objects. Keep the rectangle outline narrow so you do not "touch" other objects (see Figure 5.29).

2. With the six objects selected, select the Format menu, point to Size, and click To Narrowest. All six objects are resized to match the narrowest of them all.

3. Align all objects on the right by selecting the Format menu and then Align, Right. All objects snap into vertical alignment on the rightmost object of the six.

4. Click outside the objects to deselect them.

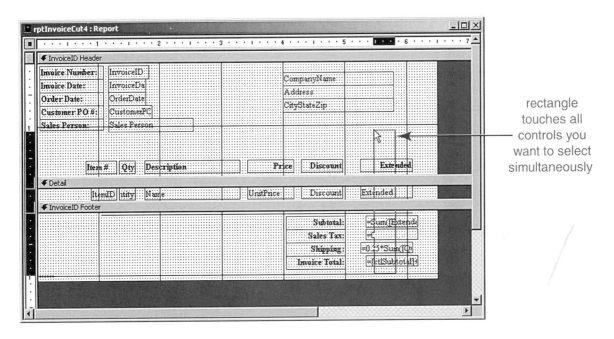

rectangle touches all controls you want to select simultaneously

Figure 5.29 Selecting multiple objects in different report sections.

Repeat the preceding four steps for the label control/bound control pairs ItemID, Quantity, UnitPrice, and Discount. However, do not narrow the Name column, so that lengthy names of coffees and teas can be displayed. Instead, size the Name label and value controls by executing Format, pointing to Size, and clicking To Widest. The Name label in the header widens to match the values in the Detail section. If necessary, you can widen both controls later to accommodate long descriptions.

Finally, place a Page Break control near the bottom of the InvoiceID Footer, below all existing InvoiceID Footer controls. Be sure to place the page break far enough down so that it will fall below the Shipping and Invoice Total controls. Save your report one more time.

Preview your Invoice report in the Report window. Your screen should resemble the one shown in Figure 5.25. There are several small embellishments you need to add to spruce it up, but you can fine tune your invoice any time you wish. So that you will have a good base from which to understand this report, we have saved the complete Invoice report and named it *rptInvoiceReport* on your Companion CD. You can improve on your design, or you can study ours.

SUMMARY

This chapter has emphasized using Access to create and modify forms and reports. You crafted forms for several tables that display a friendlier, more intuitive interface between the form user and the database. You learned how to add columns to forms and how to change the properties of fields on the form.

You have gained a lot of knowledge about Access reports in this chapter. You built a tabular-style report using a Report Wizard. You learned that reports can receive their data from both tables and queries. One of the reports you built contained a query. You also created an invoice report that tied together six of The Coffee Merchant's tables with a query. Various report headers and footers were described, including Group Headers and Footers, and you added calculated controls to the Group Footer that computed invoice subtotals, sales tax, shipping, and total invoice values. Having read this chapter, you can design and use Access forms and reports. Now that you have read the first five chapters, you are ready to apply your knowledge to build richly featured accounting database systems that serve the needs of your users.

QUESTIONS AND PROBLEMS FOR REVIEW

MULTIPLE-CHOICE QUESTIONS

1. While displaying the property sheet of a control on a form, you can change the control's
   a. size.
   b. font size.
   c. orientation.
   d. position.
2. One advantage of using a query as the foundation of a report is that
   a. a query is the only way to join multiple tables.
   b. different reports can be run from a query by changing the query's selection criteria and rerunning the report.
   c. tables cannot be used to create a report.
   d. a query is protected from unauthorized access.

3. A report can be used to
   a. change data in a table.
   b. print information found in one or more tables.
   c. input information into multiple tables.
   d. none of the preceding can be accomplished with a report.
4. What is the expression to form a subtotal of a control called Extended Price?
   a. =Sum(Extended Price)
   b. =Sum[Extended Price]
   c. =Sum([Extended Price])
   d. Sum[Extended Price]
5. Information that is unsorted can be organized into related groups in a report by
   a. creating a Page Footer.
   b. creating a Sort Footer.
   c. creating a calculated field.
   d. creating a Group Header or Footer.
6. You can align objects that lie in different sections or bands of a report. After selecting the objects to be aligned, what do you execute?
   a. Format, Size All
   b. Format, Align
   c. Format, Snap to Grid
   d. View, Align
7. When you use the Report Wizard, the report name is also used as the
   a. report section.
   b. report title.
   c. report footer.
   d. report bound control.
8. To sum up all invoice totals on each page of a report showing invoice summaries, you would place a control in the report's _____ section.
   a. Report Header
   b. Report Footer
   c. Group Footer
   d. Page Footer
9. What type of form control displays a database field?
   a. calculated
   b. unbound
   c. bound
   d. none of the above
10. What is the name of the property that allows controls to refer to a specific control?
    a. Control Source
    b. Input Mask
    c. Name
    d. Text Align

DISCUSSION QUESTIONS

1. Discuss the advantage(s) of providing a list box or a combo box in a form. How does it help a user? What possible disadvantages are present when using a list box control?

2. What are the advantages of using a form to view or update data in a table? Are there any disadvantages to using a form rather than viewing the table directly?

3. Explain why you might want to use a form to search a database. Can you change values in underlying tables through a form? Explain.

4. Discuss the differences in use between a form and a report. Where is each one best used? What advantages does a form provide when compared to a report?

5. Explain, or speculate, when it is best to use a query as the basis of a report and when it is better to use a Report Wizard and select multiple, related tables.

PROBLEMS

1. Create and print the form shown in Figure 5.2. The form displays information from several rows of the table *tblEmployee*. Include a title at the top of each form, and include your name, course number, and section in each form. Print only the first page of the form.

2. Create a report that lists employees' last names, employees' first names, and their sales in order of each employee's last name. Employee sales data is stored in the table *tblSalesTransactions*. The foreign key in that table linking it to employees is EmployeeID. Once you get the query right, produce a report showing all sales transactions for the employees whose last names are Pacioli, Hunter, or Ellison. Include an unbound control containing your name. If your instructor requests it, include other unbound controls (labels) indicating other identification information such as the course name and section number.

3. Create a form that resembles the Inventory Data Entry form shown in Figure 5.1, except that your form has a record selector—a standard form item. In addition to the fields you see in Figure 5.1, add an unbound control labeled "Country of Origin" and an associated bound control that displays each coffee's country of origin. Use the Form Wizard and base the form on tables that you specify using the Form Wizard. There is no need to first build a query and then link together the appropriate tables. The tables that you need to build the form are *tblCountryName*, *tblInventory*, and *tblInventoryDescription*. Add an unbound control with your first and last name. When the Form Wizard asks about grouping, select "view by tblInventory." Use the Filter command to locate any single coffee produced by the country of Zimbabwe. Print the form showing the Zimbabwe coffee displayed by the form. Extra credit: Remove from the form the record selector, the Minimize button, and the Maximize button.

4. Create a columnar form displaying all the fields from the table *tblSalesTaxRate*. Fields in the table include StateAbbreviation, StateName, TaxRate, Population, and LandArea. Once you or a Form Wizard creates the basic form, add a calculated control that computes and displays the population density. (Population density is the population divided by the land area and is measured, in this case, in people per square mile.) Format the calculated control Fixed with two decimal places. Change any unbound controls (labels) such as "StateName" to "State Name" so that no label is two or more words back to back. Align all unbound controls so that they line up on their right sides. Align all bound controls (text boxes showing database values) so that their values display in the left side of their respective text boxes. This is not the same as using the Format menu Align command. You must set a particular property of the control. Ensure that there is an equal amount of vertical space between all bound/unbound control pairs. Create a Form Header and place an unbound control with your first and last name. Print a form showing only one record, not several, from the database.

5. You want to mail out a large number of flyers to all your current customers. Use the Access Label Wizard to create a report. The report is, in fact, a set of Avery labels. Create a new report based on the table *tblCustomer*. Select Label Wizard from the list of report types. Then, make the following choices: Click "English Unit of Measure" and select Avery 5160 labels. Place the following fields on your mailing labels: Contact, Address, City, State, and ZipCode. Arrange the fields on the label with the Contact on line 1, Address on line 2, and City, State, and ZipCode on line 3. Place a comma between the City and State. Ensure there is at least one blank following the comma and between State and ZipCode. Sort the mailing labels by State and then by City within state. Name your report "Mailing Labels" (without the double quotation marks). Print only the first page of the report. Be careful in making your Print dialog box choices—the report is almost 60 pages long. Write your name and any other identification required by your instructor on the printed, single-page report.

INDEX